P9-DWG-804

D0037758

Caviar and Commissars

Caviar and Commissars

THE EXPERIENCES OF
A U.S. NAVAL OFFICER IN STALIN'S RUSSIA

By Kemp Tolley
Rear Admiral, U.S. Navy (Retired)

Naval Institute Press   Annapolis, Maryland

Library of Congress Cataloging in Publication Data

Tolley, Kemp, 1908–
Caviar and commissars.

Bibliography: p.
Includes index.
1. World War, 1939–1945—Soviet Union. 2. Tolley, Kemp, 1908– . 3. World War, 1939–1945—Personal narratives, American. 4. Soviet Union—History—1939–1945. 5. United States. Navy—Biography. 6. Admirals—United States—Biography. 7. Military attachés—United States—Biography. I. Title.
D764.T557 1983 940.53'22'47 83-19512

ISBN: 0-87021-741-0

Printed in the United States of America

The Russians

They were at once mystical and pagan, dazzled by God and consumed by superstition; they readily accepted the slavery of the body but sang the freedom of the spirit; they were gentle but suddenly intoxicated with fits of cruelty; they detested war but fought with insane valor; they beat their wives and respected the idea of motherhood; they hated the nobility but could not do without a master. . . . Policy was made in St. Petersburg behind closed doors, not here among the crowd. To act, one had to abstract one's self from the fragmentary reality of particular faces and characters and see people as masses. . . . In government, tenderheartedness was not a virtue.

(From *Catherine the Great*, by Henri Troyat, with permission of Elsevier-Dutton Publishing Co., Inc.)

To Vlada

Contents

Foreword

The U.S. Navy's difficulties with the Russians began when Captain John Paul Jones was persuaded by Catherine the Great to prepare her disorganized Black Sea Fleet for action against the Turks. Admiral Kemp Tolley's picaresque memoirs detail vividly the continuous tribulations with the Russians in the years of World War II. Assigned to Moscow as an intelligence officer after Pearl Harbor, he encountered extraordinary problems and pleasures that make for absorbing and illuminating reading.

In his wartime travels from one end of the Soviet Union to the other, he encountered a congeries of spies, counterspies, *agents provocateurs*, ballet dancers, fools, knaves, and innocents-abroad. Being unorthodox, waggish, ingenious, and bright, he managed to survive not only the trials but the temptations and bring forth a rollicking and insightful chronicle of the wartime honeymoon of two diametrically opposed governments.

Tolley's report to the Office of Naval Intelligence five months after his arrival can still be helpful to Americans attempting to negotiate with the USSR: "The Soviet Union and its people should be approached warily, subjectively, keeping in mind that a white skin sometimes conceals a Mongol or Tartar or trans-Caucasus mentality that does not function in the Kansas fashion." What Tolley observed after those first months make his book a cautionary tale, one that should be studied as well as savored. His account of the ordeal of William Standley, ambassador to the USSR, is both informative and admonitory. The well-meaning admiral was not only frustrated by his intransigent Soviet counterparts but undermined by another well-meaning American, Brigadier General Philip Faymonville, Chief of the U.S. Army Supply Mission. A favorite of President Roosevelt, Faymonville's wholehearted enthusiasm for the Soviet Union had begun in 1922.

The book is laced with excellent eyewitness anecdotes of the bizarre and exasperating experiences of westerners, such as the one concerning a Stalin-Churchill banquet in the Kremlin where the Generalissimus expatiated at length on the catastrophic failure of the Gallipoli campaign in World War I due to gross stupidities in concept, execution, and intelligence. Gallipoli, of course, had been Churchill's brainchild, and this was Stalin's crude but effective way of striking a knife into a former enemy he still distrusted.

Throughout the book Tolley remains irreverent, iconoclastic, bold, funny, provocative, and enlightening. That he became an admiral speaks well for the U.S. Navy since it is such original characters who irritate and provoke the nation into recognition of our perils.

John Toland
Danbury, Conn.
August 17, 1983

Preface

Until the day Hitler attacked the USSR, 22 June 1941, the Soviets had been held to be, in effect, Axis collaborators, if not allies. From then on, through the spring of 1942, Soviet fortunes were precarious, with American cooperation and assistance still in an ephemeral state.

By the time of my arrival in Kuibishev, the provisional capital, in May 1942, the American effort had begun to take shape. Ambassador Standley had just arrived. Half a dozen military and naval attachés were in place at Archangel, Vladivostok, and Kuibishev to fill a void that had existed since American recognition of the Soviet Union.

From my arrival until almost the time I departed two years later, I was the next-to-senior professional line naval officer in the capital, designated as intelligence officer. For the first year we were a tight little community of State Department and military, less than a dozen total, among whom the fortunes of war and diplomacy were discussed in deadly serious detail over tomsky collinses and lengthy dinners in the oval music room that served as a common mess in opulent Spasso House, the ambassadorial residence. I either enciphered, saw in the files, heard discussed, or personally experienced those matters about which you will read in later pages. It was a heady experience for a youngish, mid-level naval officer who had started the war by dodging Japanese forces in making an incredibly lucky escape from Corregidor.

Acknowledgments

Credit for the content of this book must go principally to several diverse sources: a country barn stashed with my weekly letters home, from 1925 to 1959, as descriptively complete as censorship and decorum allowed; a daily journal (alas! sometimes sporadically kept); a computer-like memory developed by long periods of following the doctrine, "Leave your gun and camera at home and don't write anything down!"

Filling in most generously have been Messrs John McGinnis and Theodore Grason, who lent me unpublished book manuscripts of their Russian adventures, and Rear Admiral Samuel B. Frankel and Captain George D. Roullard, who made their files available as well as setting down their personal experiences.

Greatest saver of leg work has been the highly capable information desks of the Baltimore County Public Libraries, under the overall direction of Mr. Charles W. Robinson, who recalls boyhood days of treading barefoot the hot steel decks of U.S. destroyers in Chefoo, China.

Captain Roy C. Smith III, editor of *Shipmate*, has offered constant encouragement, allowed me to draw on articles previously appearing in his magazine, and also published one advance chapter of this book.

Russian and Chinese spelling of place names and people is the Anglicized version current among Americans in the pre–World War II era.

Finally, I am much indebted to Mrs. Carol Swartz, book editor, who has the keenest eye for inconsistencies, misplaced commas, and convoluted phraseology, while generously avoiding any hint of censorship.

Caviar and Commissars

Introduction: The U.S. Navy in Russia

Over the last two centuries a long, though occasionally interrupted, parade of ill-prepared U. S. naval officers has encountered the great riddle, mystery, and enigma, as Winston Churchill described it, of Russia. Perhaps the most ironic twist of our Navy's experiences there is that the time frame has mattered very little. With rare exceptions, the newcomer has arrived open-minded, but has departed disillusioned, sometimes bitter, even if belatedly wiser. The uninitiated and uninformed American naval officer who jumps into Russia is likely to be shocked by experiences that he should have been taught to expect. Instead of accommodating himself to an alien culture, making an effort to understand its motives and even turning it to his own benefit and enjoyment, he often comes away frustrated, damning the culture and the people.

Perhaps we can forgive Captain John Paul Jones, Continental Navy (Unemployed) for being trapped by the Russian syndrome, because he was the first of thousands of U. S. naval personnel exposed to it. Denied flag rank by the Americans, the Continental Navy in near limbo, Jones came to Catherine the Great's notice while he was in Paris in 1788 being knighted. He would be just the man to whip her polyglot Black Sea Fleet into successful action against the Turks. So via Sweden, over the half-frozen Baltic, Jones arrived shivering at Reval (now Tallinn) in a 30-foot open boat, then galloped off to St. Petersburg. Catherine's prodigalities in the amatory field rivaled Jones's exploits on the sea, so legend suggests the latter's success in the imperial boudoir. But such was not the case. The lady was a fat fifty-nine. Her earlier romantic attachment, Prince Grigori Potemkin, was Jones's military boss. After jolting over the 1,200 near-roadless miles in his white *contre-admiral's* uniform, Jones found himself displacing a Greek, who became his highly disgruntled deputy. The new admiral's strategy of lying defensively in the Dnieper estuary awaiting attack by the superior Turkish fleet brought victory, but an international adventurer who commanded a flotilla of Russian gunboats, Rear Admiral Prince Nassau-Siegen, protegé of Potemkin, earned all the credit by adroit self-promotion. Unrewarded, Jones returned to St. Petersburg to await in vain a new command, his hopes dashed by blackmail, the alleged rape of a twelve-year-old girl.

Was it the Byzantine Russian deviousness we have come to know so well? The record is unclear. At any rate, Catherine, who took a dim view of others' peccadillos, true or false, curtly bade him farewell in June 1789, and as have so many other would-be departees over the years, he waited two months for an exit visa.

Although diplomatic relations between Russia and the new American Republic had been established in 1809, it was seven more years before the sloop USS *Prometheus* put into Kronstadt, port of St. Petersburg, for something more than a courtesy call. In a mirror image of Jones's imbroglio, Russia's consul general in Philadelphia had been jailed for allegedly raping a 12-year-old girl. The basic issue was not amatory indiscretion but violation of diplomatic immunity, for which the Czar threatened to withdraw his ambassador while quarantining the American chargé d'affaires in St. Petersburg. Presidential communications carried by the *Prometheus* mollified the czar, who withdrew his threat to break relations and allowed back into circulation the quarantined U. S. chargé d'affaires.

Next, in August 1830, came the USS *Concord*, bearing aged, quarrelsome minister-designate John Randolph. Skipper Matthew Calbraith Perry had flogged two of his crewmen en route, inspiring Randolph to write the Secretary of the Navy that the *Concord* was a sort of hell afloat. But Perry's views on discipline must have suited the czar right down to the ground, as he ended a long discussion with Perry by suggesting he join the imperial service.

In July 1837, the USS *Independence**, first U. S. ship-of-the-line, arrived carrying more diplomats. The Russians were impressed. Nicholas I "found his amusement in wandering alone among the seamen enquiring and conversing with the utmost freedom."† He'd like to send some of his most promising officers to the United States to study ship construction.‡

*2,259 tons, 188 ft. long, 24 ft. draft, 56 32-pounders, 4 8-inch, an amazing 750 complement.

†Log of *Independence*, National Archives.

‡The appreciation lingered on; in 1902 Cramp's Philadelphia shipyard built Russia the battleship *Retvizan*. About the same time, some Lake-type submarines launched Russia's undersea warfare program. In the mid 1930s, Stalin asked Roosevelt to have two 60,000-ton, 18-inch gun battleships and some quintuple-tube destroyers designed and built for the USSR.

In 1866, an attempted assassination of Czar Nicholas I provided a good excuse to send a U. S. warship to Russia, partly to congratulate the czar on his escape, and partly to express thanks for Russia's support of the Union during the Civil War, countering Britain's sympathy for the South. Secretary of the Navy Gustavus Fox was sent in the monitor USS *Miantonomah*,* of the type which had so recently changed the face of naval warfare. Awash most of the time, water sloshing over her turtleback deck, the ungainly ship finally arrived in the Baltic to be escorted by eleven Russian warships for a tumultuous welcome at Kronstadt. Some Russians were surprised to find that the Americans were not red-skinned, and they demonstrated much curiosity about skipper Beaumont's black steward. One hopes that Fox had a stout chest: the gold medal presented him by the czar weighed three-quarters of a pound.

Twenty years later, the aged 1,400-ton steam sloop USS *Enterprise*, Commander B. H. McCalla, creaked into Kronstadt for one of the most hectic fortnights experienced by any U. S. naval contingent before or since. The *Enterprise* entertained the officer corps of the elite Cuirassier Guards, who took to port wine "like kittens to new milk," as executive officer Lieutenant R. R. Ingersoll described it.† The return engagement was strenuous. After a lavish two-hour dinner at the Guards' bivouac, the American party and Russian hosts moved off to the exercise field. While Ingersoll was innocently applauding the magnificent horses parading by, a group of cavalrymen suddenly rushed toward him, grabbed him with many pairs of hands, and tossed him high in the air—"caught me gently . . . then hove me up again."‡ This was a rare honor, one that any prince of the blood would be happy to receive, the colonel said, as Ingersoll readjusted his badly ruffled feathers. Champagne and sakuski in the field were followed by a near all-night dinner at the Guards' mess. After a sleepless, nonstop 24 hours of conviviality that would have flattened lesser men, Ingersoll and companions dragged themselves aboard the old hulk that was home, now blooded veterans of a Russian hospitality that so many of us have come to know.

The new century, the twentieth, burst forth with portentous moves worldwide: China's Boxer Rebellion; Kaiser Wilhelm's *Drang Nach Osten*; Russia's move into Manchuria; new King Edward VII's attempts to charm

*Built in 1865, 259 feet long, 15-foot draft, 52-foot beam, wooden hull, 7 inches of side armor, 2½-inch-thick deck. Two 21-foot-diameter turrets, each housing two 15-inch Dahlgrens. Engines of 4 cylinders, 30 inches in diameter.

†Rear Admiral R. R. Ingersoll, *Cruising in the Old Navy*, Naval Historical Foundation Publication, Series 11, No. 19, winter 1974.

‡Ibid.

an old enemy across the channel; and most interesting of all, the emergence of the United States as an imperial world power.

In European eyes the United States Navy had been seen as a collection of largely wind-driven museum pieces. Then almost overnight a shiny new U. S. battle fleet appeared, its European squadron starting a chain of events unparalleled in American history. At banquets, Rear Admiral C. H. Cotton commanding, successively sat next to President Loubet of France, King Edward VII of England, and Kaiser Wilhelm II of Germany, the latter outdoing himself to put on a good show.

The old, pragmatic U. S. affinity for the Russians was waning, however. A late nineteenth century flood of Poles and Russian Jews had fled to America, bitter at Russian oppression. "Russia is a menace to modern civilization," cried Congressman J. O. Pendleton, " . . . a threat to the peace of the world!"* words which today seem strangely familiar. It was a lively protest against free transportation of grain to alleviate the Russian famine of 1891–1892, Pendleton declaring that real friendship could come only when Poland was free and a halt made to the persecution of opinion and religion.

George Kennan's 1891 book, *Siberia and the Exile System*, plus the growing Jewish and Polish ethnic clout, turned U. S. sympathies toward Japan in the 1904 Russo-Japanese War. Our first U. S. naval representative accredited exclusively to Russia was thus not cordially received when he arrived to report on the war.† Denied an audience with the czar, which was granted to all other attachés, Lieutenant Newton A. McCully shared none of the special privileges of his colleagues at the front. "No Russian official records or statistics were ever placed at my disposal," he wrote, continuing in a vein that could have been lifted *in toto* for use in a 1942 attaché report: "Few opportunities were given for personal observation, particularly with the Navy. To a direct question invariably an untrue answer would be given . . ."‡ It was all vile and abominable, he complained.

McCully considered the Russians a paradox. While the high command clumsily vacillated in its use of ships, the single-tracked Trans-Siberian Railway had miraculously transported more than a million men and all their supplies 3,500 miles overland. A mixture of chivalry and stupidity seemed to guide naval decisions: when in doubt, blow up your

Congressional Record, 6 January 1892.

†Previous attachés and assistants had been assigned primary duty at Paris, additional duty at St. Petersburg.

‡Newton A. McCully, Lieutenant Commander, USN, *The McCully Report: The Russo-Japanese War, 1904-05*, Richard von Doenhoff, ed. (Annapolis: Naval Institute Press, 1977), p. 256. The extraordinary detail in this report brings out the idiosyncracies of the Russian character, equally valid for today's "Soviet man."

Newton A. McCully, twice naval attaché in Imperial Russia, then later commanding U.S. naval forces in North Russia and Black Sea during the Revolution.

ship. When bombardment threatened men-of-war in the harbor, they were scuttled. They could be raised later.

In 1911, the Russians had refused several dozen American Jews permission to return to Russia to establish businesses in contravention of Russian law. Congress was being hotly lobbied by Jewish groups to repudiate the 1832 Russian-American trade treaty. So in keeping with Oliver Cromwell's reputed opinion that warships make the best ambassadors, an impressive display of American might showed up at Kronstadt in June 1911: the powerful new Second Division, battleships *Louisiana, South Carolina, New Hampshire*, and *Kansas*.

The Russian aim then as now was *détente*. There were glittering receptions, with lavish entertainment ashore for all. The czar himself doubled his expected stay in his inspection aboard the flagship.

But *détente* was not to be. In 1912 Congress repudiated the treaty and the American ambassador came home, at last ending the incongruous "alliance" of democracy and autocracy. It was not until 1914 and World

War I that an American ambassador once more appeared in the Russian capital, and McCully, now a captain, returned as naval attaché. Until the American entry into the war in 1917, McCully meticulously kept the Navy Department informed on the Russian forays against the Turks and the skirmishes in the Baltic, all characterized by the same erratic command performances he had observed in 1904.

American sympathies in World War I, enhanced by clever and sometimes unscrupulous propaganda, lay with the two great democracies, Britain and France. When the intended German blitz degenerated into a stalemated slaughterhouse, it was a sea attack, the sinking of the SS *Lusitania*, that drew America into the war. When the United States declared war on the Central Powers on 7 April 1917, it became not an *ally* but a *power associated with* the Entente, which included Imperial Russia, to whom U. S. war material and loans were soon en route for a total of $192,599,324.37. Not a dime was ever repaid: in effect, the money was "traded for Siberia," as we shall see later.

March 1917 was a momentous month. From the 8th to the 11th, riots rocked St. Petersburg. On the 15th, the czar abdicated. Captain McCully's relief, Commander Walter S. Crosley, coming in the back door via Harbin, Manchuria, in April, and accompanied by the spunky, unflappable Mrs. Crosley, already had found things deteriorating. Although Crosley had been advised in advance to wear his uniform once he was aboard the Russian train, it was clear that officers were not popular. "There is a look on the faces of the soldiers that almost frightens me . . ." wrote Mrs. Crosley, whose husband in short order had doffed his uniform.* Service was surly in the international car, where candles substituted for the disabled dynamo. Train personnel at first kept roaming soldiers out by locking the doors, but soon they simply broke into all the cars except the wagon-lits. At Vologda "White Guardists" appeared, and partly by persuasion and partly by force, ejected all soldiers from the train. It was early evidence of the fratricidal struggle that, for the next five years, would embroil Russia, eventually involving the United States in its first war with that country.

The Revolution staggered on through the summer, starting spontaneously, bereft of any identifiable leadership—in effect, anonymous. Only Lenin's Bolsheviks had a plan, surprisingly simple in a complex land: "Land, bread, peace! All power to the Soviets!"

In this anomalous situation, the Crosleys entertained Russian aristocrats and fellow diplomats, avoiding areas where shooting was in progress. They scrounged for food and wood, and went frequently to the magnificent

*Pauline Crosley, *Intimate Letters From Petrograd* (New York: E. P. Dutton & Co., 1920).

ballet, where soldiers, sailors, and peasants now occupied the royal boxes. Idle soldiers sat by the thousands in the parks eating sunflower seeds. Others rode street cars or crowded aboard a train to no particular destination.

In mid-October 1917 the front collapsed, and the German war in effect ended for Russia. The final revolt that overturned the provisional government was touched off by the cruiser *Aurora*'s guns aimed at the Winter Palace, and on 7 November Lenin's Bolsheviks assumed complete control.*

On 16 February 1918, the Crosleys experienced the new egalitarianism first hand—they were ordered to shovel snow like any other comrade. It clearly was time for departure, which entailed a wildly hectic two weeks of bribing and preparation for the touch-and-go train ride to Finland, during which their passports were checked nineteen times en route by the already infamous Red Guards.

Even more fabulous were the experiences of assistant attaché Lieutenant Sergius M. Riis, son of a Danish immigrant fur merchant, who had accompanied his father to St. Petersburg where he had acquired a good knowledge of Russian. Riis was appointed a second lieutenant in the U. S. Marine Corps in 1907, transferred to the Navy, took part in laying the North Sea mine barrage, then was ordered to Russia. Riis was in Petrograd, the former St. Petersburg, when on 30 August 1918 Socialist Dora Kaplan put two bullets into demigod Lenin, wounding but not killing him. The frenzied reprisals were bloody. When Captain F. N. A. Cromie, British naval attaché, was assassinated by Bolsheviks, Lieutenant Commander MacGloin, British assistant attaché, telephoned Riis, urging him to leave. Riis found the railway station swarming with people, corpses stacked by the dozen. MacGloin meanwhile had turned up. The two of them bribed the crew of a locomotive towing one box car, and off they went via the main line to Moscow.

A dozen or so miles later, Red Guards stopped the "train," putting aboard Comrades Galinski and Morosov, whose rudimentary English had been picked up in the New York garment district. Clearly divining the intentions of their watchdogs, MacGloin and Riis anticipated them by throttling the two when they dozed. Then they exchanged clothes and papers before tossing the corpses out of the careening box car.

For the next week, Comrade Commissar Maxim Galinski (né Riis) ricocheted from Moscow to Vologda to Kazan to Kiev and finally to Odessa, whence he proceeded by sea to Archangel to resume his interrupted duties. There, he reported on conditions, people, and beautiful spies who were

*Now a memorial ship moored in the Neva at Leningrad.

It was behind such a locomotive as this that the American sailors from the USS *Olympia* spearheaded the Intervention in North Russia, August 1918. Note the supply of fuel in the foreground.

seducing innocent naval officers, earning a Navy Cross for his unusual exploits.

There was more going on in Archangel than mere spying. There was America's Russian War of 1918–1919, a bizarre struggle in the frigid wilderness that soured Russian-American relations for a generation and is by no means forgotten in the USSR to this day. It started on 3 August 1918, with an elderly locomotive towing several flatcars clattering down a single track through virgin forests and tiny villages. Stoking pitch-pine sticks into the firebox or hanging on for dear life aboard the swaying cars were well-armed sailors from the old cruiser USS *Olympia*. They were on their adventurous own, spearheading an incredible campaign that would involve the United States in a year of bloody, undeclared war against the infant Soviet Republic.*

*See "Our Russian War Of 1918-1919," U. S. Naval Institute *Proceedings*, February, 1969.

Sailors from USS *Olympia*'s landing force who campaigned for months in the North Russian wilderness engaging Bolshevik bands and exciting enmity, which is still vividly remembered by Soviets.

Concurrently with the North Russia troubles, a counterpart was boiling in the Far East, where Americans were again involved, though not as combatants. In June 1917, a U. S. mission under Elihu Root, including Rear Admiral James H. Glennon, USN, arrived in Vladivostok, then crossed Russia in some splendor aboard the deposed czar's special train, their task to determine how best to help the new Provisional Government continue the war. Glennon, who visited all the principal naval bases, found chaos, the naval forces controlled largely by committees of workmen and sailors and the fleet clearly no longer a fighting entity.

The mission got back to Vladivostok with difficulty, finding conditions in Vladivostok tranquil, ". . . no shortage of food, business as usual," according to Lieutenant Bruce Flood, who reveals some interesting Russian characteristics: "All citizens and foreign travellers are required to carry passports . . . bribery a necessary adjunct to anything slightly out of the ordinary . . . gracious and generous to a fault . . . but the most long-winded, procrastinating and time wasting people in the universe."* To which those who have experienced the modern Soviet bureaucracy would breathe a heartfelt Amen!

President Wilson's reluctant decision to send a U. S. Army division to Vladivostok was based on both a desire to prevent the huge quantities of war material on the docks from falling into Bolshevik, thence enemy, hands, and to facilitate the evacuation of some 50,000 Czecho-Slovaks, former prisoners, to be shipped half way around the world to fight Germans. The American troops had stern Washington instructions *not* to meddle in Russian politics, to which they tenaciously held.

American cruisers lay in Vladivostok throughout the Russian Revolution, landing Marines on occasion. Sailormen promoted romances with white refugees, and fire fights ashore went on in plain view of the ships. "Who the hell hit me with that spud?" cried out one USS *Brooklyn* sailor, then fell dead from a stray bullet. In the Baltic, American warships sailed on errands of mercy, bringing food to stranded countrymen in an area where, in spite of the Armistice, German occupying troops were still cocky.

By July 1919, Commander F. H. Sadler, commanding the destroyer USS *Evans* at Libau, Latvia, described his functions as, "(a) a yacht for the American Relief Administration; (b) a radio station; (c) a boating agent. Tennis, baseball, fine swimming beach; liberty to 11 P.M. Being the possessors of soap, cigarettes, chocolate and sugar, we are rather popular."†

But as late as 1920 there still were Baltic alarums. When the USS *Pittsburgh* got word of two Red subs off Estonia, she sent a priority dispatch to Washington: "URGE THAT I BE DIRECTED TO TREAT AS HOSTILE BOLSHEVIC [sic] SUBMARINES AS IT IS THE ONLY WAY TO DEFEND AMERICAN SHIPS"† The attitude in Washington was more calm. For God's sake, cool it, the CNO in effect told the excitable gentlemen in the USS *Pittsburgh*, assuring them that the United States definitely was not at war with the Bolshies.

So, at last, ended World War I, with Great Russia sealed off behind the Cordon Sanitaire, dismissed as a pariah among nations by the vengeful old men who framed the peace treaties that guaranteed the even more cataclysmic war to come.

*From Captain Bruce Flood's unpublished narrative furnished to the author.
†Record Group 45, National Archives.
†Ibid.

1 / *The Road to Muscovy*

The sporadic parade of U.S. warships to Russia over the nineteenth century provided only a passing glimpse of the Russian scene for the naval personnel embarked. It was not until the establishment of the naval attaché system by act of Congress in 1888 that naval officers became residents and observers on a long-term basis.

On 1 March 1889, the first U. S. naval attaché was posted to Imperial Russia, Lieutenant Aaron Ward. As continued to be the practice until 1904, he was accredited to Paris and Berlin as well as St. Petersburg, visiting the latter generally only on those occasions of special audiences or celebrations where the military officer's cocked hat, gold epaulettes, striped pants, and sword lent a touch of color to the otherwise funereally garbed American delegation.

In 1904, the outbreak of the Russo-Japanese War suggested the usefulness of a full-time naval attaché at the front, so 37-year-old Lieutenant Newton A. McCully, Jr., was designated, commencing the sequence of naval attachés accredited exclusively to Russia.

Between 1889 and the end of World War I, eleven U. S. naval attachés had served in Russia, including in addition to Ward and McCully such well known names as R. P. Rodgers, W. S. Sims and H. H. Hough. Of the eleven, five became flag officers, suggesting the fallacy of the general pre–World War II belief that service with the Office of Naval Intelligence (ONI) was the kiss of death.

During World War II, the number of U. S. naval officers in the USSR outnumbered over two to one those who had served there until that time. Since the end of World War II, approximately one hundred U. S. naval and Marine officers have been attached to the American embassy at Moscow, generally for a tour of two years, for a grand total of two hundred years' collective experience in attempting to unravel the mysteries of the Russian soul and land.

How did they get there? What did they find? How well were they prepared? What was their motivation? Or did they simply "get sent?" The answers in most cases lie in the archives of ONI, plus on rare occasions in a book, such as Vice Admiral Leslie C. Stevens's *Russian Assignment*, the story of his tenure as naval attaché at Moscow, 1947–1949. (Boston: Little, Brown & Co., 1953).

How, indeed, does one become involved in the Russian syndrome? In my own case it was not something that happened overnight. It was, in fact, sparked in early youth, launching a career in this special field that probably predated any other similar one in the U. S. Navy.

While the guns of August 1914 thundered in Europe, echoes reverberated in the Far East. On 1 August the Russian cruiser *Askold*, the Austro-Hungarian battleship *Queen Elizabeth* and the USS *Saratoga* were lying in the port of Chinwangtao when news came of the war. The *Askold* made it out of port 15 minutes ahead of the Austrian *Queen*, managed to escape the crack German cruiser squadron and headed for Europe, where the real action was, stopping at Manila en route. Her officers were entertained at a Ft. McKinley *thé dansant*, where their unusual uniforms—dark trousers topped by white jackets with brilliant gold epaulettes—charmed all with their exotic elegance. Those ladies who spoke French, the Russians' second tongue, were in great demand as dancing partners. The *Askold's* skipper, whose store of languages extended to fractured English, delighted in remarking that he was captain of *Askold*, "but varm heart!" pleased with himself at this exhibition of what he felt to be sharp American wit.

On the edge of the bandstand sat a gaggle of small boys, who can be highly impressionable at that age, especially if memories are reinforced by family reminiscences, plus daily headlines six years later of White Russians against Reds, fierce cavalry battles, murder and mayhem.

So, sparked by these earlier memories, the once small boy now at the Naval Academy, where only French and Spanish were taught, was struck by the idea of studying Russian on his own. He asked his French professor for advice.

"Meester Tolay," said Paul Lajoie, his blue eyes a'twinkle, "ze Meedsheepman in ze fairst seksion are zo afraid to make a *mee*stake, zey say nossing. In ze anchor seksion [last or bottom], zey do not know enough to say anytheeng. In your meedle seksion, you know a leetle somethee ng and you are not afraid to make a *mee*stake. You weel speak to many people in many languages."

In the 1928 United States, Russian was a non-language. We had to send to London for a grammar, an outmoded tome aimed at the British commercial fraternity once predominant in Imperial Russia. By graduation in 1929, "Meedsheepman" Tolley could painfully write, and slowly read and speak, simple Russian. It had been like Tarzan of the Apes, up a tree, learning English from a book found adrift in the jungle.

My first sea assignment as an ensign was the elderly battleship USS *Florida*, recently converted from coal to oil burner. Life in such a ship for a young bachelor was humdrum: Monday to Friday at sea, anchored a mile out on weekends at Norfolk or Newport, New Year's to April in Guantánamo, Cuba. Was there *any* adventure in the Navy? "Yep!" said the Old China Hands. "Just apply for the Asiatics." They spun tall tales of the Russian girls on the China coast—young, debonair, dressing with flair on a pittance. Some were salesgirls, telephone operators, or office assistants, but most were cabaret dance hostesses in a land where labor, skilled or unskilled, was rewarded with little more than a bowl of rice. In June the girls migrated to the summer resorts of Tsingtao and Chefoo, whither the Asiatic Fleet's heavy cruiser, thirteen destroyers, six submarines, and various auxiliaries "came up to China in the springtime," in the words of a favorite drinking song, to relax and train. The younger officers, predominantly carefree bachelors in those days, found it easily possible on an ensign's pay of $143.25 monthly to maintain a private, brass-mounted rickshaw, a Manchurian pony, several club memberships, have a *pied à terre* for late nights, drink premium whiskey, plus in many cases establish a temporary liaison with one of those throaty-voiced, lissome Russian "princesses." It all sounded very good indeed.

After the *Florida*, there was a year on the staff of the Commander in Chief U. S. Fleet, and then time to move on in the rotational plans for young officers. From such a springboard, orders to "the Asiatics" were merely for the asking. Thirty days aboard the Dollar liner *President Adams* drinking champagne out of teacups (the line was officially "dry") brought me to Manila, where in nearby Ft. McKinley my childhood bungalow still stood, the *Askold*'s Russians only a dim memory.

In the spring, the submarine tender *Canopus*, my new home, lumbered northward with her brood of ancient S-boats to Hongkong, Amoy, then Shanghai.

At a Japanese sukiaki restaurant in Shanghai, we chanced to meet two Russian girls dining alone. Charming, witty, worldly—in a few words, wholly fascinating—they showed us Shanghai by day and by night. We saw the cabarets, the clubs, hotels, dog races, jai-alai, the good, the bad, the wicked, and the magnificent—all the beauty and squalor of a tiny island of 50,000 "Europeans" (euphemism for "white") in a great, milling sea of 3,000,000 Chinese. Ten thousand of the "Europeans" were Russians, emigrés swept from their homeland by the Bolshevik Revolution.

"You must come to Peking," said our new friends. "There you will see the real majesty of China. There, also, is baby sister. You will like her. She is eighteen."

White Russian General Horvath, former governor-general of Manchuria, lived in slightly down-at-the-heel splendor in the big, old ex-Austro-Hungarian legation in Peking. There, at a gala affair for local Russians, younger sister, standing on a candle-lit balcony in a flowing, white organdy ball gown, was a ravishing picture of what one might imagine to be the heroine of a Tolstoy romance. What were they *saying* in that gush of jumbled, sibilant jargon? *Bondar's Commercial Russian Grammar* was no help.

In Tsingtao, I advertised in the paper an offer to exchange English lessons for Russian. "Thank God you have come for your replies!" the clerk had said. "Otherwise we should have had to hire a warehouse to contain them."

"Kennot pronounce your fairst nem," said Nina P., the one finally selected. She had tried, but it always turned out to be "Camp," which even she had laughed at. "I weel call you 'Neeka!' " she said. "Eeet ees goot Roshian nem." And to all my Russian friends so I have been ever since.

Unlike Anglo-Saxon debutantes, so many of whom can be bare half way to the waist without exposing their nipples, Nina's bosom was pure Slavic, well up on her chest, pointed and ample. Neither stocky nor leggy, she probably was somewhere between small entrepreneur and peasant in ancestry. This was the traditional rosy-cheeked, well-rounded village beauty that in the old days would have been scooped up by the local petty nobility in the kind of haystack romance that has enriched Russian literature for centuries and the Russian race for millennia.

From late 1931 to mid-1934, submarine squadron, cruiser, and river gunboat duty had showed me most of what was to be experienced on the China station. But the Russian lure was uppermost; younger sister had spent a summer in Tsingtao. Indeed, those Old China Hands in Norfolk had been right.

For many years, Japanese and Chinese language courses had been available in the Navy. In 1931, when Russian was added, I applied. Dated 5 May 1934, the blessed order came, ". . . to duty on shore beyond the seas, acquiring a knowledge of the Russian language."

I was attached to the 4th Regiment, USMC, at Shanghai. "Come back every three months for an exam and to tell us where you've been," said the major. The year was divided between winter in Shanghai, summer on Tsingtao's salubrious beaches, autumn in Harbin. By the end of it, *Bondar's Russian Grammar* was in the trash can, while that "gush of jumbled, sibilant jargon" was no longer a mystery. Indeed, it was this sequence that marked my entry into something a bit beyond mere observational intelligence. My boardinghouse maestro in Tsingtao once had been a soldier of the Czar. An earthy, powerful, mustachioed proletarian, he harbored distinctly Red leanings. In the cool of the evening we sometimes sat in the yard drinking toasts to Stalin and War Commissar Voroshilov as he told me tales of his adventures in the Revolution. With Tsingtao-made vodka at 30 cents a pint, the toasts could be numerous. Then, back in Shanghai at the end of the specified three months, I went aboard the flagship, where over coffee, the chief of staff, Asiatic Fleet, gave me permission to spend the autumn in wholly Japanese-controlled Manchuria. "But leave your gun and camera in Shanghai," he said. "And *don't* write anything down. I won't give you any instructions. If you get into trouble, you are on your own; we can't help you."

Passing through Tsingtao en route, I checked in with old friend landlord. "Here is a ham I'd much appreciate your taking to my cousin in Harbin," he said. I reluctantly made room for the greasy ham in my meager hand baggage. "I might as well tell you," he added, "this ham is your passport. It guarantees my cousin will accept you as wholly OK. I would not like to write him anything. The Japs could well search you."

I was still shaking the snow from my overcoat when there was a tap on the hotel room door in Harbin. The visitor was a small, scruffy-looking Russian. *"Zachem vwi priyehali?"* (For what purpose have you come?) He was an agent of the Japanese gendarmerie, he said. "I have come to study Russian," I replied. "Come in and have a smoke. I'll show you my notebooks." Accepting my bona fides, he settled in a chair. "It will soon be 40 degrees of frost," he said with a grin. "You will need a fur coat. Also, you will want to meet some nice girls. I will help you in these things."

Neither of the kind offers of the agent was accepted, nor did I see him again, but it was a clear indication of Japanese interest and the need for circumspection.

The ham and I were cordially received, a manifestation reinforced over the years of my experience in the very strong ties that bind Russians to friends and family. "I know what you are here for," he said cheerfully, "and I will help you."

The two months passed swiftly and pleasantly. Until heavy snow fell, I played golf with British and American friends, accompanied not only by the usual faultless caddies, but by a trio of heavily armed White Russian bodyguards as a precaution against free-lance kidnappers. There was no mention made to White Russian friends of my Red contact. At the English Club, members were reminded to check their sidearms along with their overcoats at the entrance; in the past there had been some slight contretemps involving random shots after a few too many of those 6-cent gins. For mixed socializing, there were the daughters of the White Russian

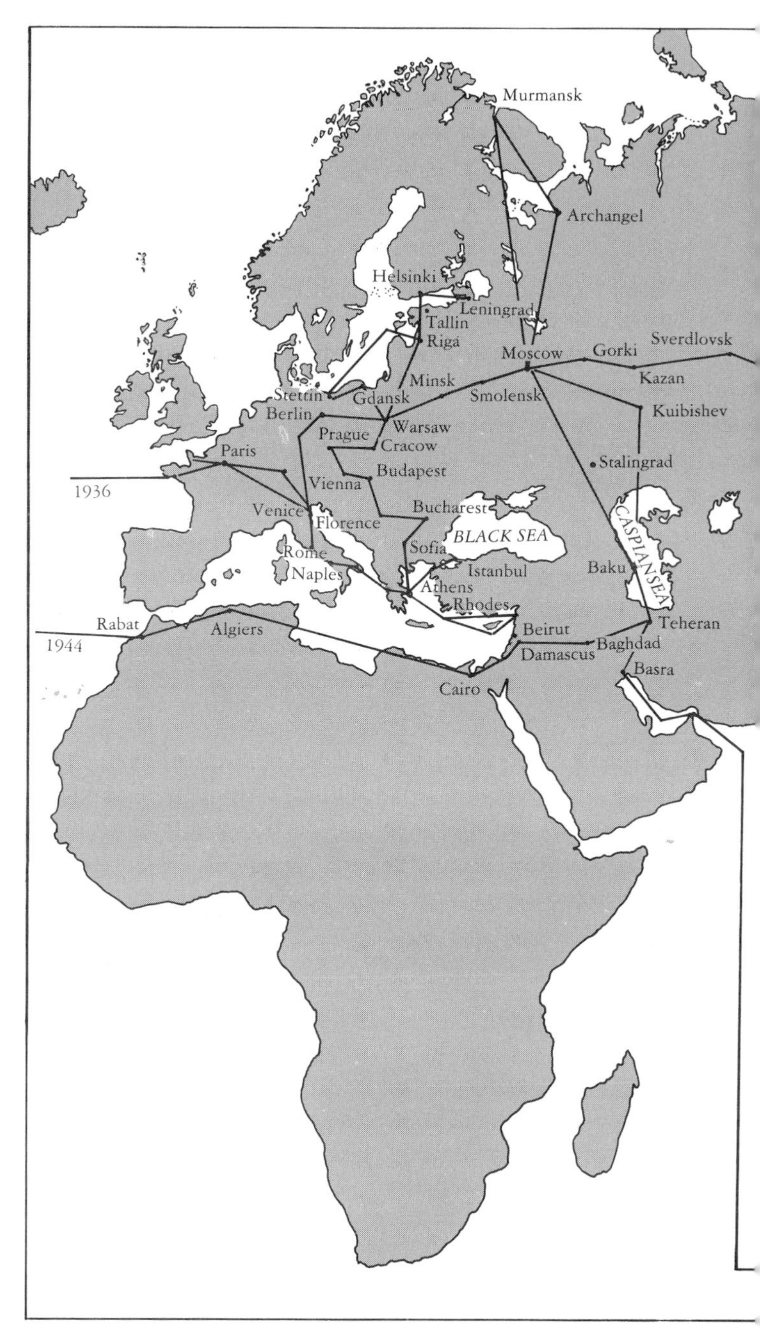

The routes of my many travels through Asia, Russia, and Europe from 1934 to 1944.

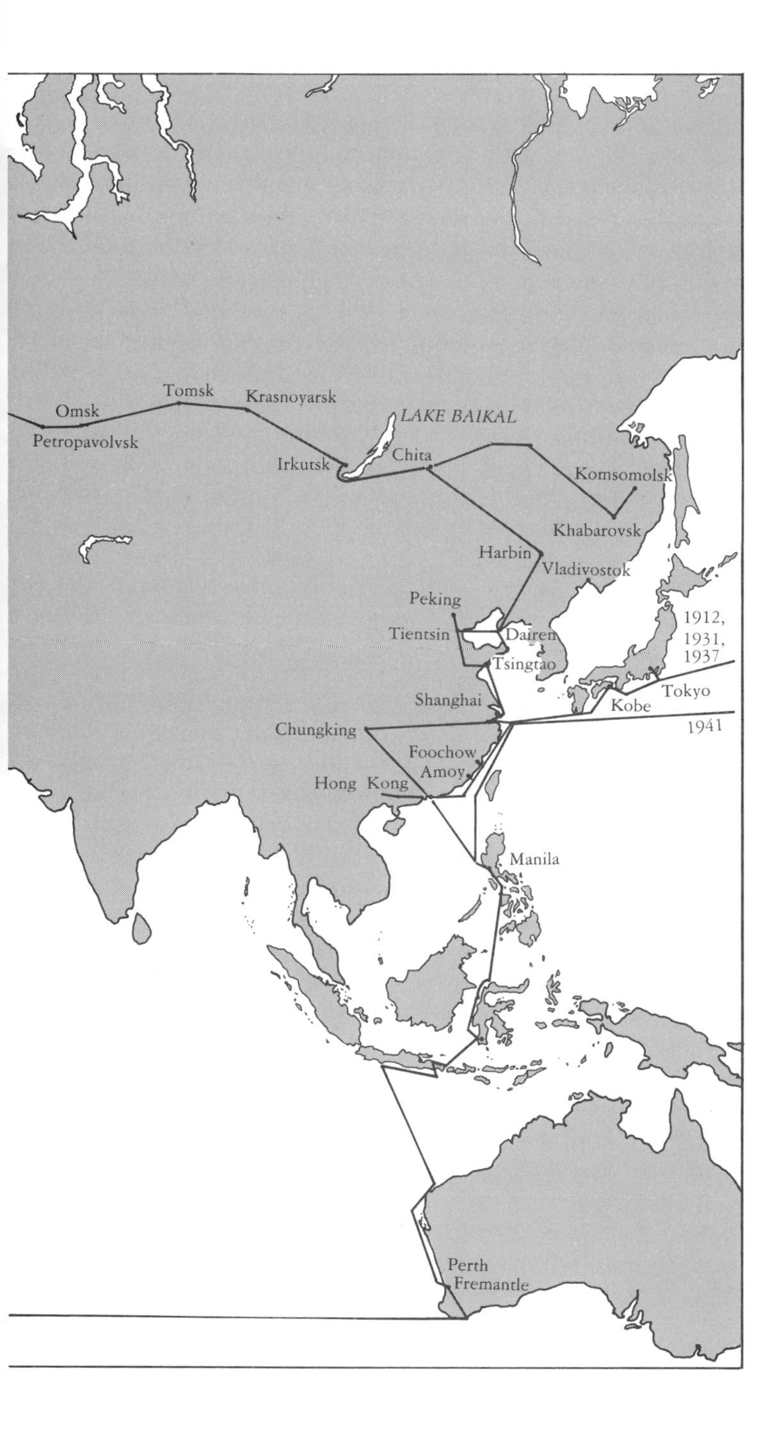

Tomsk
Krasnoyarsk
Omsk
Petropavolvsk
LAKE BAIKAL
Irkutsk
Chita
Komsomolsk
Khabarovsk
Harbin
Vladivostok
Peking
Tientsin
Dairen
Tsingtao
1912,
1931,
1937
Tokyo
Kobe
Shanghai
Chungking
1941
Foochow
Amoy
Hong Kong
Manila
Perth
Fremantle

émigré aristocrats, well educated, devilishly keen, but desperately afraid to be naughty. On the other hand were the gamines of the cabarets, offspring of spikedriving Russians who had pushed the railway through to the sea a generation earlier. Jolly, interesting, pretty, many of them close to illiterate, they somehow managed to survive on a pittance—free dinner plus a Manchurian yuan (8 cents US)—for sitting at the table to provide a dancing partner and light conversation. Some were more than just close friends of the young foreign consuls and businessmen.

Then the great cold arrived; it was time to retreat to Shanghai. My Red Russian friend bade me a fond farewell. "Here are some figures," he said. "Memorize them carefully. They are the Japanese order of battle in Manchuria—men, tanks, guns, aircraft." They looked pretty skimpy to me, I commented. "Never mind," he replied. "And by the way, I've got a ham to send to cousin Ignatius in Tsingtao. I want to show him I can cure a better ham than he can. Tell him it weighs exactly four and a half kilograms." He added with emphasis *not* to forget *that*.

The ham was in due course delivered to Ignatius, including news of its weight. "You have some figures perhaps?" he wanted to know. I recited the figures. "Just multiply that by four and a half," he said. "If the Japs had pushed a burning match or two under your fingernails they wouldn't have got much out of you that made sense."

In the *Hoten Maru*'s steerage, a space about sixty by ninety feet was divided into eight-foot cubicles surrounded by waist-high partitions. In each a family—mostly Russian—parents, gabbling children, sedate grandparents, camped out, lying on spread-out bedrolls on deck, eating, sitting, or leaning over the partitions socializing with neighbors. The air carried a heavy burden of odors—smoked fish, trash tobacco, vomit, urine.

In 1935 the fare to Moscow via ship to Dairen, Manchuria, thence rail, was $235. What better way to test my White vernacular on the Reds, get to Europe in half the time and a third of the price of a ship via Suez? The rickshaw coolie shifted from one burning sole to another as the hot asphalt gave beneath his bare feet, waiting at an intersection for the Sikh policeman's wave through. A few blocks away the sickle and hammer waved lazily in the blue July sky over the Soviet consulate general, incongruously sharing the scene with the Nazi's crooked cross over their consulate general next door. I was en route to pick up the visa that had cost some thirty dollars in telegraph fees, when visas worldwide for special military passports were free and given instantly on the asking. It was a portent of the shape of things to come wherever Soviet communist bureaucracy was involved. Indeed, it was a second frustration on my part vis-à-vis that same consulate. Some time before I had called their commercial section to inquire where in Shanghai one might buy Narzan, a natural Russian mineral water superior to Vichy. "*Chort vozmi!* (The devil take it!) What do you think this is? A liquor store? This is the Soviet consulate general!" And bang went the receiver.

Again I found myself aboard one of the three fast little passenger-freighters of DKK, Dairen Kisen Kaisha, that sailed from Shanghai to Tsingtao to Dairen, a fast milk run made in fog, typhoon, or balmy blue at the ship's maximum speed. Groundings and collisions were commonplace. We sat in the saloon after dinner chatting, playing dominoes, or watching magic tricks performed by one of the British passengers. Then a Japanese ship's officer came in. Clearly a little the worse for wear, he joined the beer drinkers, his conversation progressively more incoherent. Then he unsteadily rose. "Gooby! I go on watch now!" he said, and tottered off.

Demonstrating the extraordinary range of the Far East Russian, one of the passengers was a Russian-speaking young lady of Baghdad-Jewish extraction who had silky black hair tied in a tight knot, a long, delicate neck, a fine nose, olive skin with high coloring, and green eyes—altogether such a striking resemblance to ancient Egypt's Queen Nefertiti that it was a pleasure just to look at her. Later, on the train to Harbin, she came into my compartment. Like many things Japanese, their railways early recognized women's lib at least physically, in that both sexes shared toilets and train compartments. Nefertiti's compartment mate was a Chinese general, she said agitatedly. He had had his bunk made up, had peeled down to his underwear, and was heavily nipping out of a bottle of what smelled like *maotai*, a 120-proof blood relative of varnish remover.

"For God's sake, get me a swap with your roommate," she said earnestly, indicating the innocuous brown gentleman in long gown perched apprehensively on the edge of his seat, taking it all in. The trade was accomplished neatly and with dispatch; one learned early the British way of dealing with the "natives," an air of casual superiority so clear that a baring of fangs is rarely necessary.

I went into the corridor while Nefertiti readied herself for bed. Then it was my turn while she stood outside in her dressing gown. After that, there was the muffled, lulling clickety-clack of the wheels, an occasional shriek of the locomotive whistle far up ahead, and a blink of light in the darkened coupe when the train thundered by some village platform. This was a sort of space capsule. The real world soon drew very far away.

Leaving Harbin for Moscow in those days could be compared to Columbus departing Spain for the unknown. Harbin was a safe, known haven where a young man's heart could be tugged many ways. The Soviet Union was *terra incognita* for almost the entire world, and certainly for the majority of the 50,000 Russians of Harbin, most of whom had never set foot in their motherland. The Soviet Russians who had run the Chinese

Eastern Railway across Manchuria had been an isolated group, keeping largely to themselves and their club until the railway was sold to Japan in 1934. Then they left for the uncertain fate awaiting Russians who had been abroad, generally Siberia or the firing squad. There were Red-inclined Russians in Harbin too, such as the helpful ham fancier. But they kept a low profile.

Many of my friends were at the railway station to see me off, a custom I found universal in the USSR. They were there to reinforce me with items not yet common, they said, in the Worker's Paradise, such as toilet paper, decent soap, flea powder, and a universal bathtub plug, plus canned goods to supplement the "vagon restauran's" greasy borshch and black bread.

The Japanese had just taken over the last vestige of Soviet railway in Manchuria, from Harbin to Manchouli. The new owners had not yet had time to manifest their typical Japanese solicitude for passengers by furnishing sleeping kimonos, workable toilets, hot water, or windows clean enough to allow a glimpse of the passing scene. These minor deficiencies were in part compensated for in my car by the presence of a rather comely young lady, who if found aboard a present day airliner would be known as a stewardess. At that stage of the Manchurian Railway game, today's rigid job classification in this area had yet to be worked out. As a "Radiska," (radish) red outside, probably white inside, the young lady had been included in the inventory passed on by the Soviets.

It was insufferably stuffy in the little windowless cubicle she inhabited at the end of the car, she said. Could she join me in my relatively airy coupe? She brought tea, washed the outside of the window at the next stop, tidied up the lavabo adjoining the coupe, and dredged up a fairly clean towel. Then she unwound the cloth from around her hair and mopped her face and neck.

"Teplo! Mojhno?" ("It is warm! May I?") And without awaiting a reply she began to take off her clothes. My year of "instruction in the Russian language" had ended, and my trip halfway around the globe had commenced.

Outer space began at Manchouli/Otpor. Soviet customs officials spent three hours meticulously shaking down the luggage of the dozen-odd foreigners. My toilet paper was inspected sheet by sheet. A Britisher's twenty-five phonograph records were played end to end. No clandestine messages were turned up on either, so we were allowed to board the Wagon-lits coach, a relic or replica recalling French commercial enterprise in Imperial Russia.

My roommate was a caricature of a German as represented in World War I horror propaganda posters, with heavy wrinkles in the back of a neck so thick that his collar possibly could have been slipped unbuttoned over his head. Unlike most Germans I had known in China, he was less than congenial, having immediately deduced that I was a Soviet agent put in his coupe to worm out secrets, as I learned later from a mutual train acquaintance.

The *vagon restauran*'s reputation for grease fully justified the forebodings of my Harbin friends. The beer was even worse, a cloudy, orange-colored liquid smelling strongly of hops. Meals were prepaid in Shanghai, but liquor cost roubles at the wholly ridiculous rate of 1 rouble = $1, with a real exchange value of about 75 to 1.

Those who have seen the film *Doctor Zhivago* got a good representation of the Siberian landscape—a sea of waving wild flowers in summer, barren, windswept, endless rolling prairies or gloomy *taiga* (forest) in winter, with the double tracks of the Trans-Sib merging into a thin black pencil line on the distant horizon.* Like islands in an endless sea, small towns strung themselves along the tracks at intervals of twenty or thirty miles, tiny-windowed log huts scattered at random. There the train stopped fifteen or so minutes while passengers in the "hard" cars scrambled out with their pots to the tap that supplied free boiling water, "*kipyaitok*," for that essential component of Russian life, tea drinking. Peasants on the platform offered pitiful little items in exchange for bread: cups of forest berries, a single hard-boiled egg, bits of cooked chicken. The choice was so unappealing that my own little stock of trade goods: needles, thread, cheap scissors, and buttons went untouched.

Russian gregariousness on trains was at full flower in the dining car, crowded with military men spending their kopeks for the abominable beer and insisting that I accept their hospitality or grievously offend them. All were initially interested in an American, taking as a matter of course that I could communicate in their language. One or two even volunteered the information that they were grateful for the American famine relief after World War I, which had saved thousands of lives. "Ah yes! Indeed that's a fact!" chorused several others, anxious to show their appreciation and a knowledge of what was what, even though they might never have heard of it. Mostly apolitical peasants joyfully going home to shuck their baggy uniforms at the end of military call-up, they were more interested in telling about their villages, proudly exhibiting family pictures and talking about the future—fishing in the pond, strolling on Sunday with Katya in the forest to pick mushrooms, helping with the pigs and chickens—than they were in enlightening themselves on overseas affairs in a world beyond their ken.

*Filmed partly in Spain, partly in Finland. The masses of "wild flowers," in the movie were daffodils, a flower that does not exist in Russia.

The Trans-Siberian skirts all the principal cities en route by five to ten miles, so Moscow was the first glimpse of anything other than primitive countryside. Arriving there rolling like a sailor after eight days aboard a train, half sick from green beer and greasy food, my first impression was one of all-pervading drabness. Women innocent of makeup, monochrome clothing, no colorful advertising, all produced a black-white-and-gray image like a 1925 movie.*

American embassy secretaries, as isolated from friendly contact with the people as the lepers of Molokai, were happy to see a stranger from outside the boring closeness of the tiny diplomatic colony. Secretaries' wives took me shopping to the peasants' market, a vast open-air array of little stalls with gorgeous vegetables, to the meat market, where cuts were wholly unidentifiable in pools of blood, and to picnic at the embassy country *dacha*, or summer cottage. Tourists were rare in that pre-airline era, so as I was escorted by a young lady from Intourist, I was an object of considerable interest in the Park of Culture and Rest, attending a court in session, and at the bureau where Russians signed the book to become man and wife—little dreaming that seven years hence I would be standing there myself, depositing fifteen roubles. ("A divorce will cost you fifty," the cheerful damsel behind the desk had added.)

Hearing I had come from China, Ambassador Bullitt invited me to "tea" to learn the latest news. (In those days of sparse international telegraphic reporting, one often saw at the beginning of news items, "A traveler reports. . . .") Spasso House, the embassy residence, once the mansion of an opulent sugar baron, gave one the impression of entering an opera house, with its marble columns, huge crystal chandelier, and vaulted ceilings. "Chiang Kai-shek will be forced to make some sort of deal with the Communists," I observed over the second or third martini. "Oh, *nobody* believes *that*!" countered Bullitt, and shortly after this the interview came to an end, my image as a seer undoubtedly tarnished. Five months later, when Chiang was captured at Sian by Chang Hsueh-liang and forthwith made a deal with the Communists, I wondered if the ambassador remembered. As to Spasso House itself, I was not so prescient, not remotely imagining that this magnificent pile, with its seven-foot marble bathtubs, oval music room, fifty-place dining hall with huge fireplace, and mahogany-walled billiard room would one day be my wartime home for a year.

As for Bullitt, his roseate expectations of 1918 had become a cautious optimism by recognition, which quickly soured to frustration. Coached by

*By 1981 the scene had flipped; Muscovites were in colorful clothing, much of it from the satellites, or "puppets" as some Russians call them, while Americans paraded in sloppy jeans.

master Sovietologist George Kennan, Bullitt began sending dispatches to the State Department lifted in toto from the pages of State's archives of the nineteenth century, fitting the situation so letter perfect that only names had to be changed. By 1952, Bullitt's glass was wholly clear. In a conversation with veteran "communistologist" Karl Baarslag, he told him that, "The great tragedy of the West is that its leaders are simply congenitally and psychologically incapable of grasping or even dimly understanding the nature of our enemy openly bent on our destruction. Don't get me wrong that they are dim-witted or lack intelligence. They are all fine Christian, patriotic men, but I repeat they are hopelessly incapable of understanding the cold horror of Communism."*

The intimate story of the Americans' adventures in Red Never-Never land was told to me by embassy secretary Bert Kuniholm during the long summer twilight that lasts until near midnight, as we sat on his *dacha* porch overlooking the rolling, open countryside outside Moscow. In his terse, no-nonsense manner, a legacy of his West Point days, his story was one of high hopes and frequent frustrations.

After Roosevelt took office in 1932, he very soon commenced negotiations with Foreign Minister of the USSR Maxim Litvinov on recognition. War debts were a stumbling block. "But what about the enormous damage the American interventionist troops did?" Litvinov countered.

The conversation wandered on. Then the president mildly inquired what Litvinov felt was the value of Siberia east of Lake Baikal. Litvinov replied it was impossible to estimate off the cuff, but certainly in the billions. With a pixyish grin, Roosevelt drew from his pocket a scrap of paper signed by Tchicherin, Commissar for Foreign Affairs of the USSR, immediately post-Revolution. It was dated shortly after the Japanese, under heavy American pressure, quit Siberia in 1922. In effect, the memo said that the Soviet Union was indebted to the United States in that eastern Siberia was not Japanese. He handed Litvinov the note. "There, sir, is your receipt for Siberia. Now how many *billions* did you say it was worth?"

"You are a better Jew than I am, Mr. President!" chuckled Litvinov, whose real name was Meier Moisevich Wallach. "Let us say that all claims on both sides are settled."

In 1919, the wealthy, starry-eyed, liberal young graduate of Yale (1912) and of Harvard Law School, William C. Bullitt, was sent by the State Department to the fledgling Soviet Union for a look-see. His enthusiasm for the great new experiment and his recommendation to President Wilson that we adopt a friendly attitude toward the Bolshevik regime got nowhere. Soon the two countries not only turned away from each other, but

*Karl Baarslag, in the *Manchester Union Leader*, Manchester, N.H., August 29, 1979.

inward on themselves. America became isolationist and Russia found herself in as deep a quarantine as any household with the smallpox.

But now, with recognition, perhaps things would be different. Still somewhat starry-eyed, Bill Bullitt sailed from New York on 15 February 1934, with enthusiastic high hopes, as first American ambassador to the USSR. Among those in his suite were Captain David Nimmer, USMC, six Marine enlisted men and two U. S. sailors, one a pharmacist's mate, the other an electrician's mate. The Marines were to be embassy drivers, messengers, guards, and handy men. The pharmacist's mate was standing by to dole out aspirins and sundry simple remedies to the diplomats in darkest Russia. The electrician's mate was brought along to ensure expert maintenance on the embassy's American refrigerators, electric irons, and other such exotic equipment. More importantly, the electrician's mate carried a little black box designed to sniff out electronically any microphones buried in the ambassadorial plaster.

As for Nimmer, he was the first formal U. S. naval representative to set foot in Russia since Rear Admiral Newton A. McCully, Commander Naval Forces, Black Sea, quit that revolution-, famine-, and cholera-infested area in 1919.

In 1931 Nimmer was serving in the cruiser *Pittsburgh*, where the charm of the White Russians in the ship's Far East bailiwick beguiled him to the point of his requesting and getting duty as a Russian language student in Harbin, Manchuria. So when Recognition came in 1934, Nimmer was the first and only formal Russian language expert in the U.S. Navy or Marine Corps and was ready for Moscow.

Whether Moscow was ready for Nimmer is something else. The honeymoon period of USA-USSR relations was short. Bullitt's 1919 contacts were all either dead, in exile, or in Siberia. Oriental style doubletalk soon made it clear that the promises given Roosevelt by Litvinov would not be matched by deeds. It was a sad disappointment to find that the eager American salesmen who flocked to Moscow found themselves and their wares up dead ends; the Soviets had their own buying agencies abroad. Commissar for Foreign Trade Rosengoltz either made belittling remarks to Bullitt at diplomatic functions or pointedly ignored him. In a reflection of his pique, Bullitt telegraphed the State Department that, "Extraordinary numbers of Jews are employed in all the Commissariats." (Rosengoltz, of course, was a Jew.) "Only one out of each 61 inhabitants of the Soviet Union is a Jew; but twenty of the sixty-one Commissars and Vice-Commissars are Jews."*

Bullitt's and Roosevelt's disenchantment soon reached such a point

***USSR-USA Relations*, 1933–1939, Department of State, vol. 1, page 294.

that it was decided that what the Soviets needed was a stiff jolt. So, on 6 February 1935 the State Department announced the withdrawal of our naval and military attachés and that the consulate general would be abolished.

The Soviets were no more upset by these moves than was Br'er Rabbit when Br'er B'ar tossed him into the briar patch. Loy Henderson, outstanding Soviet expert and diplomat, remarked later that it should be considered as axiomatic that the ruling forces of the Soviet Union have always considered and still take the view that the presence of foreign diplomatic representatives in the Soviet Union is an evil which world conditions force them to endure.

To ensure that the full import of this U. S. blockbuster was sufficiently appreciated, a farewell audience for Nimmer and his U.S. Army Air Force opposite number, Lieutenant Thomas White (later Chief of Staff, U. S. Air Force), was requested with Czarist ex-cavalry sergeant Defense Commissar Klimentiy Voroshilov. Nimmer poured out his tale of frustration in his attempts to make normal contacts with Soviet citizens or officials. He also carried a verbal message from Roosevelt over the debt stalling.*

Such an audience with Stalin's right-hand man and favorite drinking companion was a notable event when one considers Nimmer's modest rank. Voroshilov's frank and unconcealed surprise at Nimmer's complaints was either magnificent acting or something of a revelation, the latter possibility suggesting that the defense commissar was operating at an altitude where layers of thoroughly frightened bureaucratic underlings would keep him insulated from the doings of Moscow-based Marine Corps captains.

Voroshilov professed to be very sorry that Nimmer felt he had been short-circuited, and stated that under the circumstances, the withdrawal of Soviet attachés in Washington seemed appropriate.

Perhaps Nimmer was known to Voroshilov, through an equally close chum and also a confidant of Stalin: hard-drinking, hard-riding ex-Czarist sergeant, Marshal Simeon Budenny, famous for his six-inch mustachios. At a very large official banquet, Mrs. Nimmer, on Budenny's left, who in turn was on Ambassador Bullitt's left, was using her Harbin-acquired Russian to translate. After many toasts and three or four hours at the table, everybody's syntax understandably became a bit confused and vague. "I am going home on a small vacation," Mrs. Nimmer told Budenny. "Only I hope that the same thing doesn't happen that took place when I went home on vacation from Harbin. When I returned, I found my husband living next door to the most beautiful Russian girl in town. Only instead of saying "next door to,"

*Personal letter from Major General Nimmer to the author.

she said, "*next* to." Immediately Budenny's mustache bristled and he said, "Your husband must be a villain to do such a thing to a young, charming lady as you. Show me the wretch!" Mrs. Nimmer wrote that by then she was quite beyond making any explanation in Russian, merely pointing out David, at about which time the signal came for the ladies to withdraw.

"Before that," Mrs. Nimmer wrote, "I had been told that Budenny had strangled his first wife . . . and married an opera star from the Bolshoi."*

The withdrawal of Nimmer and the six enlisted Marines suited the State Department and the U. S. Navy as much as it did the Soviets. The Office of Naval Intelligence, on a tight budget and getting no information out of Moscow, was glad to use the money elsewhere. State and Navy had been squabbling over the enlisted Marines' tab, and both agreed that Nimmer had about as much chance of making any normal personal contacts as he had of shaking hands with Lenin's corpse in its marble mausoleum over on Red Square.

As for the pharmacist's mate and the electrician's mate, the embassy judged them to be essential members of the Moscow team, even to the agonizing extent of picking up the tab for their pay.

In February 1935 Nimmer departed. He would not be replaced until 28 July 1941, when Lieutenant Commander Ronald H. Allen, USNR, was cleared by the Soviets as assistant naval attaché—portentously a mere six days after Nazi bombs had started to rain down on the USSR, soon to be a de facto ally of the USA through the agency of Lend-Lease.

If Nimmer had not created much of a splash in Moscow, the same could scarcely be said for his opposite number who turned up in Washington, a former czarist warrant officer named Paul Yurevich Oras. Along with his assistant, Oras appeared at ONI, rushing up to the Marine sergeant-major who in full dress blue regimentals guarded the portals. "I am so hoppy to see you, Keptin!" cried Oras, all but embracing the startled Marine. The latter politely disengaged himself, explaining that the director was inside. Introductions were made all around and coffee produced. The Soviets were wearing a monastic, high-collared uniform something like that of the World War I U. S. Navy.

"I see you are wearing no rank insignia, sir." said the director. "May I ask what is your rank?" Oras exchanged a few words in Russian with his assistant. "What is the usual rank for naval attachés here?" said Oras. The director explained that it usually was captain for major powers, commander for lesser. Oras digested this over a few moments. Then he looked up. "I am a vice admiral!" he said brightly. "My assistant here is a rear admiral." This

*In a personal letter from Mrs. Nimmer to the author in December 1975.

made Oras senior to every U. S. naval officer in Washington with the exception of the Chief of Naval Operations. Far too sticky a wicket for the Navy to handle, the problem was turned over to State. "Rank means absolutely *nothing* to us!" declared the new Soviet Ambassador Troyanovsky, without the flicker of an eyebrow. But Oras could not be demoted to four stripes without insufferable loss of face since the foreign attaché corps had just tendered him a dinner and by virtue of his exalted rank proclaimed him dean of the corps. So he was eased back to rear admiral, to rank with, but below, all U. S. rear admirals. The assistant was reduced to commander. On the diplomatic list, both appeared as just plain "mister."

The following year, Oras was guest on a Potomac yachting cruise. "Hey! Where the hell did that Rooskie get to?" somebody wanted to know. He had quietly disappeared. Overboard? A search turned him up in the engine room, exhorting the bemused black gang on the glories of a classless society. Shortly thereafter, in August 1935, he was on his way home. The following month officer ranks were established in the USSR, so that Oras's assistant, Alexander M. Yakimichev, who had remained, became a captain second rank, four stripes. So passed the minor storm.

"A strange, paradoxical people," mused Bert Kuniholm, after we all had had a good laugh at the Oras episode. "It's a sort of love-hate relationship. We love the people and hate the rulers." Looking out over the beautiful, rolling countryside below us—open fields, copses of trees, a small, winding stream, it could have been Maryland.

The drabness of Moscow, the wretched food, even worse beer, were strong inducements to hurry on. After five days of soaking up all the information possible and grateful for the hospitality of the embassy, I headed for Warsaw. The final annoyance was being forced to hire a porter to carry my suitcases from the Soviet to the Polish train at the border, at the rouble equivalent of five U. S. dollars each.

The language of Warsaw *sounded* something like Russian, but was enough out of focus to be unintelligible, a lispy, hissing delivery suggesting a Muscovite who had lost suction on his upper plate. But it was a colorful, gay, vital comparison to dull, forbidding, gray Moscow. Houses were in blue, pink, gray, and other pastels, in good repair, grass cut, flowers blooming—indications of pride in ownership lacking in the communist paradise.

The U. S. military attaché, Colonel Gilmor, took a strong fancy to my detailed report of the Trans-Siberian, written with an expertise grounded in many happy childhood summer days on the railroad that ran through our country village, keeping the trackwalker company on his otherwise lonely grounds.

"We have no naval attaché in Poland," lamented Colonel Gilmore, whose extremely pretty eighteen-year-old daughter would certainly have provided any bachelor an inducement to sign on. "Come back if you can," he said, as he put me on the train at the end of a very pleasant week for a "cruise" that would include Prague, Budapest, Vienna, Bucharest, Sofia, Athens, Istanbul, Beirut, Damascus, Rhodes, Naples, Rome, Florence, and Venice.

I was being introduced to a new area for me in naval intelligence, which would include some "firsts" and some revelations. There would be a minor "loss" and some minor "pluses." Was this a more sophisticated intelligence arena than the Far East? Not really. Simply a different accent, a different milieu.

The one "loss" was peripheral. In our *wagon-lits* from Moscow to Warsaw had been four of those rare birds in the USSR in those days, independent sightseers: a charming, aristocratic papa and mama, with two equally charming, sophisticated young ladies burnishing their education with exotic travel. We agreed we would renew our friendship in Prague and Vienna under more romantic circumstances. The pursuit was interrupted by a small contretemps, through my having ignored the basic aphorism that a fool and his baggage are soon parted. I had got off the train for some fresh air at the Polish border town while the international train was being put together for the trip across a mile-wide strip of plowed ground and barbed wire to Czechoslovakia. (The Poles and Czechs were not speaking.) To my horror, without a warning tootle, the train, my car attached, my two suitcases aboard, started and picked up speed into the unknown, leaving me on the platform. Half a day later I made it across to Czechland, the only passenger on a local train—several four-wheeled caricatures of people-cars. At the tiny border station, the baggage hunt began. Obviously, it would have been taken off the express by the Czech customs. Nobody spoke English. *Or* Russian. *Or* French. Fifty miles away, at the other end of a telephone line, the stationmaster had a friend who spoke bad Russian. By this tortuous exchange we finally managed a meeting of minds. A great light burst on the stationmaster's face. "Ah! Ba*gash*! Ba*gash*!" he triumphantly shouted. And there, sure enough, behind the door of the room in which we had been struggling to communicate for an hour stood my two suitcases. Once more the chase was on.

This was independent duty as its very best, headed where, when, and how fancy took me. It was only months later that I learned the full story behind the U. S. Navy couriers working out of Paris, whose peregrinations matched my own. But by instinct perhaps I fell into the thought process that was in part the couriers' *raison d'etre. And that was an evaluation of our own people!* In effect, internal espionage. It was amply clear that our attachés were subjected to pressures to which they were neither accustomed nor trained to weather. In western Europe, they were constantly associated with clever, sophisticated contacts who turned them on. In xenophobic Russia and (in those bad old days) Turkey, churlish and confining tactics turned them off. By knowing the prejudices, pro, con or neutral, of the various attachés through the couriers' on-the-spot conversations at overnight stops, attaché reports could be accurately evaluated as to direction and degree of slant. Thus, along with carrying the secret mail locked to their wrists, plus personally gathering such intelligence as their constant travels all over Europe afforded, the couriers, lieutenants, were in effect spies on American officers, mostly far senior, for the benefit of their superiors at Paris, hub of the naval intelligence effort in Europe.

It was in Vienna that I finally gave up pursuit of those fair damsels of the Moscow-Warsaw express. The trail had blown warm, then cool, but never hot.

Balkan trains were wretched, said Colonel Chase, U. S. military attaché at Vienna, reflecting the views of any good Austrian regarding those scruffy neighbors of the once-great empire. I would find my seatmates to be anything from goats or crates of chickens to unbathed characters reeking of garlic and trash tobacco. By all means go via air. So, as one of two passengers in a German Lufthansa plane that would have seated 30, I commenced my first-ever commercial flight, aboard a tri-motored Fokker sheathed with corrugated metal resembling the stuff on our barn roof in Maryland.

Perhaps the goats would have been better; my lone companion was a beefy, florid German who immediately broached a wicker hamper of sausages, salad, beer, and cheese which he attacked with gusto, vociferously insisting that I share the goodies. His enthusiasm soon waned as the plane bucked and rolled at low altitude. This was his first plane ride, he gasped between upchucks, and would certainly be his last.

Next stops were Belgrade, Bucharest, and Sofia. Balkan Slavic food not much less greasy than Russian soon had me back aboard another drafty Lufthansa plane headed for Athens. We let down at Saloniki for fuel, where the thought struck me to climb off this rattletrap and go into town to check on a friend, Consul General George Hanson, whom I had met in Manchuria. He had won a warm spot in my estimation by having given most favorable comments on my Manchurian intelligence reports when he had popped in at ONI on a Washington trip years before. Perhaps he would be glad to see an Old China Hand. The tales I had picked up from Bert Kuniholm in Moscow suggested George could stand some cheering up after a more than severe shafting by the State Department.

Hanson was a huge bear of a man, well over six feet, admiringly described by Japanese friends as a "strrrong drinkah," able to put any possible diplomatic opponent under the table even if he had to knock back a fifth of scotch himself. Graduate of Cornell, 1908, the year I was born, he had become a Chinese language officer in the then Consular Service, rising from vice consul to the top, in various Chinese cities from 1909 to 1921. From then until 1934 he spent an unprecedented 13 years at Harbin, an all-Russian city of some 50,000 White Russian émigrés plus several thousand Red Russian employees of the Chinese Eastern Railway, eastern end of the Trans-Siberian that stretched across Manchuria's middle. When the USA recognized the USSR in 1934, Hanson was the logical choice for consul general at Moscow, having become adept in the ways and language of the Russians. A year after recognition, the Great Freeze and disillusionment set in between the two new "friends." Hanson, meanwhile, had made a trip to New York, where he gave a rousing speech to a group of businessmen, laying on the line in his characteristically straight talk the perfidy of the communists. The consulate general was abolished. Nevertheless, the State Department clucked agitatedly at Hanson's forthrightness, deciding he must be punished. So in February 1935 he was ordered to the well-insulated isolation of Addis Ababa. But, oh my God! How the plot backfired! Mussolini attacked Ethiopia before Hanson ever got there. Overnight, it became the very centerpiece of action in the world's headlines. Hanson must not pick this beautiful, ripe plum! So his orders were immediately changed to Saloniki, Greece, normally a consul's post and a junior one at that.

On telephoning the consulate, they said not to come in; Hanson was too ill to be seen. Later, at the U. S. legation in Athens, the nature of his "illness" was clarified: an overdose of sleeping pills. Hanson managed to complete the job aboard ship on 2 September 1935 while on the way to New York. In a short eighteen months, a unique, though perhaps a bit too outspoken, expert in a field where experts were few, had fallen from the pinnacle to a sad end. China had been Hanson's life. The understanding and appreciation of the importance of "face" had become as ingrained in his way of existence as with any top mandarin or wretched coolie. In China, the emperor did not dirty his hands by directing the execution of an erring subordinate; he merely took action that left the accused no recourse except "eat opium." In Japan it is called "seppuku." ("Cut stomach.") But the mentality behind it is all the same.

The Mediterranean sweep that followed Greece diverges so widely from the Russian theme that it must be treated in some other vehicle. It should suffice to summarize it by saying I came out of it somewhat poorer in funds but far richer in experience. Via ship and railway it at last brought me to Venice. There, a young American vice consul taking leave joined me in hiring a tiny Fiat, which we drove up through Switzerland and the Black Forest. There, my black shirt (to ease laundering problems) and Italian license plates brought friendly greetings of, "Heil Duce!" with comments on how well an Italian spoke English. My companion furthered the mild deception through her fluent command not only of Italian, but French and German as well.

At the Paris American Express, a steamship ticket to Baltimore was waiting, and also a note from the Office of Naval Intelligence. Forget the ticket, ONI said in effect, and check in next week for a letter of further instructions.

In a week we were back from a glorious investigation of the Loire valley's chateaux, wine-tasting pavilions every few kilometers and country inns where guests were handed a cake of soap and a towel and shown the path to the river bank for a pre-dinner bath. At the American Express, a letter from ONI was waiting:

"Proceed to Berlin, Germany, and report for duty to the U. S. Naval Attaché, for assignment on shore beyond the seas . . ." again for a "study of the Russian language." The locale would be Riga, Latvia.

The Fiat, companion, and I parted company in Venice, whence I headed north, once more on the old, familiar rails. German efficiency was immediately apparent. There were no twenty-minute stops for tea water. Passengers could buy red, yellow, or green tickets, which when announced by color, meant the holder should go to the dining car for a hearty *table d'hôte* dinner plopped down from serving dishes by beefy frauleins onto already set plates. When the gong sounded in twenty minutes, it was time for the next color. Pick your teeth elsewhere.

Captain Benjamin Dutton, naval attaché in Berlin, was wholly amenable to my proposal to take a long detour via Warsaw, then double back to Stettin to take the steamer to Riga. Perhaps something useful could be picked up; the Polish Navy was a grab bag of ex-German, French, and British-built ships in a day when our allies-to-be were not too free in allowing us to inspect their men-of-war closely. Furthermore, sandwiched between two ancient enemies, Germany and Russia, the Poles were likely to have some good information on both.

Before departure for Warsaw and Riga, there was ample time in Berlin to augment my meager traveling wardrobe with a new suit and overcoat cut on the proper Prussian square-shouldered style and to wet my feet in the autumn social whirl of the diplomatic colony. Martha Dodd, the ambassador's flamboyant daughter, had a number of handsome young blond Aryan contacts, some of them high up in the Nazi government, who had been inducted into the American attaché cocktail circuit.* They seemed genuinely compassionate on hearing of my impending eastward odyssey, in which they termed the Polish border, "the flea frontier." "They will afflict you the moment you start hearing that mushy mouthing they call 'Polish,' " my young "von this" and "von that" new acquaintances assured me. "Especially along the belt line; [the fleas] have to brace themselves against it to get a good bite. The only way to catch them is in bed with a cake of wet soap, to which they stick, unable to leap." Armed with this knowledge and a cake of soap, I soon found their predictions all too true as far as the small beasties were concerned, but the efficacy of the soap routine open to question. Even unto Riga the fleas were still aboard.

At Warsaw, Miss Gilmor was her charming self, *père* the Colonel most cooperative in arranging my week's stay at the Gdynia Naval Base. The Poles were hospitable to a fault, going to such extremes of thoughtfulness as speaking only Russian or French among themselves when in my presence. They described in detail the German experiments with homing torpedoes and Russian parachute mine drops†, furnished confidential Baltic charts, and led me on thorough inspections of any ships I cared to see.

From the Grimm's fairy tale port of Stettin (now Polish Szczecin) to Riga was a three-day gustatory bout with five large meals a day plus midnight snack aboard a small, very *gemütlich* German steamer, the passengers mostly German Balts getting in the last "heil Hitlers" aboard this splinter of the Fatherland before feeling the chill of chauvinistic White Proletarian Latvia.

Arriving at Riga stuffed like a Strasbourg goose after three days of "sea duty," *schnapps und wurst*, I was taken in hand by an earlier-arrived language student, Lieutenant Carroll Hervy Taecker, whose Naval Academy nickname of "Caesar Hannibal" still stuck. He soon had me established in a Russian household, distinguishable as such the instant one set foot inside by an atmosphere heavy-laden with the mixed aroma of boiled cabbage, old boots, and fried meat on a background of wood smoke.

Lying on a lumpy bed that first night, listening to an occasional droshky rumble by on the cobblestone street, the thought struck me: *what* the *hell* am *I* doing in this backwash of a tribal society? *Why Riga?*

In the autumn of 1934, the big three-masted Polish training ship *DAR POMORZA* visited Shanghai. Without a by-your-leave from anybody, fellow Russian student Marine Lieutenant August Larsen and I

*See *Through Embassy Eyes*, Martha Dodd, printed in Taiwan.

†Sad to relate, it took World War II to convince the Bureaus of Ordnance and Aeronautics that my report was not based on lox and vodka.

Lieutenant (jg) Tolley, "language student" in Baltic area, 1935–36.

climbed into our seldom-worn uniforms, strapped on our swords, and called aboard. We were so warmly received by the universally Russian-speaking officers that several days later, after having recovered from the effects of the hospitality, I wrote the Navy Department suggesting that the Russian course be moved to Warsaw. Whether or not the arrow struck home, I cannot say. But I became the last student to be posted to China, the new locale not Warsaw, but Riga, Latvia.

The Baltic states, Estonia, Latvia, and Lithuania, with a total population of less than that of New York City, harbored a small number of White Russians who were there or had fled the USSR when these vest-pocket countries gained their independence through the German-dictated Treaty of Brest-Litovsk.

Riga was a more effective listening post for Soviet affairs than Moscow itself, where foreigners were segregated in a quarantine that heavily restricted travel or any association with the Russian people. It would have been useless to send language students there even in the unlikely event the Soviets would have permitted it. U.S. naval and army air attachés had left in disgust in 1935, not to be replaced until World War II.

Riga could thus furnish the American language students an opportunity to live in a genteel, if threadbare, Russian household, with its appropriate atmosphere of borshch, vodka, and Saturday night baths when the "kolonka" that heated the water was fired up. There might even be a mild flirtation with the landlord's highly nubile daughter, to whom an American, *any* American, was a way out.

Since its independence in 1918, Latvia had been a tight little entity desperately fighting for self-sufficiency through confiscatory import duties, currency control, clinging to the gold standard, using gasohol to save on imported oil half a century before the word was invented in the USA. Its people, largely of peasant stock, were somewhat dour, chauvinistic to the point that even though German or Russian was widely understood, one had to show a foreign passport or speak Latvian to do businesss in the post office or bank.

Those once lords and masters, the German Baltic barons, heirs to the thirteenth century Teutonic knights who founded Riga, had largely been dispossessed. Most were liquidating the rump estates left them by land reform to return to an ancient homeland, now Nazi.

The morning guard mount of a company of heavy-booted troops in German-style steel helmets, bayonets fixed, was a mixture of Teutonic stolidity and Imperial Russia; the troops sang as they tramped along, the thunder of massed voices a stirring sound in the frosty dawn. One remembered it was four regiments of Latvian troops, the only reliable force under Bolshevik command in 1917–18, that had saved the Revolution in Moscow when things hung in the balance.

The routine at Riga was no less open-ended than that in China. The boss was hundreds of miles away in Berlin. Our local godfather, Minister to Latvia, Lithuania, and Estonia, was Felix Cole, whose legendary predictions on the shape of things to come when he was a young consul in Imperial Russia had sent him to this prime listening post for the neighboring USSR.

In selecting Riga, Captain William D. Puleston, one of ONI's best directors ever, decided that ". . . the preponderance of the population is Russian or Russian speaking, and the social life there is Russian in character, as well as the fact that it is the focal point for intelligence on the U.S.S.R., Poland and Central Europe."*

He was part right, part wrong. There were 2 million Latvians, 12 percent of them Russian, mostly poor or near it. Any Latvian's second language was most likely to be German, a culture heavily reflected in Latvian life and thought. The language students had little or no social contact with Latvians. Their Russian acquaintances were not numerous—

*Puleston to Bureau of Navigation, 4 March 1935, D25, day file.

probably the boardinghouse family, professor, and a few others. It was the large diplomatic colony concentrated at what Captain Puleston characterized as "the focal point for intelligence" that provided most of the playmates and social life outside the American legation crowd. Their *lingua franca* was French. (This was a factor so enhancing to my Naval Academy fundamentals in the language that I would one day go back to Annapolis as an instructor in French, presumably partly on the debatable Navy Department logic that anyone who could speak Russian could teach *anything*.)

But alas! There were none of the feisty cabarets of Shanghai's Blood Alley, with the lissome Russian "princesses" whose worldly views found ready acceptance by the young bachelors. Riga's few cabarets were staffed by meaty local blondes whose only tongue was Latvian, a combination of grunts and whistles that can be mastered only by taking the precaution of being born and raised in Latvia.

Four hours by train lay the charming little city of Tallinn, capital of Estonia, hotel room the equivalent of $1.36 a day, large dinners 50 cents, and a half liter of the best vodka in the world a quarter. Lighthearted, gay, loving song and story, wholly unlike their near neighbors the Latvians, the Estonians are racially related to the fun-loving Hungarians, to whose immensely difficult language Estonian bears resemblance.

I went often to Tallinn. On the Dome, the ancient mini-mountain walled citadel, lived émigré Peter Baranov, direct descendant of Alexandr Andreevich Baranov, Chief Administrator of the Alaskan fur trade, 1799–1818 and founder of Sitka. Peter administered a typical pre-Revolutionary-style Russian household of stairstep children, several maiden aunts, plus a clutch of vaguely identified individuals who came and went like the characters in a Dostoyevskian novel. Also of interest were Peter's boarders, half a dozen British Army and Navy Russian students who lent a Slavified Oxford-cum-vodka atmosphere that for a visiting American taking his meals there made a lively break from stodgy Riga.

Estonia was my jumping off place in the spring of 1936 for a tour with Major William Shipp, U. S. military attaché accredited to all three Baltic states plus Finland. Ferrying to Helsinki through the rapidly disintegrating ice, we found little to suggest that the country once had been a reluctant grandy duchy of Imperial Russia. Officially bilingual in Finnish and Swedish, one could get along well enough in German, Germany having been Finland's fairy godmother in World War I (and would be again in World War II). But Russian? Ei! Nej! Nein! NO! in four languages.

A great pianist once said that one day's hiatus in practice and he would notice the difference in his touch; two days and his wife would notice it; three days and the public would be onto it. Language study is much the same. So during the week that Shipp was checking out Finland's military posture, I managed to locate a Russian language instructress. Her small flat was crammed with lavish furnishings, suggesting that they once had enjoyed more appropriate surroundings. Perched on a grand piano was a portrait of two men in naval uniform. "Excuse me," I said. "but isn't that the czar?" "Yes," said the lady. "And the other gentleman?" "That is my husband, Lieutenant Prince Potocki," she replied. "He was the czar's aide de camp."

Aside from honing my Russian and getting measured for a magnificent $150 fur-lined *shuba* (overcoat in the long, heavy Russian style to combat the Baltic winter), a legation secretary had put me onto a group of about a dozen Japanese officers sent to pick up some of the superlative Finnish expertise in winter warfare. This was to correct grave deficiencies the Japanese suffered in Jehol, Manchuria, the winter before. Now, isolated in a land of boiled reindeer, spuds, and schnapps, they were delighted to find a kindred soul who appreciated chopsticks, raw fish, and saké. As a result, I came off with several magnificent hangovers achieved while absorbing some excellent information on Japanese operations in China. Like Japanese prisoners in World War II, under release from discipline, they sang like birds.

Meanwhile, Major Shipp had completed an exchange of amenities with his military hosts. We rehabilitated ourselves by being steamed like a lobster in the sauna while taking a beating with birch switches. Then the blind, elderly ladies who perform this ritual scrubbed us from stem to stern with harsh loofa sponges, following which we were flung into a pool of ice water. It was quite enough to fit a man to tackle a bear, or even the Bolshies on their own turf, this time purely as tourists. We were off to Leningrad.

Only three or four cars made up the Leningrad express. Even in season, tourists were not common in those pre-airplane days. The inspection at the Soviet border was meticulous. Car seats were pulled up to be scrutinized from below. The overhead sleeper bunk was let down, bedding removed and mattress pummeled. Each item in my baggage was unfolded to be shaken out. Russian grammar and notebooks were gone through page by page. The major, with diplomatic immunity, looked on with quiet amusement, his own baggage unmolested. This was just as well, as it contained a bundle of black market roubles that would see the two of us through six or seven days of ballet in the glorious old Marinskiy and others, following champagne and caviar dinners at the aging but still deluxe Astoria Hotel.

Intourist, the agency for foreign travelers, supplied us with Citizen Natasha Sivers, a comely lass of about twenty, for a nominal sum in roubles, to act as guide, companion, and indispensable negotiator for theatre tickets, trains, taxis, and general advice.

At the absurd official rate of 1 rouble = 1 dollar, the expense would have been affordable only in a package deal paid in "valuta," foreign currency, carefully monitored on a precise schedule. Actually, we had committed no great transgression. The Soviets, in their usual devious way, had got around the exchange impasse without losing face by shipping bundles of currency, ink fresh, the USSR State Bank wrappers still intact, to Warsaw, where diplomatic couriers added them to their pouches of goodies: Danish hams, Dutch butter, Strasbourg *paté de fois gras*, and a bit of official mail. At the realistic black market rate thus-obtained, American diplomats could live comfortably on what the poor markets of Moscow provided, supplemented by the embassy commissary.* On the way out, the couriers' bags would be heavy with caviar, ikons, and antique silverware bought by the kilogram in commission shops—treasures of better days turned in by hard-pressed comrades.

Leningrad has the reputation of being more sophisticated than any other Soviet city. But even there, like wild deer, Russians are on the alert for something not understood or outside the usual routine, a healthy curiosity as useful for survival in the USSR as in the forest. Thus, the sight of two men dressed above the norm, accompanied by a well-turned out, attractive young woman, caught the eye of personnel in museums normally visited only by organized groups. "Excuse me, Comrades," an attendant would ask after a deferential approach (could be top commissars!), "may I ask from which organization you come?"

A week was spent doing the miles of Hermitage corridors, the extensive naval museum, St. Isaacs Cathedral, Tsarskoe Tselo, and just strolling along the snowy, broad avenues of a city laid out on grandiose lines by that eccentric genius, Peter the Great. Close to Catherine the Great's drafty confection, the splendid Peterhof Palace, its fountains still for the winter, sat a small ten- or twelve-room frame house used by Czar Nicholas the Last. It could have passed for any middle-class Pennsylvania country farmhouse of the late nineteenth century, furnished in homely bourgeois style, family photos on the mantel and piano, antimacassars on overstuffed chairs. It was a "lived in" house, restored to how it once was as a reflection of the simple, uncomplex man and his brood of five ingenuous children who loved it.

Across the still-frozen Neva, the fortress of Peter and Paul, infamous prison for earlier dissenters, hunched grim and grey. The cruiser *Aurora*, symbol of the Revolution, lay moored in the river. She had fired the shots that signaled the opening of the attack on the Winter Palace, tocsin for the

*25.5 to 1 vs. the official rate of 5.3 to 1. See *Foreign Relations*, 1941, vol. 1, p. 870.

end of a regime so hated at the time that mutineers aboard her and others of the emperor's ships pushed their officers through holes in the ice or fed them into the fireboxes.

The great St. Isaacs Cathedral had become an antireligious museum. Grotesque caricatures of the saints lined walls where once ikons had been illuminated by holy candles. From the dome, 185 feet up, a wire weighted with a basketball-sized pendulum swung over a concave pit of sand. On the end of the ball, a spur of wire etched in the sand an ever-progressing spiral line as the earth revolved on its axis. Symbolic or scientific? One could take one's choice.

For Comrade Sivers the week must have been unusual and pleasant: chicken, caviar, champagne, ballet nightly; a present purchased at a special store where only "valuta," foreign currency, was accepted, thoughtful gentility in a land where crudity of manner was the norm. And a certain tenderness. After all, she was very pretty, gracious, and charming. Also, was it really just "Sivers," Shipp wanted to know. His background in the history of those parts was good. "Von Sivers" was a famous name when Leningrad was St. Petersburg. Yes, she said. It was indeed once *von* Sivers. But there were no more counts and princes in America either, were there? The Americans had had a revolution too, hadn't they? The two Americans, and the Russian with fond, dim memories of other days, had become friends in a land where friends are picked with care.

The return to Tallinn revealed an embarrassing contretemps. There had been a mini-revolution, unreported in the Leningrad newspapers. The conspirators had struck at morning commuting time, removing the public's shoes in the railway station and at the tram stop sheds. One does not charge forth barefoot in the snow in defense of a political party. By the time the footwear had been returned and sorted out, the "ins" were out and the "outs" were in. But poor Shipp! His annual reception for the leading figures, the "bol'shiyeh shishki" (big pine cones), the big shots, had all been laid on when we first had passed through—invitations sent, entertainment arranged, hall hired. What now? His guests had all "gone to the country," or were "unfortunately detained."

This was the history of the Baltic: wars, coups, revolutions, whole peoples bottled in by ice in winter and the narrow neck of the shallow Baltic Sea's exit year round. The tribulations of Shipp thus fade in comparison with what had gone on a mere dog's age earlier, the only reminder being half a dozen ancient crocks in Tallinn's harbor, ex-German destroyers from World War I swag that largely made up the Estonian Navy.

With their eight-hundred-year-old apothecary shop still doing business as such, their transportation being sleighs in winter and droshkies in summer, the citizens of this charming little city of Tallinn probably never knew that 148 years earlier, almost to the day, the first American naval officer ever to land in Russia had struggled ashore here en route to a rendezvous with Catherine. Many hundreds more U. S. Navy and Marine officers would follow John Paul Jones in the course of three wars and one revolution, some by methods no less perilous than Pavel Ivan'ich's incredible trip from Sweden to Reval. The Russian students among them would have paid their keep. Of the fourteen total students, seven served in an area where there was a desperate shortage of adequate linguists: as assistant naval attachés at Moscow, D. R. Nimmer (USMC), C. H. Taecker, C. J. Zondorak, S. B. Frankel, Kemp Tolley, and H. E. Seidel, Jr. W. M. Sweetser served as naval attaché, Belgrade, where Russian is a kissing cousin to Serbian, widely understood, and later as naval attaché, Moscow.

2 / *The Revolving Door or Back to China*

I left the cobbled streets and Hanseatic architecture of Riga with mixed emotions. It was a city of strange contrasts—storehouse of antiquities, refugee Russian princesses (*real* ones, not the Shanghai variety), outings to the rundown, rump estates of down-at-the-heel Baltic barons, who somehow had managed to survive in the face of the chauvinistic White bolshevism of the Latvians, the latter masters at last in their own houses after centuries of foreign subjugation.

There would be no more delicious suppers in Heidelberg-like beer kellars with balalaika music, followed by a Hollywood movie dubbed in German, translated to me in close-up whispers by a vibrant, pixyish damsel, the daughter of the Swedish military attaché. No more baked beans and champagne at jolly diplomatic parties, all in good fun twitting the Italians about their stumbling in Ethiopia, or the French about German reoccupation of the Rhineland. No more breakfasts of smoked salmon, black bread, cheese, eggs, and a quart of thick milk served in front of a blazing fireplace. No more daily sessions with Major General Schmidt, late of the Czar's household cavalry, his huge mustache neatly combed, cheeks glowing pink from the zero cold outside. His Russian lessons came in the form of tall tales, adventures against the Caucasian mountaineers, World War I Germans, and as adviser to Bolshevik sergeants commanding regiments or divisions during the Revolution.

It had been a disappointment not to meet any Soviet diplomats, but they kept a low profile, not mixing with non-Latvians. Their military officers recently had been given western-style ranks—captain, major, and so forth, replacing their proletarian *comrot* (*comandir rota*, company commander), *compolk* (*comandir polka*, commander regiment). But "general" and "admiral" still were too hard to swallow. They remained *combrig, comcor, comandarm*, and for the Peasants' and Workers' Red Fleet, *flagman flota*. Such tidbits of gossip, some fact, some fancy, enlivened the diplomatic cocktail gossip. "What next in Sovietland?" people joked. "Epaulettes? The St. George's Cross?"

Yes, it was time to go home. Five years ago, I had bid a sad farewell to my affianced at San Francisco. (She was married five months later.) Time to go home for a nice stateside tour for rehabilitation in American ways. Via Berlin.

There definitely is something special about Swedes, including Swedish military attachés' daughters. At a cocktail party in Berlin during my week's debriefing, my first view of this particular one was from astern, following her gently undulating form up a stairway as she balanced a large picture hat on her exquisite blonde head. This was Riga's Anna Lisa all over again with embellishments. The party over, we repaired to a remarkable establishment for members and diplomats only that had started out as a small bistro. The proprietress had grub-staked many an indigent student in years gone by. As time went on, the students prospered, remembering and subsidizing their benefactress, transforming her modest bistro into an exclusive club of really magnificent appointments and cuisine. The walls bore signatures, caricatures, and sketches of the famous—once hungry recipients of the founder's handouts. Now, current students filled the air with joyful stein songs. Plump waitresses scurried about with trays of foaming beer mugs. Hollywood would have been hard put to duplicate it. And in the midst of all this gaiety it suddenly struck me that I was lonesome—at twenty-eight a bachelor with nothing on which to hang my life and ambitions, with my classmates raising families and receiving warm welcomes after a tour at sea.

"Maude," I said. "We have known each other only an hour, but being a good judge of form, figure, character, and intelligence, I have an unusual and sincere offer: if you will agree to say yes within thirty minutes, I would like to marry you." She looked at me long and thoughtfully, but said nothing. More out of instinct than design, we both looked at our watches. Then we carried on our chatter as before, sipped our beer, and watched the antics of the crowd, both occasionally glancing at our watches. At the end of thirty minutes, Maude had not said yes. At the end of the evening I dropped her off at home with a farewell kiss and shortly thereafter left for the United States, not seeing her again. Many years later I happened to bump into the widow of Captain Benjamin Dutton, who as naval attaché had been my boss in Berlin. "A strange thing happened in those days," reminisced Mrs. Dutton. "The Swedish military attaché mentioned to me that some young American naval officer proposed to his daughter, then disappeared and was never heard from. Who in the world do you suppose it could have been?" In the art of diplomacy, one early learns how not to say yes without prevarication, to which I now plead guilty, dear Mrs. Dutton.

Assigned to the old training battleship USS *Wyoming*, I was immediately back in Europe on a midshipmen's summer cruise: London, Paris, Gothenburg. At the latter, those friendly Swedes were at it again. Unattached girls sat at tables in the coffee houses, males at other tables. One asked a young lady to dance, then escorted her back to her table. An old gentleman spectator taking it all in got into conversation. "The Yapanee training skvadron vas here last year," he volunteered. "Dey hat about tree hundret men aboard. Ven a year go py, ve haff a lot off leetle hoff-brown babies. By de vay, how many men in your skvadron?" he added. "Oh, about a thousand," I said. "Yeesus!" he gasped. "Vee haff a new city!"

It was fun for an old rifle team buff to shoot the big twelve-inch turret guns, but bridge watches and division school come best in small doses. In nine months I was once more headed China-wards, ordered to the Asiatic Fleet. The Dollar Line tender steamed an unswerving course up the brown Whangpoo, scattering shoals of sampans and junks. Many of these tatterdemalion craft, intent on cutting demons off their trail, darted dangerously close across the tender's bow, so that her wide-eyed passengers, coming from the just-arrived SS *President Harrison*, felt sure a fatal collision was imminent.

In April 1937 we landed at a pontoon opposite the Shanghai Club and scrambled up the brow to the Bund. This was home. I felt a powerful urge to drop down and kiss the street. None of the passing, jabbering throng would have paid much attention had I done so. In blasé Shanghai a woman could have walked topless, or given birth on the sidewalk, or a coolie drop dead between the shafts of his rickshaw, and very few would have paused to watch.

By November 1939 my cruise was about up. War had rolled over China as far as the Yangtze Gorges, leaving my river gunboat USS *Tutuila* beleaguered in Chungking. Good friend ONI was amenable to an offbeat suggestion: Could I spend six months in Shanghai "studying Russian?" Attached once more to the 4th Marines as "liaison officer," my Chungking beard still intact, the name on my apartment listing, in the telephone book, and amongst my growing coterie of Russian acquaintances was Luigi Passano. In Shanghai one was not questioned too closely on connections, origin, or business. Not for nothing was it called the paradise of adventurers in a book by that title. Bona fide Italians had either long since gone home to war or disappeared into the woodwork, so that none surfaced to put the acid test to my less than fluent Italian.

For some years my fitness report block indicating proficiency in

Lieutenant Kemp Tolley (alias Sr. Luigi Passano) as a Soviet seaman, with friend, China, 1939.

foreign languages had contained my entry, "3.4," on a scale of 4, justified by the honing my Naval Academy French had got in the Far East and Riga, where French was the diplomatic *lingua franca*. This, perhaps, plus the somewhat debatable logic that anyone who could speak Russian could teach *anything*, caused the Navy Department to assign me as an instructor of French at the Naval Academy, where I managed to keep one lesson ahead of the plebe midshipmen. Living in bachelor officers' digs in the Officers' Club, noisy Bundles-For-Britain parties in the ballroom below produced such a din that, unable to sleep, I sometimes dropped down, wearing a Nazi, Italian, or Soviet lapel button of the type one commonly wore in Shanghai as a point of pride, but in this case, simply for the hell of it. An occasional party in my modest two-rooms-loo-down-the-hall usually generated quite a commotion, due perhaps to the then unfamiliar vodka served in proper Russian bottoms-up fashion, the atmosphere enhanced by colorful Russian tail-out blouses furnished the guests. A large swastika banner, souvenir of Berlin, hung on the wall, the latter containing some bullet holes where I had shot out Japan from the framed Geographic map.

At the 22 June 1941 outbreak of war between the USSR and Germany, it seemed logical that a Russian language speaker's place was in the USSR, to which end I approached ONI. The detail officer, Commander von Heimburg, recently transferred from the Naval Academy, was aware of my minor peccadillos. The quota for Russia was filled, he said. If I wanted adventure, why not go to China? Through a mutual friend I learned that von Heimburg had observed to his colleagues that concerning young Tolley there was already enough shooting going on in Russia, not to mention certain doubts as to what the hell side he actually was on.

So for the third time, which the detail officer remarked was something like the drowning man—generally fatal—I applied for and instantly got orders to China; since families had been banned from going along, there were no longer any lieutenant volunteers.

In capsule form, the months of July through November 1941 saw me across the Pacific, then three months as executive officer of the river gunboat USS *Wake*, 600 miles up the Yangtze at Hankow, surrounded by Japanese. With war obviously imminent, we dropped downriver to Shanghai.

At a ghostly silent two in the morning of 29 November, the river gunboats USS *Luzon* and *Oahu*, in which I was passenger navigator, slipped down the Whangpoo. Ashore, a handkerchief waved briefly from the window of a small red Ford I had brought over on the *Harrison*. Then the car slowly drove off. It was the poignant end of a personal epoch.

The dash to Manila was through a typhoon and squadrons of Japanese warships doing their best to divert us into Formosa, the thought of a rear admiral slipping through their fingers no doubt galling, but not sufficient for them to tip the hand holding the royal flush soon to take place at Pearl.* When war broke out on 8 December (7 December Pearl time) I was commanding the two-masted schooner USS *Lanikai*, hastily commissioned and manned largely by Filipinos on the direct order of President Roosevelt. On that momentous day, we lay at the entrance to Manila Bay, awaiting dawn to commence what almost certainly would be a one-way mission.†

Of the 75-odd naval and Marine officers who rode the SS *President Harrison* with me to China, none volunteer, I was one of the handful to miss capture or death. The short renewal of my romance with China in general and with one of her daughters in particular, culminated in the hairbreadth escape to Manila, thence to Australia, seeing me free of the prison camp, internment, or death suffered by those who remained.

One morning in early April 1942, Captain John M. Creighton, staff of Commander Southwest Pacific, looked down on the USS *Lanikai* as she lay alongside dock in Fremantle, West Australia, 4,000 perilous miles, 90 days out of Manila. Creighton had been the U. S. naval observer at Singapore, escaping very shortly before its capture. Over the years he and I had established a good professional rapport; he had been naval attaché at Peking, and later manned the Far East desk in ONI, when I used to fracture the rules by sending him intelligence reports direct (at his request) instead of through the chain of command.

Lanikai had become something of a conversation piece through her propensity for turning up after being long overdue. Aside from her unlikely role as a man-of-war on the president's clandestine business, she had had several very narrow escapes from Japanese task forces as well as typhoons, my family having been notified twice of my probable loss or capture. So Creighton had come down to see her for himself.

"Tolley! Hello there!" he called down, seeing me puttering around topside. "The ghost seems to be very much alive." He climbed aboard. In comfortable wicker chairs atop the after deckhouse, coffee in hand, we talked about *Lanikai*'s next mission—reconnaissance up the Australian coast looking for Japanese infiltrators. The Filipino crewmen were practicing stiff-armed grenade throws from down on the well deck amidships, using stones for dummies. "I know you love adventure," said Creighton, "but what the hell is an experienced intelligence officer like yourself doing in a backwash like this? You belong in the USSR. I'll send a message right away."

*Kemp Tolley, *Yangtze Patrol: The U. S. Navy in China* (Annapolis: Naval Institute Press, 1971).

†Kemp Tolley, *Cruise of the Lanikai: Incitement to War* (Annapolis: Naval Institute Press, 1973).

Creighton was true to his word; on 24 April, the *Lanikai*'s radio watch on Perth's broadcast schedule intercepted a transmission that for me would bring the *Lanikai* idyll to a close:

> LANIKAI PROCEED IMMEDIATELY TO GERALDTON X LIEUT COMDR KEMP TOLLEY RELIEVED COMMA ORDERED AMEMBASSY
>
> MOSCOW USSR AS ASSISTANT NAVAL ATTACHE AND ASSISTANT NAVAL ATTACHE FOR AIR X LIEUT COMDR CHARLES ADAIR
>
> ASSUME COMMAND* X PLANE WILL ARRIVE GERALDTON 27 APRIL TRANSPORT TOLLEY TO FREMANTLE

(The "air" bit generated considerable amusement among my Fremantle contemporaries, who knew I had never flown anything more pretentious than a kite.)

When the *Lanikai* reached Australia, a swarm of refugees had arrived ahead of her. Like those in the *Lanikai*, they had seen their proper uniforms go up in smoke or down with a ship, and so were generally reduced to a pair of ragged khaki pants. By the time the tailors in Western Australia had fitted out everyone in new blues, there was no more blue cloth for the latecomers. Admiral Glassford, top U. S. commander, ended up with a dress uniform of RAAF sky blue. Needless to say, I ended up with khaki.

For thirty days, my transportation, the old tanker USS *Trinity* crept her way west, too weak to fight, too slow to run, until due south of the Persian Gulf, then north, clear of normal ocean routes where enemy subs or raiders might be in wait. On her bridge as guest watch stander, I whiled away the dull hours on an empty ocean, Russian phrase book in hand, preparing for the great adventure.

Trinity arrived at Basra after nightfall. My journal recorded it as ". . . looking like the Garden of Eden for sure, with palms, palaces and Ayrabs in bed sheets all over the place." But daylight brought different impressions: "Woke up in the heat of the morning to find the Eden atmosphere more convincing during darkness . . . smells equal to anything China could offer. What filth!" The place was stiff with British and Indian troops toting their sidearms. Everybody was edgy after the recently attempted Nazi coup, the pubs buzzing with rumors and filled with Tommies swilling beer.

I spent several sweltering days in Basra, awaiting a plane ride to Teheran. The flat rooftops were flooded—little lakes of several inches of

*Adair, who had been Admiral Hart's flag lieutenant, had ridden *Lanikai* as a passenger from Manila to Australia, in each stop his contacts enabling him to have the ship released for the next leg. On the reconnaissance trip, he was acting as "squadron commander," to avoid replacing me as commanding officer, as he was senior.

water to ameliorate the 120° noontime heat, which must have spoiled the breakfast eggs almost in the laying process, as they distinctly were in the category described by the Chinese cook as "no can fly, can sclamble."

In the evenings, my host, the U. S. naval observer,* a 40-year-old self-described former "bone digger" (archaeologist) pinned lieutenant junior grade shoulder boards on his short-sleeved, open-necked white shirt, climbed into black trousers, wrapped a black cummerbund around his middle, and took me off to the nightly bash. There, similarly attired British officers and half a dozen pretty "cypherettes" attached to the large British mission danced and drank the night away. It was probably the first American introduction to this sensible hot weather formal evening dress that has since become part of the U. S. Navy uniform, the black cummerbund exchanged for one of gold.

Teheran was a short hop from Abadan airfield across the Shatt al Arab River from Basra. On the field I saw my first Soviets—aircrews checking out American Lend-Lease planes headed for the Russian front. It gave one a feeling of already being in the western war.

Teheran was a sleepy, semi-Oriental, oversize village, with horse-drawn, Russian-style droshkies for transportation. Gutters ran with a stream of water from the nearby mountainside that provided both garbage removal and household supply. But there were tailors and shoemakers. It was a good place to take a few days out—have some civilian clothes made, enjoy the plentiful, cheap black caviar washed down with excellent Persian vodka, while socializing with the bosomy, rosy-cheeked damsels in the Polish brigade being formed with ex-prisoners of war from the USSR.

Normally, one could have expected a considerable wait for the Soviet visa. A U. S. major general with several dozen staffers attempting to get to Kuibishev to advise the Soviets on how to run the war had cooled his heels at Teheran for several weeks. Then the general and several others had been let in for a temporary visit only, the remainder not admitted at all. So it was with considerable astonishment at the U. S. embassy that my visa was handed over immediately.

Until the unlikely event of the Lubianka's files being opened through the Freedom of Information Act, we can only speculate. However, in 1937, in that extraordinary entrepot of gun runners, smugglers, secret agents, and questionable characters, Hongkong, I had met and become friendly with a Finnish communist, one of the most powerful men physically I have ever met. (He could grasp a chair with one hand by its top back slat and hold

*On my earnest recommendation after arrival in the USSR, measures were instituted to promote this able officer immediately to lieutenant commander, a rank more appropriate for his responsibilities and American prestige.

it out horizontally.) We had discussed the USSR and my interest in visiting there again. "There is a certain photo shop in Canton," said Comrade W, "which has connections. A Chinese tailor will make you up a Soviet uniform blouse and cap for a few mex. Next time you're up in Canton, have this fellow photograph you." I not only did this, but the following year in Chungking gave a copy to the Soviet assistant military attaché, whom I had cultivated in order to practice Russian and enjoy caviar and vodka to offset the poverty of China's wartime capital.

In spite of the speedy visa, I had expected to spend some time in Teheran, principally to have some civilian clothes made. But second secretary Minor of the U. S. embassy had other ideas. "Haven't you heard there's a war going on?" he snapped. "There is some mail for our embassy in Kuibishev. Get cracking with it!"

Dear, good secretary Minor, my unpremeditated benefactor! On arrival at Kuibishev, the provisional capital, it was revealed that I had been scheduled to relieve Lieutenant Commander C. H. Taecker at Vladivostok, a place which, if one were called upon to give Mother Earth an enema, would unquestionably be the appropriate spot. The bottom line, of course, was that civilian clothes were required to support the fiction that the naval officer concerned was a clerk in the consulate general. As a clandestine member of the consulate, in mufti, the Japanese would never know, thus not press for equal treatment. Thanks to my quick ejection from Teheran, I had no civilian clothes. It was hardly likely that I would have been able to masquerade as demanded while wearing my quasi-Australian get-up.

The trip up from Teheran in a Soviet "Dooglas," their version of the DC-3, was an introduction into the ways of Russia, with typically what appears to be utter confusion, everybody gesticulating and shouting suggestions as to what should be done. But somehow, matters seem to get sorted out.

There was the usual interminable session with the customs at Baku, first stop, where a glass of boiled plums at the equivalent of 50 cents substituted for lunch. Two "king's messengers" shepherding several dozen bags of British mail added their bit to the already lively scene by loudly but fruitlessly demanding tea, deigning to speak not one word of Russian, even so much as a "pojaluista" (please). "The blighters understand English perfectly well," they said. "They're just being bloody stuffy."

Next stop was Stalingrad, which in a few more months would occupy center stage in the world's headlines for its life-and-death struggle as the key to the Volga. In a clammy, foggy sunset we filed into the airport lounge for a dinner of fish, fried eggs, and sour cream. The king's messengers, who gave a strong suggestion of being cockney constables in civvies, were in a greatly improved frame of mind; tea by the gallon was on tap. Accommodations for the night were iron cots, three to a room. What probably were the only sheets in the establishment were still damp after efforts to iron them dry. I spent the night fully clothed.

Everybody at Stalingrad was very solicitous for our comfort and anxious to please, which must have included the chickens, as again for breakfast there were ample eggs. Glasses got instant refills of tea, that prime concomitant of Russian existence.*

Finally arriving at Kuibishev in a deluge of rain, the King's messengers, really decent chaps at heart, offered me a lift on top of their truckload of mail. The ancient vehicle lurched, swayed, bumped, and rattled over ten miles of what had to be the worst road that side of Poland, to finally deposit me at the ex-schoolhouse serving as temporary American embassy. There, Australian finery bedraggled by the vicissitudes of the trip, I was presented to Captain Jack Harlan Duncan, naval attaché. "*What* the *hell* are *you*!?" gasped Duncan, whose wholly justifiable exclamation in this case was typical of the man who could confidently be counted on to say exactly what he thought.

This was my introduction to wartime Russia.

The roommate who drew up Duncan's biographical sketch in the 1917 *Lucky Bag*, the Naval Academy class yearbook, certainly knew his man. By 1942 "Dunc" hadn't changed a whit, excerpts suggesting he had only accentuated the traits noted a quarter century earlier: "He is an abject slave of Old Dame Fortune," his dossier reads. "Briefly, he loves to sit behind a pat full house or four of a kind. When so situated, he assumes a sophisticated and worldly air . . . Dunc knows where to go, what to do, and as for how to do it, his blasé manner and air of perfect sangfroid always secure obsequious attention on the part of the pilot of popping corks . . . Adept at the gentle art of repartee, fluent stock of satirical wit . . . generous and sympathetic." The accompanying photo of the man from Missouri (Ozark) suggests a note of whimsical sadness; the less formal snapshot below, a confident, straight-backed young man astride a horse. I remember him with great affection, pride, and keen recognition of his forthrightness and ability.†

*Tea in Russia is served in glasses, held in a metal outer jacket with a handle.

†In 1943, reverting to the rank of captain from his spot rank of rear admiral, Duncan went to command cruiser USS *Phoenix*, earning a Navy Cross in operations off the Philippines. Then he returned to Washington, where he heard the post of Chief of Naval Mission to Peru was open. Approaching Admiral Ernest King, Chief of Naval Operations, "Dunc" volunteered for the assignment. "But that is a rear admiral's job, Jack." said the crusty CNO, who had known Duncan during the latter's years as Admiral Standley's aide. "*I* don't mind being a rear admiral," replied Duncan, flashing his whimsical smile. King's faced cracked into a rare grin. "O.K., you old bastard, you're a rear admiral," he said. Duncan

How had "Dunc" got to Kuibishev, the first naval attaché ever accredited to the Soviet Union? His sole naval predecessor had been designated "assistant naval attaché," Captain David Nimmer, USMC, who had been withdrawn in a huff in 1935.

Even before the outbreak of World War II, it was not clear whether the Soviet Union was potentially hostile, neutral, or a possible future ally. The Soviets had dangled the British on a string during the summer of 1939 until they were sure of a pact with Germany, signed 23 August. Was it a cynical deal on Stalin's part to divide the swag? A frantic effort to hold off the deluge until better prepared? Or was it simply a risky balance-of-power act in hopes of European capitalism's collapse—Germany and the Anglo-French beating each others' brains out? Whatever the motive, Russian supplies to Germany brought not only Anglo-Russian but American-Russian relations to a near deep freeze.

Typical of British uncertainty was the reaction of HMS *Gannet*'s skipper, 1,300 miles up the Yangtze at China's wartime capital, Chungking. Half a mile downriver lay the USS *Tutuila*, who on 17 September 1939 received the following priority message:

> STATE DEPARTMENT INFORMS THAT SOVIET GOVERNMENT UNDER PRETENSE OF RESTORING ORDER AND PROTECTING WHITE RUSSIAN MINORITY ENTERED EASTERN FRONTIER OF POLAND AT DAWN

In a Yangtze gunboat, informality reigned; I personally manned the big bridge searchlight and flashed out the message to *Gannet*. Back came an instant reply:

FOR GODS SAKE ON WHOSE SIDE ARE THEY

On 22 June 1941, although repeatedly warned by Washington, through information received from Japanese intercepts, that Hitler was planning to attack Russia, the Soviets were caught with their planes and their pants down. The flip-flop in Russo-American relations was a wonder to behold, including the New York *Daily Worker*, overnight switching the role of villain from Britain to Berlin. Two Soviet assistant military attachés homeward bound from the U. S. as personae non gratae for espionage were turned around, reinstated, and given carte blanche to travel where they chose.

The Soviet embassy in Washington responded in kind; on 23 June, the day after the invasion, they indicated they'd be happy to have a U. S.

---

retired from this assignment as a vice admiral, by virtue of the act then in force elevating the holder of a decoration for gallantry in action against the enemy one rank on retirement. As far as the author knows, Duncan never was formally selected for any rank beyond commander. It was pure JHD all the way.

naval attaché in Moscow. The Navy had asked for one in April 1941 (about the time I had made my request), but State had batted it down; living space was very tight, rations slim, situation volatile. There already was a military attaché on hand, Major Ivan Yeaton. He could take care of naval affairs, which State apparently considered didn't amount to much anyway. But with the war, things were different. "Send him via Chungking," urged Soviet Ambassador Oumansky. "It is quicker that way."

Unlike Stalin, able U. S. Ambassador Laurance Steinhardt had taken the war warnings seriously, setting up contingency plans. A *dacha* (summer residence) had been obtained, an elderly, 10- or 12-room western-style frame house in the country at Tarasovka, 20 miles from the chancery. It had been stocked with tents, food, beer, and 25 sets of everything from sheets to eating utensils. The day of the Nazi attack, on the theory that the Germans liked to hit capitals first, Steinhardt moved the whole embassy to the dacha, where all hands enjoyed the exhilaration of roughing it in the gentle Russian spring countryside.

By 1 July, the Navy Department had requested *four* naval officers for Moscow and one for Vladivostok, with the Soviets genially agreeable to accepting *any* officer the U. S. might designate. But the one at Vladivostok must carry no title and wear civilian clothes, attached to the consulate general as a clerk.

On 27 July 1941, Lieutenant Commander Ronald H. Allen, USNR, was named as the first naval assistant attaché since the unfortunate experience of Captain Nimmer in 1935. "Ronnie" Allen was a six-foot-one, black haired, erudite, urbane, diplomatic type who had been a reserve ensign in World War I, assigned to Eastern Europe after the war. There he had picked up a speaking knowledge of Russian, an intimate understanding of the ballet and opera, and a deep appreciation of the Slavic soul. All these attributes would be of great comfort to his ultimate boss, Captain Duncan, naval attaché-to-be, as some of these talents were in rather short supply among the professional naval officers rounding out the staff.

Concurrently, Lieutenants Samuel B. Frankel and George "D" Roullard were ordered as additional assistants. But it was not until 20 December 1941 that Lieutenant Carroll H. Taecker was recalled from physical retirement for duty at "Vladi." To the Russians there, other than the NKVD, and the 30-odd foreigners—Chinese, Japanese, and a few others—Taecker would be just another consular clerk, assuming they were denser than probably was the case.

My welcome at Kuibishev was warm, everybody hungry for news of the "outside," *any* outside, even Western Australia. Navy radioman Stannard's meager, spotty press copy, plus the fables handed out by the Soviet news agency to correspondents, left the world at large a near total blank to the little cluster of diverse souls making up the American embassy. As is usually the case in times of adversity, uncertainty, and what is presumed to be hardship, people draw closer together. Acquaintances become friends. Once distant superiors become associates rather than bosses, their human qualities, bad and good, more clearly understood. This is what happened to the diplomatic colony in general as well as to the American embassy staff itself.

The provisional capital was a sleepy Volga river port, named Samara in Czarist times, when it would have been considered a place of exile by imperial officers. Little had changed since. The streets were still dirt or cobbled. Paint peeled from the huge, ornate opera house, opulent survivor of the old days. Beggars lounged at the cathedral door, where Sunday services were still held for the few elderly faithful.

The "new" American embassy was an ex-schoolhouse, with the generally ill-used, pock-marked, pocket-knife-carved aspect of that species. For furnishings there were nondescript iron bunks with mattresses of dubious ancestry, boxes for chairs, and very little else.

Steinhardt had left to become ambassador to Turkey. Former Chief of Naval Operations Admiral William H. Standley, USN (retired), who replaced him, was living in a small house with his secretary, Edward Page, Jr., and his four "YMCA" (NKVD) bodyguards and sometime tennis partners. In the "upstairs" mess at the schoolhouse-embassy, the meager rations of British "bangers" (sausages heavily laced with cornmeal), cabbage, half-rotten potatoes, and an occasional meatball of undetermined origin, all washed down with large quantities of weak tea, were shared by embassy secretaries and the service attachés. Yeaton had gone home, disgusted. For a century it had been accepted military practice for foreign attachés, including neutrals, to be near or at the fighting front. Evasiveness met Yeaton's preliminary efforts to go where the action was. Finally pestered beyond endurance, the Red Army liaison officer peremptorily told Yeaton on 15 July 1941 that neither the British Military Mission nor American military attachés would be permitted to visit the front, "now or hereafter." And indeed, in this the Soviets kept their word with one exception, about which more later.

Yeaton, who had told Washington he expected the Soviets to last about two months, had been succeeded by his thoroughly anti-Soviet cavalryman assistant, Major Joseph A. Michela,* West Point 1928. Pro-

*As military attaché in Czechoslovakia, Michela died in 1950, mysteriously, suddenly, and alone. It was a heart attack, the Czechs said. At about the same time, Lieutenant Colonel Andrew Wylie, USMCR, naval attaché at Warsaw, disappeared while returning to his post from a conference in London. Concurrently, Captain Eugene S. Karpe, naval attaché

Admiral-Ambassador William H. Standley.

fessorial in his steel-rimmed glasses and trim mustache, "Mike" Michela was a perfect foil for Jack Duncan's tongue-in-cheek wit. Fellow West Pointers Captains James O. Boswell and Richard Park, Jr., both class of 1933, and Robert E. McCabe, '36, completed the Army contingent. All three were "Army brats," sons of Army officers, as was I, all four of us having been born in the Philippines, a further bond.

On the Navy side, Duncan and Allen were strangers to me. But Sam Frankel and I, 1929 Naval Academy classmates, had been fellow members of the gym team. We had served together in China, and he had relieved me in Riga. George Roullard, USNA '34, also was an old China hand and friend. Added to these were two State Department embassy secretaries, one of whom I had known well in Riga. It was a very congenial atmosphere.

The "downstairs" mess harbored a team of seasoned Navy enlisted

in the Balkans, fell to his death from that paragon of spy thrillers, the Orient Express, near Salzburg.

men who in spite of the haphazard selection process for those supposed to be best fitted for Russian duty, could not have been better chosen. Chief Storekeeper Byron Uskievich was a two-fisted, motorcycle-riding whiz at getting things done so often characteristic of career men of the pre-war Navy. He had ridden transatlantic with George Roullard to set up the office. Chief Yeoman John McGinnis, a six-foot ex-Yangtze veteran, traveled from New York to Archangel with Boswell and Frankel.

The embassy had moved to Kuibishev in October 1941, by which time the jubilant Nazi columns were in sight of the Kremlin's bulbous domes. There had been only a few hours' advance notice of the government's withdrawal. One first-class railroad car had been provided for chiefs of mission. The rest rode four to a room or in "hard" cars with uncushioned wooden slats. There was no water. NKVD troops with rifles heavily guarded the train. The night after departure, a small quantity of soup, cabbage, black bread, and eggs appeared. Thirty hours later, at 5 A.M. another meal was produced, there having been no other food for the five nights and four days en route the 600-odd miles to Kuibishev. The wonder of it all was that anything whatever could have been resolved out of such last-minute chaos. Soviet information on the state of affairs heretofore had been so vague that Ambassador Steinhardt had apprehensively sent a scouting party to the Volga port of Kazan, once the capital of that earlier scourge of Russia, the Tartars.

When the foreign embassies moved to Kuibishev, so did the branch offices of the various commissariats that dealt with them. This included the Soviet Navy liaison office for dealing with naval attachés. New and disorganized, it was further confused by the arrival of Chief Yeoman John McGinnis, one of the outriders coming in from the north before Standley's and Duncan's arrival from the south. Old-timer McGinnis, six feet of solid Irish blarney, with sixteen years' service, much of it in China, made only feeble efforts to disabuse the Soviets in their supposition that the four gold "hash marks" (service stripes) on his left sleeve represented a captain, U. S. Navy, and that he was thus the expected attaché himself. Language difficulties compounded this innocent deception.

Quartered temporarily in the Intourist Hotel, tired, hungry, and dirty after a grueling train and boat trip of ten days, Mac was happy to be offered a welcoming feast befitting his supposed rank: half a goose with enough vodka to have floated it. Did he want more? inquired the hospitable, smiling, solicitous hotel manager in Russian, assuming Mac understood the language through his use of half a dozen fractured Russian phrases. "Da!" Da!" Ochen mnogo!" (Yes! Yes! Very much!) replied Mac, by then stuffed to the gills and feeling very pleased with himself at the turn of events, believing he had been asked how he had enjoyed the *pièce de resistance*. In very short order, in came the other half of the goose. It was a typical, honest error brought about by language difficulties and would by no means be the last one.

How had McGinnis got to Russia? The Bureau of Naval Personnel had assured naval attaché-designate Duncan that there would be no problem getting him an adequate staff, explaining that if one wanted, let us say, a left-handed seven-footer, adept at driving a motorcycle, who wore a purple goatee and could recite the multiplication table backwards, the punch-card machine would clatter through several hundred thousand records and turn out half a dozen suitable candidates. And what came to Moscow? Ruthenians and Poles, Irishmen who loved Russians, Slovaks, speakers of Yiddish and Ukrainian. But nary a Russian. There was nobody in BuPers who knew any Russian to check them out.

At least McGinnis had had a crash course in Navy accounting in an atmosphere of mystery and secrecy, with no clue as to his ultimate destination. Public knowledge of a military mission to help the Russians would have been met with cries of anger at collaborating with "those damned communists."

Chief McGinnis hauled his lanky frame aboard the SS *Ville d'Anvers* on 9 September 1941, accompanied by some exotic baggage: half a dozen each, 45-caliber automatic pistols, gas masks, World War I model wash-basin tin hats, sheepskin coats, jungle cloth winter wearing apparel, American flags of the size used for draping coffins. In the hold were a big motorcycle with sidecar, a Ford sedan, office supplies, and miscellaneous items the Office of Naval Intelligence felt appropriate for a place it knew nothing about except that it could be blistering cold, was remote, and was smack in the middle of a hot war.

In New York, it was clear the secrecy veil had some rips. While hunting down the mooring of the *Ville d'Anvers*, McGinnis's taxi driver stopped to ask a policeman the way to the Lehigh Valley Docks. Before the cop could reply, an urchin piped up, "You wanna get to that ship that's goin' to Russia?"

Flying the Belgian flag, her name and registry changed to avoid neutrality complications, the *Ville d'Anvers* was an ex-U. S.-flag passenger-freighter with a crew of some 17 different nationalities and British officers. Below were Studebaker trucks, drums of toluene; on deck, crated aircraft.

The toluene drums were leaky, deeply concerning the Coast Guard officer charged with clearing the ship. No sailing until those fumes were stopped! A generous application of scotch whiskey smoothed over this little contretemps to the point that not only was the release signed, but amid convivial group singing with the ship's officers of "The White Cliffs of Dover," "Bless 'Em All!", and such, the gentleman was reluctant to leave the ship, declaring a strong desire to sign on. Leaky drums, the Soviet Union, German torpedoes—none of them scared him now, so that it was only with some strong physical persuasion that he was put ashore.

Close to sailing time, Lieutenant S. B. Frankel and Captain James Boswell, respectively assistant naval and assistant military attachés, Moscow, came aboard. Both were *rarae aves*—fairly fluent speakers of Russian.

The *Anvers* sailed without fanfare, with no crowds shouting goodby, no confetti, no leis. People at the rail waved at workers ashore, but nobody waved back. As the pilot quit the ship, he looked up at the three military men, but gave no farewell greeting. One began to suspect that the ship and the people in it were not popular. Crew members seldom spoke when spoken to. They had no stomach for this voyage, the steward told McGinnis. In dangerous waters, the ship would sail unprotected to Halifax. Some crewmen had spent time on life rafts after their ships had gone down. They smelt the leaking toluene. Most came from countries unfriendly to the Soviet Union. With incipient mutiny developing, the skipper strapped on his pistol, suggesting that the three military men do likewise. In half an hour he was back from the crew's quarters. "All is cricket," the intrepid Britisher announced. "No need for anxiety." Then he tossed a switchblade knife on the chart table. "Had to take it from one of the men," he said.

In Halifax, huge three-stackers of the Canadian Pacific Line, hulls now battle grey, were loading Canadian troops. Their escorts would include some of the old U. S. four-stackers traded to the British for bases. Aboard the little Panamanian freighter *Capira*, its holds full of Soviet-bound war material, rode two more Moscow-bound: Lieutenant George D. Roullard and Storekeeper First Class Byron Uskievich.

George Roullard continues the story.

Everything McGinnis found aboard the *Ville d'Anvers*—the war cargo for Russia, the attitude of the crew, the unfriendly atmosphere, the wide variety of nationalities, and "bad trips" in the war zone—was the case with the SS *Capira*. Even to the chief engineer, also a Scotsman. The Yugoslav skipper, no friend of the commies, didn't relish his job, but felt his place was at sea, where his forbears for generations had extracted a livelihood.

Since Roullard and Uskievich were incognito, listed as "supercargo" and bunked in the dispensary, they were looked upon with some curiosity and speculation.

Ships of all types, sizes, nationalities, and colors stretched out as far as the eye could see as the convoy sailed from Halifax. Without escort, the expected happened south of Iceland at what was known as "Torpedo Junction," where several ships were sunk. At Hafnarfjördhur, Iceland, the *Capira* and consorts at last saw some support in the form of battleships USS *Mississippi*, *New Mexico* and HMS *King George V*, along with cruisers USS

Tuscaloosa, Vincennes, and many destroyers. It looked like something big was cooking, even though the USA was still only fighting the president's "undeclared war."* There was much grousing by the merchant crews that such a fleet should be swinging around the hook instead of at sea protecting the convoys. Perhaps they would be with them en route Russia. But as matters turned out, no battleships were needed. The escort of cruiser HMS *Suffolk* and several destroyer escorts were more than sufficient; no enemy opposition developed. (Such a respite would be short. This convoy was designated PQ-1. By the time the PQs had reached their teens, half the ships were being sunk by U-boats and aircraft, PQ-17 losing over two-thirds of its cargo vessels.)

PQ-1 entered the White Sea ten days out of Iceland, and true to its name, the water had a dirty gray-white color accentuated by the snow flurries and cold wind that whipped up whitecaps.

Finally up the narrow Dvina River channel and ashore, the newcomers were not quite prepared for the shock they were to receive at the sight of ramshackle, frontier-style log buildings, board sidewalks, unpaved muddy streets, and vintage trolley cars. Equally a surprise, even shock, was the appearance of the people. Poorly dressed, giving no sign of welcome, unsmiling, they suggested that life in wartime Archangel was scarcely a lark.

It was half-expected that a U.S. embassy representative would be on hand to greet the first supplies and personnel from the U.S. East Coast. But no one showed. Stevedores and dock workers, guarded by sentries and police dogs, were political prisoners forbidden to communicate with anyone. Ships' radios had been sealed, and no small boats were allowed launched. Armed sentries stood at the foot of each brow. In this unfriendly and noncommunicative atmosphere, Roullard and Uskievich, Frankel, Boswell, and McGinnis—rendezvousing more by chance than by good management—stumbled on the town's flea bag of a hotel, the Intourist, where they found three equally confused and confounded British colonels, a Navy captain, and a civilian who had come over with the Beaverbrook Mission and stayed on to greet the first convoy. Their very sketchy news was not encouraging. The Nazis were knocking on Moscow's gates whence all the diplomatic corps had been evacuated, to where they knew not, since all radio and telephone communication had been cut for several days. Better jump back aboard and return to Iceland, they advised. Russia's chances of survival looked dim, and the probability of the Americans reaching Moscow or their embassy, wherever it might be, even dimmer. That was the

*Patrick Abbasia, *Mr. Roosevelt's Navy; The Private War of the U. S. Atlantic Fleet, 1939 to 1942*. (Annapolis: Naval Institute Press, 1975).

course they themselves were planning to follow, with the exception of the civilian, Mr. Monk, an adventurous fellow, excellent linguist, and one whose connection with the British military contingent remained a mystery.

Monk believed that the Russians would survive even if Moscow were taken, and volunteered to join Frankel, now in charge by reason of seniority, and party in a search for the new location of the embassies, even if it took them to Vladivostok, which events indicated was by no means improbable.

Now Frankel takes over the story. Making his basic tactical error in believing the train would start on time, he, plus one and a half tons of baggage and five fellows, assembled at the station in late afternoon for the 10:30 P.M. "express" to Moscow. With no train in sight and the station swarming with humanity, the NKVD was importuned to open the snack bar (empty of snacks for months before) so the group could bed down for a fitful, frigid night on chairs and table tops.

It was noon next day when the travelers finally were under way, the two enlisted men, Uskievich and McGinnis, with baggage and food in a "hard" car, the officers in a "soft" one, first of the many anomalies in the classless society.*

After two days of slow, stop-and-go travel, Yaroslavl appeared to be the end. Everybody out, the line to Moscow had been cut, they said. Thousands milled with their mounds of baggage on the station platform. What to do? Should they press on? Conditions at the station were fast becoming chaotic with the arrival of trains from Moscow carrying huge crowds of raggedly dressed refugees who carried rumors that the prisons had been opened. McGinnis, tallest and most imposing member of the American party, checked his 45-Colt to be prepared, the refugees eyeing the big, armed foreigner with curiosity.

Frankel, like Roullard in full uniform, soon was back from the NKVD with news that the U. S. embassy had indeed been evacuated, probably to Kazan, 380 miles east of Moscow on the Volga. Take a river steamer, advised the NKVD, who, feeling responsible for foreigners, spies or not, undertook to book passage and provide a truck to haul the baggage.

Three first-class cabins housed the party of six, in a little ship rated at 350 passengers but which now carried no less than 800. Frankel, meanwhile, had struck up a fortuitous friendship with a man who threw real weight—a Soviet naval flier who had shot down 22 enemy planes and was wearing the gold star of a Hero of the Soviet Union. Just out of the hospital, "every inch an extrovert," as Frankel described him, the two became

*"International," French-type wagon-lits: "soft," four padded bunks, upper & lower; "hard," four or six wood benches, barely room to turn over.

inseparable. At every stop, he would dash ashore to come back with unexpected and "unobtainable" items—tomatoes, watermelon, and once even a chicken, which he cajoled the ship's cook into preparing after he himself had plucked the feathers and done the cleaning.

Since they had tickets only to Gorky, a judicious combination of persuasion, browbeating, cigarettes, and whiskey retained the three cabins against almost overwhelming odds. The ship was a shambles: at night not a square foot of space not covered by a human body and three toilets for this throng, suggesting that perhaps a shortage of food did have some compensations.

At Kazan, 430 kilometers downriver from Gorky, the travelers met a British embassy party, scouts who had sat around the abominable hotel a week waiting for the expected arrival of the evacuated British embassy. Now both Britishers and Americans were happy to learn that the target at last had been fixed—Kuibishev. Roullard had his pocket picked, but the young culprit was nabbed and the loot returned.

Ten days later—exhausted, jostled, and dirty, aghast at the suffering, starving refugees they had seen, ten pounds lighter in spite of the sausages, cheese, and tinned provisions requisitioned from the ships, all abetted by the largesse provided by the Hero of the Soviet Union—the Americans arrived at last in Kuibishev, latter-day pioneers in a land as strange and in some respects as forbidding as the Great Plains and its savages.

The quarters of the American embassy were no Comrade Hilton. But it was a real American welcome, with hot water for a bath, coffee, plus one egg and toast for breakfast. Frankel shaved in water collected from the drip of the eaves, presumably soft snowmelt. But it didn't work up much of a lather. "That is from the pigeon droppings," explained a veteran resident of one week. "It tends to make the water hard." This, for a spell, would be home.

3 / *The Settling In*

In 1853, the U. S. Minister to Russia, Neill S. Brown, wrote the State Department that he was of the opinion a Minister to Russia from the United States ought to be a military man, because the government of Russia was a military government. Over the century, matters had changed little; "Czar" Stalin wore a marshal's uniform, while the military enjoyed special status. But even in the unlikely event President Roosevelt was familiar with Brown's views, it is probably for another reason that in the spring of 1942 he appointed retired Admiral William H. Standley as his ambassador at Moscow.

The new envoy was widely experienced in the Navy, had held some prestigious positions in business after retirement, and had brushed up on his Russian by accompanying the Harriman Lend-Lease Mission to Moscow in the autumn of 1941. As Roosevelt's Chief of Naval Operations, 1933–1937, he had resigned in protest over his boss's having named a new CinC US Fleet without consulting him, while he was at a disarmament conference in London. But he continued to support Roosevelt's foreign policy, including backing the 150-destroyers-for-bases deal with Britain.

Immediately after Pearl Harbor, the president, with the hot wind of public clamor on his neck, forestalled the peril that Congress would order an investigation by setting up one of his own, headed by Supreme Court Justice Owen J. Roberts. FDR astutely directed that the investigation's purpose was to determine if any derelictions of duty or errors of judgment lay on the part of *United States Army or Navy personnel*. This clear definition of the target effectively spared from jeopardy any civilian member of the administration, *including the president himself.*

Standley, appointed as one of the four supposedly "tame" members, turned out to be a maverick, denouncing the proceedings as incompetent whitewash and Roberts as crooked as a snake, telling Navy Secretary Knox that if Admiral Kimmel were court-martialed for his alleged malfeasance at Pearl, he would act as his counsel and get him acquitted.

Obviously the crusty old gentleman was too dangerous a character to allow to remain in highly politicized Washington. Rocket him off to the moon. Or a reasonable facsimile thereof—remote, hermetically sealed Moscow.*

On 5 November 1941, Roosevelt had proposed Major General James H. Burns, USA, a strong Russophile, as ambassador to the USSR to replace incumbent Laurence A. Steinhardt. But in January 1942, he reviewed the bidding; Burns was more useful in the United States, while Standley was just the man for Russia.†

Standley's membership on the Harriman-Beaverbrook Mission had given him some solid experience in the whipsawing tactics, the alternate cheer, chill, freeze, and thaw the Soviets used to gain their objectives. Even the trip itself had corroborated the advice of a British general at Murmansk a generation before: "Never believe a Russian when he says, 'It is done.' Go see for yourself."‡ The Harriman mission was to fly to London in a seaplane outfitted to carry VIPs. Why not take that big, comfortable flying boat on to Moscow, suggested Standley. Ambassador Litvinov said, "Da! Permission granted!" Luckily for the flying boat's tender bottom, the leg from London to the USSR was by cruiser to Murmansk, as Litvinov's lake near Moscow did not exist.

For his new mission, Standley arrived at the provisional capital, Kuibishev, in April 1942, via Africa, not exactly a neophyte, to take over a bobtailed embassy in a former schoolhouse. By the time of his arrival the war had been on for almost a year. Swarms of hungry refugees from the west shambled along Kuibishev's streets with colorless faces, eyes red-rimmed. There were signs of incipient scurvy even among the embassy personnel, reflecting the sorry diet. More alarmingly, Commander F. R. Lang, the Navy medical officer, was recuperating from typhus.

Twenty American diplomatic clerks and all the women had been sent home, leaving a rump staff of about seven. Captain Duncan, naval attaché, a quick-witted, poker-playing Irishman, had been Admiral Standley's aide for years before the latter's retirement. As the first naval attaché in Russia

*Another highly knowledgeable potential leaker was Chief of Naval Operations Admiral Harold Stark. "I don't give a damn what happens to Stark," Roosevelt told Admiral King, "as long as you get him out of Washington as soon as practicable." Stark took his four stars and Distinguished Service Medal to London for the duration, considered by many as being heavily responsible for the Pearl disaster. See, *On The Treadmill to Pearl Harbor*, Admiral J. O. Richardson and Vice Admiral George C. Dyer, Naval History Division, 1973.

†*Foreign Relations*, vol. 1, 1941, p. 853.

‡General F. C. Poole, Royal Army, commanding Allied Forces North Russia, 1918.

since 1917, he had little tradition and no turnover notes to fall back on. (Captain Nimmer, in 1934, had been designated only as "assistant naval attaché.)

The new ambassador found little to do professionally. Only second-string Soviet Foreign Commissariat people were in town, and they were restricted to a reply of, "Nyet!" or occasionally, "Zavtra budyet!" (tomorrow it will be), a phrase mutually understood to be empty. This was a land where only the dictator himself could say, "Da!" to any but the most piddling requests.

The new attachés made calls on their only opposite numbers in town, the British, Swedes, and Japanese. A good bit of their time was laboriously spent over the Navy coding device, by which most of the State Department's highly verbose traffic came to the ambassador. The old gentleman also got in a lot of tennis, his partners often being drawn from the four NKVD bodyguards who stuck close by. It was after such a warming set or two that the ambassador noticed a tiny kiosk recently set up a few steps from his quarters. A long queue stood awaiting turns at the tincup on a chain and a swig of orange-brown liquid purported to be beer. "No! No!" protested the bodyguards. They would bring him some. It was not proper for him to stand in line and drink out of a tincup. Nothing doing, the ambassador retorted. He was going to do it just like any citizen, and so he proceeded to do. Next day the kiosk was gone.

The ambassador also went to church, whether out of curiosity or religious persuasion not made clear. At any rate, he was accosted at the door by the usual knot of ragged, elderly beggars, holding out pans. Standley, rather well known for his parsimony, had only a bill he felt too large to contribute to charity, so asked one of his accompanying staff to change it. An NKVD bodyguard, taking it all in, handed Standley's bill to one of the beggars, who pulled out a roll big enough to choke a horse, from which he made the necessary change. Every day was thus a small bit in the education of an ambassador who by the time he left had come to understand very well the oriental bazaar mentality of the Russians.

Admiral Standley renewed his acquaintance with Stalin for the first time as ambassador on 23 April 1942, having first met him during the October 1941 Lend-Lease conference. Stalin showed considerable strain, as well he might. The Germans, after having been pushed back from the Moscow suburbs in mid-winter, were taking advantage of the springtime drying out of the roads and fields to bounce back to the offensive. Relations with Britain were poor. Stalin was pressing London to agree to his demands for a postwar USSR frontier the same as that just prior to the German attack. This would include the Baltic States, a third of Poland, and a chunk of Romania. The British were being pressed by Washington not to accede, but Ambassador Halifax cynically told Under Secretary of State Sumner Welles that weighing the two on balance, he did not feel that enjoyment of self-government by the Baltic peoples could be compared in importance to the assurance that the Soviet Union would loyally continue until the end of the war.* There was obvious fear that Stalin would make a separate peace. The possible scenario was nothing less than bone-chilling: the British government would fall, and Sir Stafford Cripps (then the British ambassador in the USSR, and a communistically inclined socialist) would replace Churchill, following which a frankly pro-communist, pro-Moscow policy would be pursued.

Opinions were being voiced in Allied councils that the *real* reason the Soviets were violently agitating for a second front was to draw the new allies in so inextricably that they would never be able to entertain any thoughts of a separate peace with Germany.

It was in this harried atmosphere of mutual suspicion that the new Ambassador Standley donned his diplomatic spurs. And they could be sharp, directed not only at the recalcitrant Soviets but at Washington. In May 1942, he complained to the president that the first information he had had of a General George Marshall—Harry Hopkins visit to London to discuss with the British problems of supplies for the USSR—was when he read about it in *Pravda*. It was embarrassing when discussing this episode with Stalin, "because he presumed that I had not been taken fully into your confidence."† It was not the last time the old gentleman would have the ground cut out from under him.

As for the Soviets, Standley sent a blast to Secretary of State Cordell Hull on 5 July 1942 describing the uncooperative attitude of the Russians, already having voiced the same views to Premier Vyacheslav Molotov. Stalin was equally hard-nosed, needling Standley with his special Georgian-type humor. "What's the matter, Mr. Ambassador?" queried the Generalissimus, sucking on his briar. "Why are you staying in Kuibishev? Are you afraid?"

It was heady stuff for a youngish naval officer of 34 to be a party to such high-level matters—hearing them discussed, helping encipher and break the messages that we now see engraved in State Department archives. Only weeks before, this same naval officer had been thinking more in terms of how to catch sufficient fish, to better store rainwater, choose a hideout for the day, or outguess the Japanese on their next move, sailing the *Lanikai* out of harm's way.

*Welles-Halifax conversations, *Foreign Relations*, 1942, vol. 3, p. 538.

†*Foreign Relations of the United States*, Department of State, U. S. Government Printing Office, 1942, vol. 3, p. 551.

There were, of course, diversions other than high-level diplomacy. My journal, kept in contravention of wartime regulations, records, for example, that 13 June was a gorgeous, balmy, cloudless day that wound up with cocktails—the ambassador, Boswell, and second secretary Charley Dickerson—then hurrying off to dinner so as to be on time for *Don Quixote* at the opera house, "where met a couple of Chinese military attachés, several British ditto, a rather attractive Polish girl and several others unidentified." It was pure ballet. Don Q's horse didn't misbehave on stage, thus deciding winners and losers among embassy personnel who regularly wagered on this aspect of the performing arts. "And a Little Friend walked home with us," I concluded, "one 'Rita' (for 'Margarita'), who does it because she likes it and silk stockings. One of the few not fenced off by the YMCA." (The latter, was, of course, the euphemism common among foreigners for "NKVD," and obviously enough, Rita was not "fenced off" by the NKVD because she *was* the NKVD.)

It was Hitler's bad luck that the Russian winter of 1941–'42 was the worst in a century. His troops shivered in thin clothing, their feet frostbitten in boots that had room for only one pair of sox.* Eating their frozen horses, their tanks stalled with burst engines, they had been unable to withstand Marshal Giorgi Zhukov's slashing counterattack. Soviet pincers were already starting to close in on Stalingrad, so that by June 1942 the trickle back to Moscow of the foreign embassies commenced. Most of the Americans joined their rump staff left in Moscow: second secretary Llewellyn E. Thompson, Jr.,† and three others. Remaining in Kuibishev were Ambassador Standley, Minister-Counselor Walter Thurston and large boxer dog, and second secretary Edward Page, Jr., a socialite favorite of the ambassador who acted as a sort of flag lieutenant.

On 16 June, Captain Richard Park, Jr., assistant military attaché, and newly arrived assistant naval attaché Tolley were up at 2:30 A.M. and off to the airfield for a ride to Moscow in a Soviet Douglas. It was loaded to the marks with passengers and baggage, everybody scrambling and shoving. Also aboard was British Ambassador Archibald Clark-Kerr. As a morale-boosting indication of Allied confidence in ultimate Soviet victory, his return to Moscow was heavily covered by newsreel crews. Soon on screens

*Soviets wrapped their feet in long cloth strips in oversize boots. Their heavy overcoats were double-folded in back to open into a blanket. Trigger guards and bolts were made to be used while wearing mittens.

†An unprecedented twice ambassador to the USSR: 1957–1962, 1967–1969. A tight-lipped, poker-playing realist on Soviet affairs, "Tommy's" close wartime liaison with a member of the Moscow ballet provided a pipeline through which he could try out and receive suggestions that could not safely have been made officially.

throughout the country one heard the debonair trio described as, "the British Ambassador and his military staff, Majors Tolley and Park. One can forgive them; Dicky Park was in U. S. Army khaki and I was in my Aussie jacket and boots.

Frankel had been sent to the north, while Roullard had been left in Kuibishev to clear up loose ends and, along with Ronnie Allen, crack the ambassador's coded traffic. Included in Roullard's chores was sending the naval attaché's Ford sedan back to Moscow. Put on a barge, it sat there a week, obviously going nowhere. So Roullard went to reclaim it. "Your receipt says you are to receive the car in Moscow," said the young woman behind the wicket. "Let me remind you that you are *not* in Moscow but in Kuibishev. You cannot have the car without a letter requesting its return in *Kuibishev*. And don't forget the *pechat* [official seal], otherwise we cannot honor it." No amount of explanation had any effect. No letter and *pechat*, no car. Roullard's blood pressure mounted. He furiously threw his hat on the floor. "There!" he shouted. "Do I need a letter and a *pechat* to get my hat back?" He danced around in a fury. People came running from other rooms to see what the commotion was all about.

If indeed there was such a rule, certainly not beyond the realm of possibility in that bureaucratic land, the young woman was too flabbergasted at Roullard's outburst to invoke it. But, let us add, he got the car back.

The moral is that in dealing with Russians, especially petty functionaries, it may be more productive to take the offensive straightaway; a hundred years earlier, an American had observed that Russians were infuriatingly overbearing to inferiors and cringingly servile to supposed superiors. So operating on these lines, just-promoted Major James Boswell, assistant military attaché, wandered over to a parked plane at the Moscow airfield while awaiting someone's arrival. A sentry immediately sprang up out of the ground and warned him away.

"What are you doing, allowing a foreigner to get so close to a military secret?" stormed Boswell in his best parade ground manner. "What would have happened if I had been a German? I could have blown both you and the plane up!"

The by now thoroughly browbeaten and alarmed soldier, mumbling excuses and apologies to "the comrade commander," followed Boswell around as he circled the plane, taking in all the details, meanwhile carrying on a running commentary on the gruesome future awaiting sloppy sentries. When he had satisfied himself, Boswell walked off, first having extracted from the quivering guard an obviously heartfelt promise to be more careful in future.

There was a distinct deference shown foreign officers in the USSR, perhaps a hangover from the imperial tradition of employing foreign military to advise or even command Russian troops, but undoubtedly basically due to intrinsic Russian hospitality. The Soviet respect for rank also played a part. "This is a funny situation," said Captain Lieutenant Pancratov to Sam Frankel, who had given him a lift in his jeep in Murmansk. "Here you are, a captain in the important, powerful U. S. Navy, acting as chauffeur to me, a two-and-a-half striper." Frankel, one of the most informal of men, replied that he could not only be Pancratov's chauffeur, but his friend. "No, you could never be my friend," said Pancratov. "You are a captain and I am only a captain lieutenant."

The Soviets, adept at the quick switch in political tilt, were equally adaptable in re-shufflings of nomenclature and the roll of honor. World War I was known as "The First Imperialist War. World War II was "The Second Imperialist War" until Hitler attacked the USSR, then it instantly became "The Second Fatherland War," Napoleon's foray having been the "First." Along with this patriotic, nationalistic fervor came a dusting off of earlier, almost forgotten heroes. Military high schools became "Suvorov schools," after Napoleon's nemesis. Marshal Barclay de Tolly, a Scotsman in imperial Russian service against Napoleon (called "Bonapartay" by the Soviets), also was rehabilitated. Was I related to the marshal, Soviet friends wanted to know? "Undoubtedly," I would reply, with only a faint trace of blush. "We came from Scotland via Virginia to what is now Tolly Point near Annapolis in 1648." That to the Soviets I might just as well have been rattling off locations on the lunar landscape, and that somewhere along the line an "e" had been added to Tolley Point, was less important than establishing a better rapport with quondam adversaries.

(Actually, a direct descendant of the marshal came to the U. S. Military Mission in 1944: Lieutenant Colonel Nicholas de Tolly, AUS, the family having left Russia at the time of the Revolution. "Nick," with accented English and excellent Russian, was enthusiastically received.)

The last days of June 1942 were for me mostly a breaking in. There were the rounds of introductions to opposite numbers: Chinese, Swedish, Norwegian, British, Canadian, Turkish, Afghan. The Japanese were there too, but maintained a very low profile. There was the business of learning the names of Spasso's "downstairs" crew and where the passages and stairs led in that labyrinthine demi-palace. Most visible among the help to the newcomer were Edie, a wonderfully shy Siberian blonde chambermaid, and two fixtures of many years, Chinese houseboys named appropriately for a diplomatic atmosphere, "Gin," and "Tom," the latter originally, "Tonic." Edie's husband was Olaf, the naval attaché's driver, whose family, Finnish immigrants in the United States, had brought him as a teenager to the

USSR in the twenties, along with many other former Russian subjects returning to the land of freedom, prosperity, opportunity, equality, and a future, which they had come to believe the USA was not. They had torn up their United States passports in a grand celebration while crossing the Atlantic. Then came the great purges of 1936–1937, which swept into limbo anyone having had contact with the foreign infection. Olaf, speaking English with a proper East Side twang, as well as fluent Russian, was an outcast, unable to return to his birthplace, and desperately grateful for employment, temporary safety, and a ration card.

The ballet and opera were performed in the "filial," (branch) of the magnificent Bolshoi Theatre, while the latter's marble columns and facade of rampant horses were undergoing repairs from bomb damage. Tops in entertainment for the bland, blue-sky weather of a Moscow summer were such items as, *The Merry Wives of Windsor*, and the NKVD Ensemble, a magnificent extravaganza of song, dance, skit, and burlesque—no doubt calculated to soften the comrades' image of that dread institution. Admiral Standley, up from Kuibishev on one of his commuting trips, attended the Ensemble, along with almost the entire American diplomatic community, taking up the whole of "baldheaded row" (first row), soon to be derisively described as, "the second front." Gravely seated behind the ambassador were his three occasional tennis partners, sideboys, and bodyguards, the NKVD "boys," very evident in their black suits and stark white celluloid collars. On the mile walk home to Spasso in the soft summer twilight, people taking the air were friendly and curious at the variety of foreign uniforms. The military saluted, kids said "hello" with a smile, and drunks gravely if unsteadily took off their hats. Even the occasional NKVD trooper clumping by, distinguished by his sky-blue cap cover, seemed less ominous after that dream of Russian songs, dances, and spirit by the uniformed boys and girls of the secret police choir.

There constantly was somebody coming or going, with Thompson, the Spasso "manager," always somehow able to scrounge the necessary makings for a mini-banquet. Even stony-visaged old Molotov had risked cracking his face by joking with Thompson that last week there were only ten swans in the performance of *Swan Lake*, rumor having it that the American embassy had demanded a couple of large birds for a special affair.

Something after the old pre-war fashion of "a traveler reports," a British colonel dropped in from Tashkent, liaison officer with the Polish divisions being formed from ex-prisoners of war picked up by the Soviets in 1939. He had interesting tales to tell of the anti-Russian attitude of the native Moslems, and of the beauty of the surroundings. It was no longer an oriental city with flying carpets and thieves-of-Baghdad types, but had wide streets lined with mighty trees, all the trimmings of a successful

Soviet city. It was in his honor that a large duck appeared on the table, possibly one of those swans.

Frankel and Roullard, from Archangel and Kuibishev respectively, dropped in for several days, bringing news and swelling the afternoon cocktail round. The embassy bar repertoire included two mainstays: first, the tomsky collins—Navy lemon powder for pies, mixed with vodka, diluted with narzan, a natural mineral water, garnished with a sprig of a plant the Soviet agricultural fellow claimed was mint, but strongly suggested catnip; second was the iron curtain, antedating Churchill by several years, a mixture of one bottle each of vodka, dry white wine, and champagne, a cake of ice swimming on top. Even the attaché group all together could not have safely coped with three bottles at one sitting, so the iron curtain was reserved for large official parties. Its effect was dramatic.

Following routine, I went out to the military airfield to speed Frankel and Roullard on their way, stopping by the Northern Sea Route Headquarters to pick up other passengers. One was an exceedingly pretty little Red Army captain, carrying a bouquet almost as large as herself. She was on leave from Polyarnoe, naval base at the Kola Inlet entrance, to visit her mother in Ryazan. In four days' leave, she had managed four hours at home, having hiked the last 18 kilometers. It was a story repeated many times, memorialized in that touching Soviet film, "The Cranes Are Flying." "Cute as a bug's ear," I wrote in my journal, "and speaking pretty good English. In fact, too good *British*, having mentioned we were 'pulling her leg.' Sounds like the British Supply Mission's perfidy."

Russians are inveterate strollers, whether it be in the theatre foyer during the entr'acte, or summer evenings in the park. It is a prime opportunity to size up and be sized up.

Too full of the *joie de vivre* to sit at home after dinner, too stuffed to play badminton on the lawn, no ballet scheduled that day, the younger attachés often followed the Russian example of exploring Moscow's wide streets and many parks that dot the city. One such evening there was nothing doing for a long time as several of us sat on a bench in the parkway off Arbat Square. Then a young parachutist came up to ask for a cigarette. Then several others. Then more, like all humans who see a gathering knot of people, wondering what the attraction may be. Soon there was a generous crowd to share our cigarettes and exchange chat. Last to hang on as it grew dark were two high school girls of seventeen, perhaps drawn to each other through both being named Zena. We were more inclined to notice the fresh young faces unmarked by cosmetics than the stockingless legs, run-over slippers and faded but neat print dresses. Cornflower blue eyes opened wide gave an air of perpetual astonishment, understandable enough in that neither had ever before exchanged a word with someone from outer space. There was no need for those black brassieres here; ample, pointed young bosoms thrust out in high relief well up on the chest.

In the deepening twilight we talked of many things—life, the war, love, God, food, future hopes. They poured out their hearts in earnest if not eloquent enthusiasm, taxing our poor Russian to keep abreast of the flood of questions and comments on our replies.

There were other times when the scenario shifted. On another such outing, two "kholhoznitsi" joined us, typical potato-nosed farm girls eager for a smoke. One was seventeen, the other nineteen, Russian, earthy, but full of a brand of chat a tourist wouldn't hear in a hundred years. "Harmless types (probably)," I set down in my journal that night. After an hour's badinage on their boy friends, what American girls were like, and how much better Moscow was than the village, we dropped them off home, first having to push the military attaché's rattletrap of a car down a hill to get it started. "Wonder on the part of our passengers," my account records, "one of them admitting to being a mechanic and driver first class (tractor?), remarking on how wonderfully smooth the motor ran, how unlike anything Sovietski it was. Very quiet, simple and not too sweet," I concluded, "but a sound evening for ten cigarettes."

There were many such evenings, many such friends of an hour, never meaning, expecting, even hoping ever to meet again. Sad, sad that such a cleavage should exist between two great peoples.

Along with the rest of the American official colony, chief of the U. S. Army Supply Mission, Brigadier General Philip Faymonville, and his crew had retreated to Kuibishev. But he was back early to Moscow. His long previous service in the USSR, during which his sympathies had clearly been pro-Soviet, had put him in a solid position with top officials, including Stalin himself. This special entrée allowed him to establish himself in Mokovaya, the embassy chancery and apartment building, before anyone else. Several of the Supply Mission officers occupied one of the Mokovaya apartments, ensuring more privacy than Spasso's fishbowl environment. It was a convenient downtown watering hole after the opera or a visit to the liaison office, which after the Russian fashion could be anything up to midnight. There were always some prospects of a real martini or even a whisky-and-splash, the Mission having good contacts in Teheran. Another of the apartments had been partly set to rights, referred to as the snake den and used to bed down couriers passing through.

Dropping in one evening at the Mission apartment, I found a small party in progress, not an unusual event. The two guests were quite unlike anything I had so far seen in the Soviet Union—svelte, soignée, conservatively made up, impeccable hairdos, high heels, stockings, and modish dresses, both of them really beauties. They far outshone even the pick of the

Major Ivan Yeaton, prewar military attaché, and Mrs. Yeaton in front of Mokovaya, the embassy chancery. My apartment is above the flagstaff.

ballet foyer promenaders. Introductions were made, and the small talk my entry had interrupted resumed. I soon learned that Vasya was a refugee from Poland. "Oh! I know Poland well, "I said enthusiastically. "I've a number of friends in the Polish Navy." Vasya looked at me disdainfully. "Don't talk to me of that Polish dung," she sneered. "I am not Polish; I am Jewish!"

As for the other young lady, one almost was ready to conclude that standardization of Soviet life extended to first names; she, also, was Zena.

Vasya and Zena did not instantly fade into memory as had our chance park bench acquaintances. During the next several weeks, along with an embassy attaché who had taken a fancy to Vasya, we went to the ballet, to the Hermitage Park for the open-air musicale, and took walks in the city—all punctuated by jolly parties in the Supply Mission apartment. The

Zena wearing my uniform.

finale of one of these affairs was the snake den. With the two of us alone in the semidarkness, Zena was disarmingly discreet in her approach, asking the most innocent questions. Was I married? Why had I wanted to come to the Soviet Union? Where did I acquire my knowledge of the Russian language? Did I know any émigrée Russians? What were the girls like? Were they pretty? Well behaved? Whom had I met in the Soviet Union that I liked?

Then she talked about herself. She had been married, but it didn't work out; couldn't even say where the fellow was. Perhaps killed in the war. Yes, the war. That was the great burden. "This damned black underwear!" she exploded. "Just look at it. Well, you can't see it properly, but feel it. Like burlap. Its a uniform for all of us. Of course it doesn't show the dirt, which is just as well, because the soap, when you can get it, stinks of fish oil. Just have a sniff of this bra!"

Building up her ire, Zena damned the communists. It was the old game of *agente provocatrice*, sounding out, baiting, not very artfully contrived. Was she so naive or simply such an amateur as to suppose I didn't know the place was bugged, and that I didn't know that she knew it was bugged?

Poor Vasya and Zena! After a few weeks there were no more telephone calls. (We never could call them.) A year later I chanced to bump into Vasya on the street. She was haggard and ill-looking, her dark eyes deep in their sockets, a husk of what once had been a beautiful, poised young woman. She scuttled away at my approach to greet her, knowing that very probably an NKVD man was on my tail.

Vasya and Zena had done their bit as bidden. Were they shucked off as no longer productive? Or had they been judged guilty of the all too human frailty of following normal impulses?

Thus it went. Tall, slim, brown-haired Irina, met while strolling in the ballet foyer, came to my apartment half a dozen times. She was a pretty, intelligent girl of twenty, her claim to be a university student substantiated by her obvious breeding, manner, and conversation. With a display of affection that had been growing, taking a fearful risk in such a revelation, she tearfully told me on what was to be her final visit that she had been assigned to the British Mission, and thenceforth must avoid Americans. We passed again from time to time in the Bolshoi theatre foyer, but there was no sign of recognition.

Welcome help for the one-man coding detail (me), arrived in the form of Lieutenant (jg) Winston W. Cram, USNR. He and Commander Lea, RN, whom I had known in Tallinn seven years before as a fellow Russian student, arrived from Archangel stuffed into a four-place compartment along with a vast pile of long overdue, very welcome mail, plus a pair of Lea's skis, the latter whether for sport or for anticipated evacuation eastward not made clear in the confusion of arrival.

Chosen for Moscow because he spoke "Slavic," which ONI presumably felt covered Russian, Cram was a jolly, pug-nosed fellow who gave every indication, later well justified, of being good shipmate material. " 'Cram' is too formal," I said, after the hubbub of getting detrained was over. "What do we call you?" With a big grin he took off his cap, revealing a shiny pate sparsely fringed over the ears. " 'Curly' is the name," he said.

Amongst the baggage were two cipher machines, a huge step up from the slow, primitive devices I had been struggling with. The machines must have been roughly handled en route; for an anguished two days I worked on them, aided by the experience of ten years before when the machines first were being developed and introduced in the navy. Then at last they whirred and clattered, cranking out what we hoped would be something the Russians and Germans would have trouble cracking.

Curly Cram had been a newspaper correspondent in pre-war Poland, the source of his "Slavic" capability. Another spinoff of his Polish caper had been a honing of his piano-playing ability, coupled with an enhanced appreciation of Chopin's haunting melodies. Early after our moving from

Spasso to Mokovaya, Curly had contracted with Burobin, the agency that seemingly existed primarily to frustrate foreigners, to supply him with a baby grand piano, a matter requiring the posting of a several thousand roubles deposit. Primed lightly with vodka, rocking back and forth on the stool, Curly would produce chords and melodies by the hour, soothing to the soul after a day in which one wondered what the hell, if anything, really had been accomplished.

Periodically, the air raid siren would wail, announcing what usually turned out to be a German reconnaissance plane or a lone bomber at high altitude—small danger to a great city, but of considerable nuisance value in its disruption of life. The bomb might drop anywhere. More dangerous by far was the shower of shards from antiaircraft shells. Curly retreated under the big piano at such times, jokingly remarking that if the piano went, he wanted to go too, what with that 5,000 rouble deposit in escrow.

Manual dexterity inherent in a pianist, coupled with a most uncorrespondent-like ability to use the touch system on a typewriter, combined to make Curly a virtuoso at the cipher machine. Perhaps he felt he was producing a lyric, which judging from the content of most of those messages, would have suggested an imagination fertile beyond the ken of a salt water sailor.

Curly was the first of us to be licensed to drive a motor car, a by no means simple accomplishment that required undergoing an examination in the theory of internal combustion engines, the intricate traffic pattern of Moscow, and the awful penalties of transgressions of the rules—the latter more applicable to those of nondiplomatic status. More practically, being privileged to drive meant that the nondrivers were out behind in the starting process, pushing the model A Ford until the near-kerosene smokily started to fire. Only when a U. S. bomber came to town was the starting procedure less complicated; half a barrel of Soviet "gasoline" blended with half a barrel bled from the bomber's tanks made an acceptable fuel.

Later, I took the driver's test myself, passing easily. Olaf translated, as an accomplished mechanic and long time chauffeur, giving impeccably correct replies that sometimes had only marginal resemblance to mine in English. One is reminded of the stock Russian humor concerning two sons: a mother, describing them to a friend, explained that one of them was quite bright, but the other became a militiaman (policeman). If one must take recourse to mild subterfuge in a good cause, when it concerns Moscow policemen, so be it.

Duncan's Red Navy contact normally was Captain 2nd rank Zaitsev, in his office by appointment. Vodka was always produced, along with blocks of excellent Russian chocolate, seemingly a bizarre combination, but actually very good. Captain Lieutenant Mikhail Kostrinsky, formerly assistant naval attaché in the United Kingdom, one of those rare Russians who spoke good English, often was on hand. But there were unusual occasions when a more rarified stratum was indicated, such as congratulations on Red Navy Day. In those cases, Duncan would request an audience with the deputy navy commissar, tall, grandfatherly ex-Czarist captain, Vice Admiral Stepanov. Or later, jolly, roly-poly, French-speaking Alafuzov.

In one particular situation, it seemed appropriate to go even higher—to the commissar himself, Admiral of the Fleet Nikolai G. Kuznetsov. It concerned one of six Soviet submarines sent from Vladivostok in October 1942 via the Panama Canal to Murmansk. Each boat had picked up an American liaison cadre in Dutch Harbor and headed south. Aboard the *L-16* as interpreter was Chief Photographer Sergei A. Mihailoff, USN, a naturalized American born in St. Petersburg.

The Japanese submarine *I-25* had one torpedo left. About 800 miles off the Washington coast, as she was starting back for Japan, two submarines were sighted moving south on the surface about 800 yards apart. Assuming them to be American, Commander Tagami ordered the last torpedo fired at the leading one from a distance of about 500 yards. It must have hit a vital spot. Witnesses on both the *I-25* and the other Soviet sub describe the resulting explosion as devastating. Torpedoman Shoji Aizawa said that the shock broke glass covers on instruments, put out some lights and broke porcelain toilets aboard the *I-25*. U.S. officials had offered partial air cover from Alaska to Panama, but the Soviets refused it, preferring not to follow a definite course.

No American submarine was operating in the area. But the incident presented a potentially embarrassing international situation. The Soviet Union and Japan were not at war and would not be for nearly three more years. The *I-25*'s skipper, Tagami, reported that he had sunk an American sub.

Of course, none of the foregoing facts concerning the sinking was known to Duncan; merely the report of the commanding officer of the remaining submarine, *L-15*, when she appeared at San Francisco. Captain Lieutenant Vasily I. Komazov had seen the bow of the *L-16* disappear and heard two underwater explosions take place. Two periscopes of a submarine were sighted 1,500 yards to port and the *L-15* fired five rounds at them without apparent result.*

*See, "L-16—Mystery No Longer," Rear Admiral George M. Lowry, U. S. Naval Institute *Proceedings*, January 1942, pp. 115–16. Also, "L-16 Sinking—'No Mistake, Just Dirty Work,' " C. P. Lemieux, *Proceedings*, 1963, pp. 118–20. Also, Commander, Western Sea Frontier letter (SC) Serial 1363 of 18 October 1942, Naval Operational Archives.

Admiral Kuznetsov radiated the stability of a granite bridge pylon. Although he was not above average height, his broad shoulders and flat stomach, most un-Russian in a top commander, gave the impression of massive physical strength. Feet spaced apart as if on the deck of a rolling ship, face chiseled in angular lines rather than curves, his presence was too austere even for Duncan to try his dry wit. So we never had the opportunity to assess the commissar's smile, assuming he ever produced one.

Kuznetsov's reaction to the American regrets over the sinking was unexpected and perhaps revelatory of his character: "Think nothing of it." he said gruffly. "If they were so careless as to get caught napping, they deserved to get sunk. They would have been no use here!" was his rather brutal treatment of the incident.

The audience was short. There was no idle chat, no vodka, not even chocolate. Or the generally inevitable exchange of platitudes on the detested Hun. His ham of a hand was extended in farewell as in greeting—feet wide apart as if it were an approach to a standing bout of Indian wrestling. Clearly here was a man whom Ernie King would have found compatible.

July in Moscow is much like in New England: warmish days, cool nights, clear blue skies. The younger service attachés—Majors Boswell and Park and Captain Robert E. McCabe—visited the zoo, sat on park benches and chatted with citizens who drifted up to share a cigarette. I joined them when I wasn't bent over the coding machine.

The elders hung around Spasso House, reading, endlessly discussing "the situation," visiting British Military Mission colleagues, or making an occasional trip to the Soviet military liaison office to exchange innocuous information. When my boss Duncan went, I accompanied as interpreter. Constant requests to visit military establishments and armament factories resulted in invitations to inspect a chocolate factory, a hospital, and the Novodeivichie Monastery, where a lot of notables are buried. In the evenings, there was always a pool game in the big billiard room. Two or three nights a week, a party of half a dozen or so attended the opera or ballet in front row seats, the curtain rising at 6 P.M. to beat the blackout at dusk and the midnight curfew. Dinner was at the European hour of 10 P.M., the near starvation diet of late 1941 transformed by summer vegetables, an augmented diplomatic ration, and supplies sent down from Archangel, scrounged from U. S. merchant ships. The ration of fish was three kilograms a month. But there was no fish, so prime black caviar was substituted. Potato pancakes topped with copious gobs of caviar and sour cream was a staple breakfast item. An allotment of four liters of vodka per month plus more or less unlimited wine was sufficient to avoid parched throats. Sunday movies in Spasso's ballroom with new American and British films flown in via diplomatic pouch drew a crowd of twenty or more news correspondents and foreign diplomats. But no Soviets. Those we saw only at official parties or in their offices.

As the summer waxed, so did activities at Spasso House. On the Glorious Fourth, the occasion was especially marked by a reception, Ambassador-Admiral Standley up from Kuibishev for the occasion, "jubilant over the results of his session with Stalin several days ago," my journal records. After the movies, "The Earl of Chicago," Robert Montgomery up, the journal continues that, "The British, Free French, Afghan rug merchants, etc., swept out and after a polite lapse the punch trundled in. The newshawks had stayed: Robinson, Gilmore, Leland Stowe, the two Henrys—Shapiro (UP) and Cassidy (AP)—Larry Lesueur, and several others. A terrific poker game following, with skipper Duncan high man to the tune of something like 3,000 roubles [$250]. Newspapers will probably go up to 4¢ in the States after all the newshawks' expense accounts are in. On later to Colonel Exham's with Eddie Page (we both had known him in Riga where he was a British Army Russian student) for more vodka, white wine, champagne, and brandy in quantities to cement the alliance most solidly. Home in the dusk of 1:30 A.M., curfew be damned, and had no complaints from the militsia. In fact, hard to find one to show us the way."

By 6 July, the journal recalls that I was, "still feeling the effects of the Boston Tea Party, but not too far gone to join Colonel Mike [Michela], just promoted to full bird, probably the youngest in the U. S. Army, and the rest of the attachés for a few tomski collinses before dinner. A quiet day and a more quiet evening doing some late-arrived ciphers." And reflecting a certain disenchantment with some aspects of diplomatic life, I ended the day's entry with, "Naval attaché or code clerk?"

One always had to expect the unexpected. Walking back one evening from the office, I found a sizeable group in the great hall at Spasso. A long table groaning with sakuska had been set up, stretching under the monster chandelier with its hundreds of glittering little bulbs and iridescent prisms. A dozen or so people were standing around socializing, some bellied up to the table, eating, others with glass in hand, chatting. Most of them I hadn't seen before, some in British uniform, some in civvies. Joining the group, I was soon busy piling caviar on a slice of bread while exchanging remarks with a stranger likewise engaged, a tall, slim, impeccably turned-out fellow with a trim military mustache. Meanwhile, we were amiably swapping small talk—the weather, the front, and such sundry trifles. "We mustaches should stick together for mutual support," I said. "By the way, my name's Tolley, Kemp Tolley." He shifted his drink and held out his hand. "Mine's Tony," he replied. "Tony Eden." Thus, informally, did I get to know a most charming man, Britain's foreign secretary Anthony Eden, over on a super-secret, surprise visit.

Other functions reflected less international flavor, one such being an evening's entertainment set up by that indefatigable entrepreneur and diplomat Tommy Thompson. The star was Lalya Chernaya, a magnificent Gypsy of the type one imagined had set the imperial princes afire one war earlier. Reported to be married to a Soviet general and thus supporting the old tradition, "Chernaya"—meaning black—was an appropriate *nom d'étage*. She was very dark, with flowing black hair and jet black eyes, dressed in a voluminous dark skirt glittering with sequins. Accompanied by several guitarists, she sang wild extravaganzas in a throaty voice, sometimes tinged with pathos, sometimes with trilling shrieks of abandon, whirling about in flamboyant dances, castanets clacking, filling the great rotunda with reverberating sound.

Then there were stunts—Gypsy magic and tricks. Handed a one- or two-line message written by one of us in the audience, the pianist would belt out a lively tune lasting two or three minutes. Then a member of the troupe on the other side of the room would bring us the message we had given the pianist, word for word. What a way to transfer clandestine information in a crowded cafe!

There were other Gypsy tricks, too. Some members of the troupe had occasion to visit the bathroom. After the performers had departed, it was discovered that the medicine cabinets were bare of soap, toothbrushes, paste, and pills. And Tommy's favorite bedroom slippers were missing, too, though not taken from his feet, although it was later said that these worthies undoubtedly could have removed his sox without unlacing the shoes.

The weekly movies drew most of the diplomatic colony; films were air-lifted in from Britain and the USA to trade with the Soviets for their productions. Of a dozen films, perhaps three would be accepted by the Soviet censors. They would be musical extravaganzas or war films, nothing which portrayed the American scene that might be compared too favorably with the Soviet paradise. Soviet films all carried a message, a quality not likely to be paramount in Hollywood eyes. "Vot ees de poleetical seegneefi-cance of thees film?" inquired bewildered liaison officer Captain-Lieutenant Pancratov in Murmansk, on witnessing a typical Hollywood pot boiler shown in Sam Frankel's mess hall mini-theatre.

The Spasso projector operator, an embassy handyman, was paid in the only really negotiable currency—a half liter of vodka. In one of the earlier showings, the vodka was handed over before the performance, a gross tactical error. The film progressed satisfactorily enough for the first reel or two, after which matters became progressively more confused. Reels came in indiscriminate order or a previously shown reel not yet rewound appeared upside down in backward motion. Although a good many of the programs would not have suffered much from such treatment, it was henceforth felt that as a matter of principle and good order the vodka should come last.

In mid-July 1942, although the war still held in the balance on the eastern front, it was decided that the service attachés would move out of Spasso to Mokovaya. But the Spasso messing arrangement would continue for the time being, as housekeeper and general factotum Thompson could best pool all the ration tickets to produce the most efficient culinary effort. Besides, gathering all hands, diplomats and service attachés together along with the ambassador, at least for dinner allowed a broad discussion of matters affecting Washington as well as ourselves.

Mokovaya, the chancery, was a five-story Italian Renaissance-cum-Slavic overtones building, beautifully situated on a huge square looking across at the Kremlin, the great box of the Moscow Hotel at one end, the czar's riding stable at the other. Through the gap between the Kremlin and the red brick pile of the Lenin Museum, one could see a good part of Red Square. Prewar, Spasso House had been exclusively the ambassador's residence. It had enormous public rooms—great hall, state dining room, music room, billard room, and so forth—but only fifteen bedrooms leading off the balcony surrounding the great hall at the second floor level, so that the service attachés, steadily increasing in number, were more and more

The view of the Moscow Hotel (left) and a portion of the Kremlin from my apartment window.

cramped for bunking space. I slept in the code room to avoid Ronnie Allen's thunderous snoring.

Mokovaya had been abandoned, with most of its furniture intact, when dependents were sent home at war's outbreak. So there was plenty of apartment and office space for all. As a junior division officer I had learned early the art of the "moonlight requisition" from canny old petty officers. One asked no questions when a nice new rug appeared in the skipper's gig, through no effort of the Supply Department. Or a fifty-foot purple plush rope mounted on brass posts, large tassels at the ends, appeared around the quarterdeck one Saturday morning at inspection. Or a solid brass ladder suddenly replaced the old war-color steel one leading up to the captain's veranda. From such beginnings it was small potatoes for Tolley, nominated by Duncan as first lieutenant in charge of naval housing, to arrive on the Mokovaya scene earliest. By climbing over transoms or picking locks with bent nails, it was child's play to select the best of Uncle Sam's largesse in the way of furniture, bricabrac, pictures, drapes, and rugs to adorn the digs slated to be inhabited by Duncan and Allen. With the VIPs taken care of, not forgotten, of course, were the SLIPs (slightly less important persons) who were set to share an apartment, myself and my highly appreciated relief at the code machine, Curly Cram. In only one respect was my tactical cunning at fault; in the balmy Moscow summer, who would have foreseen that having the flagpole protrude from our apartment's balcony would entail the daily running out and retrieving of the national colors? On the

face of it, this might appear to be an operation appealing to any red-blooded sailorman, until realizing that the balcony's double doors could not be sealed like everything else when winter's minus 40° howled down from the north. (All Mokovaya's windows were double, the inner and outer sashes separated by about six inches. The sash edges were sealed with glued paper strips in winter. One pane of each six-paned sash was hinged, so that it could be opened for ventilation.)

Having served aboard Yangtze gunboats, where each officer wears half a dozen hats, it was no strain in Moscow to find myself code clerk, housing officer, photographer, intelligence officer, and logistician, the last a euphemism for food scrounger. During the summer of 1942 one of my regular letters to Major Andrew Wylie, USMCR, ONI's Russian desk holder, suggested some of the angles.

"I drove out to the kolhoz* this morning to pick up some vegetables. The Director said we would have to write a letter. (Every goddam thing requires a letter, even a theatre ticket.) Write a letter to Burobin (office for all deals with foreigners) saying what we wanted. They would in due course pass it to the regional directorate of kolhozes. From there it would go to the local directorate in the general area where our kolhoz was located. Those comrades would give it to our kolhoz manager, and provided it was not early winter by that time, we could collect our stuff. Bring our own bags.

Just for the fun of it, we followed the trail until the highest (Burobin) where we ran into the usual stone wall. The Director would be away for some time. Nobody else could do anything about it. This had taken all day. Trying a new tack, we wrote our letter, took it straight out to the kolhoz this morning, paid double price for everything, coming back with a carload of cabbage, tomatoes, cucumbers, plus two carrots on the house for lunch. Everybody was as fine as frog hair and a political director hollered sharp words at a local comrade who was griping about our getting ahead of him in line. Faymonville's chauffeurs and various spare pump handles were clustering around the car when we came back, wanting to know whence the windfall, but no telling. People fall out over a cabbage around here. Or a couple of tomatoes.

"Apparently the Second Front is still a subject of light remarks among the Reds. Somebody was telling me that when the soldiers open up a can of American food, one of them can be counted on to make a crack about, 'Well, boys, here is the opening of the Second Front! Hurrah!'"

"I stopped by to chat with the NKVD lad out in front of Mokovaya the other night and we got to discussing the poor state of the potato crop in our

Kollektivnoe hozaistvo, collective farm, theoretically "owned" by the members.

victory garden front yard. He on the strong, simple side, a muscle man. Said he believed there were buried steam pipes that heated the ground too much. I told him my theory—the site of Mokovaya is an old burial ground. The place is charged with old bones which give manifestations on dark nights that we have so far found no explanation for. It is well known that potatoes thrive no better in supernatural phenomena than do humans. Obviously, there were lots of old skulls and disjointed bones out there trying to get themselves reassembled after the steam shovels had messed up the place. Later, looking out the window, I noted the NKVD man was doing his patrolling well out into the street."

Curly Cram's background of foreign news correspondent had sharpened his ingenuity. Aside from being a virtuoso at the piano and code machine, he had such remarkable talents as making a large can of spam taste like a roast of pork, manufacturing Boston baked beans from scratch with far-out Russian substitutes, brewing *kvass*, a mild sort of beer, from black bread, and producing a passable wine from raisins.

Driving in the countryside one Sunday we came upon great fields of dandelions, just the stuff for vinous experiment. We were picking merrily away when an NKVD trooper appeared from out of the ground, looking very stern and businesslike, demanding our documents. What were we doing picking those dandelions, he wanted to know. To make *wine*? This obviously was too much. "You will explain please exactly how you make this wine!" he said sharply, not handing back the documents, even refusing a cigarette, suggesting he clearly felt he had got his teeth into something. Several more NKVD men had joined the party. Another of Curly's talents was a thoroughly well-developed sense of fun, in this case less inhibited than was indicated under the circumstances through the effects of the bottle of wine that had washed down our picnic lunch earlier. In Polish-accented Russian he explained with gestures the manufacture of dandelion wine, including the blessing of the hops (which one would assume even an NKVD man knew wasn't an ingredient of wine), the barefooted stomping of the flowers, then the seven rackings of the glorious golden nectar. One could only assume that we were let loose through the NKVD logic that the man had to be a harmless lunatic, who like children and drunks was to be humored as far as possible.

The bottom line, as we later discovered, was not a prohibition on picking the beautiful yellow flowers, but the fact that the road led to Stalin's *dacha*.

The first really big Soviet affair was in celebration of Red Navy Day, 25 July. There was wine for stand-up cocktails in the old National Hotel banquet room. Next, at a long table totally covered with plates of food and glassware, 50 or so people sat down to zakuska with vodka, then in turn, soup, fish, chicken, and steak, each with its special wine.

Ranged around the table were deputy navy commissar Vice Admiral Alafuzov, the otherwise unidentified general commandant of Moscow, Soviet General Panfilov, a Free French general, Colonel Yestignaev (military liaison), Captain second rank Zaitsev (naval liaison), Rear Admiral G. J. A. Miles, chief of the British Naval Mission, British Colonel Exham, all our own service attachés, and more lesser Soviets.

By my left sat the general commandant of Moscow, large of belly like most Soviet lieutenant generals. Perforce eating little and drinking nothing due to stomach problems, he was not in a jovial mood. Most of his time was spent twitting Zaitsev across the table, whose Red Navy was in a largely subsidiary role. "Look here, Zaitsev," the general boomed for all to hear. "Here is an American naval officer—from the greatest navy in the world (frowns from Miles)—and he is dressed in khaki." (I was in my Australian "horse pants" and boots.) The Red Navy soon would be in khaki, too, the general continued, as was proper and fitting for an appendage of the Red Army. "Yes! Get some zip in your appearance. Good for morale!"

The endless speeches finally intervened. Colonel Michela, U. S. military attaché, gave one in Russian. Duncan's was in English, but made up for it in wit, humor, and gentle suggestions that the more cooperation the sooner the war would be over. The French general gave a fiery dissertation, translated into Russian by Admiral Alafuzov (an unusually urbane fellow for a Russian admiral, probably as a counterweight to stonefaced, hard-nosed Navy Commissar Kuznetsov), then translated into English by General Panfilov. The speech was by now probably in a considerably macerated state, considering the number of toasts so far downed. All extolled the beautiful friendship burgeoning not only across the seas, but right here at the dinner table. Nobody mentioned the candy factory or the Novodeivichie cemetery.

The afternoon following the banquet, ballet bound, I had some papers to drop off with Zaitsev en route. He hadn't made it to the office. Winding down from the night before, he was sitting at a table in his National Hotel bedroom, three sheets in the wind, washing down a chicken with tumblers of vodka. I must join him or greatly offend the American Navy's best friend in Moscow, he declared, offering me a tumbler of vodka. "To the downfall of that sookin sin (son-of-a-bitch) of a general!" he proposed, obviously still smarting from the needling of the previous night. "We'll fix that general and his dung-colored uniforms! I'll get you a blue one." Eventually I made the ballet, rewarded by seeing more actors and horses (it was *Don Quixote*) than the program called for, everything appearing double.

Commander Tolley in Moscow in 1942, three months after escaping the debacle in Java. The modified Australian Army uniform he is wearing was the only thing available in West Australia. Earlier arriving destitute survivors had long since used up the supply of blue cloth.

The following day I was called to the liaison office. "Here is enough material to make a uniform and an overcoat—flag officer quality, gold buttons," said a beaming Zaitsev, handing me a bolt of beautiful broadcloth. "Here's the address of the Navy tailor. He'll make it up."

To the elegant, wasp-waisted, broad-shouldered ensemble thus provided, I was able to add several campaign ribbons scrounged in Fremantle.

The Russian military is very decoration-conscious. Additional awards of the same medal are added to the row of ribbons rather than pinning stars on the first award, so that elderly generals can be ribbon-plated from clavicle to belly button. Thus, even though most Soviets prudently keep their noses out of matters that don't concern them, my combination of Red Navy uniform with offbeat ribbons was too much for the curiosity of naval officers promenading around the foyer during the opera or ballet entr'acte.

"Excuse me, comrade captain third rank," one might say. "But what are those ribbons you are wearing?" A man with a certain sense of deviltry can be forgiven for giving a lengthy reply in English. Roll a mixture of apprehension, surprise, astonishment, and bewilderment into one and you have a fair description of the expressions on the faces of my questioners. One, less shaken, summed it up very briefly: "*Boje moi!*" he gasped to his companion. "*On s'uma soshol!*" (My God! He's nuts!)

Along with being decoration-conscious, the Russian is also extremely rank-conscious. Privates give up seats in trams to officers; when a senior pulls out a cigarette, juniors are there in an instant with a match. Captain Frankel discovered from a Soviet friend in Murmansk why senior officers had not come to his large party for port officials; also on the invitation list were several Soviet clerks and his own enlisted men.

Before my arrival in the USSR, Duncan had decided to send me to Vladivostok to relieve Lieutenant Commander C. H. Taecker, to be the top and only U. S. Navy man there. So he had requested the Navy Department to give me a spot promotion to commander, although I had only been promoted to lieutenant commander several months previously. The Vladi deal fell through (no civilian clothes!), but the rank was authorized, making me at the tender age of 34 probably the youngest three-striper in the Navy. The extra rank was useful in dealing with the Soviets in Moscow and the northern ports.

But still, the shoulder boards confused the Soviets. Navy sleeve stripes and star above were identical in both navies. But my three-stripe shoulder boards denoted sergeant in the Soviet armed forces; *their* officers' shoulder boards were near solid gilt, with star groupings indicating rank. In winter, wearing my tall, Cossack-style caracul uniform hat, sergeant's shoulder boards covered by a matching fur overcoat collar, Soviet colonels passing on the street would snap into a crashing goosestep while presenting a stiff salute; such hats were worn only by generals in the USSR. A soldier in a photographer's anteroom, perched on the bench next to me while we awaited our turn, came straight to the point concerning my three-stripe shoulder boards pinned to an aviator's winter jacket: "Hey, sarge!" he inquired jovially, "what the hell are you doing with a gold chinstrap?"

The official seat of government throughout the summer of 1942 was Kuibishev, even though Stalin, Molotov, and the Defense commissariat never left Moscow. Admiral Standley attempted to interpret the rules as seemed appropriate by remaining in Kuibishev, commuting to Moscow on those infrequent occasions that required an audience with the top.

Major General Follett Bradley, U. S. Army Air Corps,* had lumbered

*Ninth in the U. S. Naval Academy class of 1910.

over to Moscow in a B-24, arriving 4 August, to set up delivery of Lend-Lease aircraft via Siberia: Nome, Seimchan, Yakutsk, Kirensk, Krasnoyarsk. This would save crating the fighters and losing some on the Murmansk run, or flying the bombers circuitously via Brazil to Iran.

Bradley's B-24 was used on one occasion to fetch the ambassador to Moscow in state for one of his Stalin chats. A Soviet navigator was assigned to guide the American crew,† with me as translator. The flight was at near treetop level, after the Russian fashion; Nazi intruders were still about. The navigator, an elderly Ukrainian major whose Russian left much to be desired, gave the impression of being totally lost most of the time. When he had positively identified some landmark, he would burst into song, first having passed the good news via intercom to his Soviet radioman back aft.

The day after the B-24's arrival, the pilots and mechanics went out to the airfield to houseclean the plane. I was along as interpreter. The place was stiff with generals, wanting to have a tour of the biggest bomber any of them had ever seen. One of them was a five-star, first live one I'd so far met. He was quite a well known hero, Army General Yeremenko, quite fat, limping along on a stick, two wound stripes, and very appreciative of the pack of cigarettes as an offering from America. He and others seemed to genuinely admire the plane. "But where are the cannon?" Yeremenko wanted to know. "Only machine guns? Not enough!" he growled.

On the five-star staff, along with half a dozen others, was one equal in uniqueness to the B-24 itself: one of the cutest and liveliest lieutenants in my experience. My comments, voiced with genuine and no doubt obvious sincerity, on such a beautiful young lady's being in the army and not in the movies, where all could enjoy her good looks, was received with coy shyness, as was my admiration of the button in her well-supported lapel—a nickel-sized, smiling face of Stalin encased in glass. The general's party departed. Then, some ten minutes later, hotfooting it back came a staff major with the Stalin button as a present. "Very tender," I wrote in my journal for the day, "and wishing heartily there were a telephone number on the back of it."

There was genuine rapport at the Red Army Day banquet on 7 August 1942. A fat little lieutenant general none of us had heard of before was senior Soviet, Rear Admiral Sterling representing the Red Navy. With them at the center of the table were Ambassador Standley, Major General Bradley, Brigadier General Faymonville, Captain Duncan, Colonel Michela and British Rear Admiral Miles, the remainder of Spasso and British Mission military below the salt, interspersed with lesser rank Soviets.

†In Bradley's crew was Captain Thomas J. Watson, Jr., AUS, subsequently ambassador to the USSR, 1979–1981.

Next to me sat a most friendly Cossack, an Air Force major. It was good to see us all "fighting shoulder to shoulder," was his opener, using a favorite Soviet expression when referring to the new allies. We exchanged the usual platitudes about the excellent weather—good for air operations, the delicate situation in the Caucasus, sorry the ballet was gone for the summer, and so forth, until after about the fourth toast it seemed appropriate to get on with more serious matters. "You were speaking of 'shoulder-to-shoulder' a while back," I said. "You know, I'll have to admit that it is largely symbolic. See that bald-headed general over there? That's General Bradley, Army Air Corps. He's been here a month trying to get permission to ferry U. S. planes in via Alaska and Siberia instead of their being crated in ships to the north where a lot get sunk en route."

The major thought it a good idea. "But of course you know that there would be difficulties with your people landing on our fields—language, customs. They wouldn't like our poor food. It is really wartime. Things are not pleasant in Siberia. Besides, we have offered to send all the pilots necessary to Alaska to pick up the planes."

The major didn't know that only 11 of Convoy PQ 17's 35 ships made it to Archangel. "The British want to send a squadron of Spitfires to Murmansk," I told him. "They can protect the Barents Sea portion where the Focke-Wulfs are giving us hell. But you won't let the Spitfires in. Why?" He professed to know nothing of this, but replied they would gladly accept any planes offered. As for pilots, he continued, when the war started, through German perfidy in attacking without warning, many hundreds of Soviet planes were lost on the ground. Thus, they had a surplus of pilots. "I dare say you Americans now have a keen appreciation of surprise too," he added, with a smile that might have been described as slightly sardonic. Had he been more charged with vodka or as frank as "Mike" Kostrinsky, he would have made no bones about their not wanting British pilots flying over territory Britain had done its damndest to make a British sphere of influence in the 1919 Intervention.

"And what about the American offer to send a heavy bomber squadron to the south, to stop the German advance into the Caucasus?" I asked. "We'd love your bombers," the major said amiably, "but we really don't need the aircrews. Excuse me for saying so, but one fights harder when defending one's homeland. Our fighter pilots when out of ammunition come in behind the enemy and cut off his tail with their prop."

Had there been imperial ghosts about, they would have felt at home in the lavish surroundings of the National Hotel banquet room, softly lit by huge, glittering chandeliers over a table forty or more feet long, gold-rimmed china sparkling in the mellow light of big silver candelabra.

The speeches were short and to the point, perfectly translated by a Soviet Army captain speaking flawless English for his side and by Faymonville for the Americans. "A real love feast," my journal records, "that appears to be entirely sincere." Admiral Standley was bottoms-upping and becoming more and more jolly. "Told them off for secretiveness," I noted of the admiral, "adding a finale that he hoped we would all be one country some day not too long in the future, but diplomatically neglecting to mention under whose auspices."

Zaitsev, Red Navy liaison officer, was in rare good form, having drained his glass at each of many toasts. Then, slightly out of line for such a relative junior, he started popping to his feet to propose toasts of his own—to the everlasting friendship of the two greatest navies, the Red and the American (smiles from the Red Army types, frowns from the British), to the great leadership of that incredible genius, Stalin (all hands on their feet), to Fleet Admiral Kuznetsov, inspiration and pillar of strength (who never would have deigned to attend such a function, nor would have any top flight Soviet general).

Even Colonel Yestignaev, Army liaison, referred to in polite company by cavalryman Michela as, "that south end of a horse headed north," was the very model of amiability and friendliness. But when I tried to break the interpreter captain loose at the end of the party to join the smaller fry for a few quick ones in Major Olson's Supply Mission apartment, the answer was a polite but firm, "nyet!"

This anomaly of social apartheid constantly thwarted any real meeting of minds or normal friendships. It was in stark contrast with what I had found in that other semiclosed dictatorial society, Nazi Germany. Handsome, heel-clicking, young Nazi officers freely associated with foreign military in their homes. One, a baron, his name with a couple of "von der" embellishments, even invited me to his wedding, which I unfortunately missed, having left town.

In the afternoon cocktail sessions and interminable discussions at and after dinner, we attempted to rationalize the Russians. We were melding the pedantic lore of Harvard and Cambridge, as represented by master's degree holders Michela, Boswell, and Park, with the cold practicalities around us, just as we were mixing Russian vodka with America lemon powder to come up with a consensus called a tomsky collins.

Certainly it was not wholly the system, pontificated professorial straight-man Michela. "Russians once were free men," he declared, "roaming the forest. Then along came the Mongols in 1237, controlling the country through selected "princes" who collected the taxes for the conquerors."

"Looks like somebody beside tax collectors got around," interjected Dicky Park. "What about Olga, our Russian prof? She's a blue-eyed blonde with a Chinese face."

"Three years old and can run like a deer is the Mongol definition of a virgin," observed Boswell.

"Scratch a Russian and you'll find a Tartar," McCabe said, puffing away on his pipe.

"Oh my God!" groaned Duncan, whose appreciation of wit, humor, and epigram ran more to the subtle.

Michela got the floor again: "As the Mongols withered away, the prince tax collectors took over as lords of the land. The common people regressed into a state of peonage, slaves, serfs, fixed to the land. They were freed by imperial decree about the same time as negroes were freed in the U. S. But a tradition of second class hung on amongst the Russian ex-serfs, as it has until the very recent past with American negroes. Same fear of authority, subservience to seniors, suspicion of the unusual and of outsiders."

My own ideas on Russians had jelled years before, in the cabarets of Shanghai and Harbin, on Tsingtao's beaches, in many a humble and some not so humble Russian home. Those White emigres were a gregarious, open-hearted lot with deep feelings of loyalty to friends, church, and their country as they had known it, or as the younger generation of the born-in-China had heard of it. Many went back to an uncertain fate in the USSR in 1940 and 1941. "Send us a photo when you get there," a Shanghai Russian asked his friend about to depart on the great gamble. "If things are good, be photographed standing up. If not so good, sitting." In due course the photo arrived, the friend stretched out on the floor.

What was the "new Soviet man" all about? I had better write ONI my impression of him before too late, remembering the experience of a well-known authoress I had met in Shanghai. "Are you here to sight-see?" I asked her, making small talk at a cocktail party. "No, to write a book," she replied. "I'll be here only four days, so forgive me if I circulate." Write a book on the basis of four days experience? What an absurdity, I thought. But it turned out to be the best book on Shanghai I had ever read. She had a fresh viewpoint, not having lost her objectivity, wherein the unusual becomes the commonplace to the old-timer. Before getting stale, I must follow her example. So five months after arrival, I wrote ONI five single-spaced pages of impressions, closing with, "The Soviet Union and its people should be approached warily, subjectively, keeping in mind that a white skin sometimes conceals a Mongol or Tartar or trans-Caucasus mentality that does not function in the Kansas fashion."*

As the summer wore on, matters at the front improved only slightly, with what news was available being supplied by the Soviets. Allied attachés and newsmen were allowed nowhere near the fighting to see for themselves. "Our fine coverage of the war in Russia comes from our correspondent Walter Graebner, at the front with the Soviet armies," *Time* had trumpeted. Poor fellow! He was well known among the foreign colony. It was not his doing that the only "front" he had ever visited was the first row of the Bolshoi theatre, reserved for foreigners. He was not alone. Another Bolshoi *aficionado*, the chief of the British Naval Mission, Rear Admiral G. J. A. Miles, had established an enviable record. The cast of the ballet, some of whom were frequent visitors in foreign apartments, had planned to present the admiral with a floral wreath on his one hundredth attendance, but sadly he had been detached at about the ninety-sixth.

When it became apparent that the cross-channel invasion of *Festung Europa* would be impossible to mount in 1942, as Stalin had been led to believe by Churchill, it was felt necessary that the latter go in person to mollify the furious Generalissmus. So on 12 August 1942, four big B-24 bombers lumbered up from Teheran to Moscow bearing a distinguished company. On arrival, Churchill and staff emerged from the lead plane; from the second came Averell Harriman with a clutch of civilian and military advisers. The third was loaded with yet more brass, while the fourth, carrying British General Archibald Wavell, fell out somewhere en route and never made it at all.

From the top of the ladder, Churchill greeted the welcoming crowd with two fingers held up in his characteristic "V for Victory" sign. Moscow's superefficient bamboo telegraph instantly got the word around that Churchill had come to announce the imminent opening of the second front. This unfortunate, totally false interpretation would of course compound the delicate contretemps the P.M. had expressly come to arbitrate.

A band played "God Save The King," then raced twice through "The Star Spangled Banner," winding up with the "Internationale." The later, more chauvinistic Soviet anthem had not yet been written. Then the honor guard stomped by in a crashing goose step. One almost expected to see a charge of the colorful Cossack troop in tall fur hats and red-lined capes, mounted on magnificent grays, that had trotted through the square in front of the U. S. embassy the same morning. (Along with God, the dread Cossacks—the Czar's knout-wielders—had been resurrected as part of proper Russian tradition in support of "The Second Fatherland War." Next to be brought back, in 1943, would be shoulder boards, once ripped from officers' tunics by Bolsheviks in 1917, or in more extreme cases, nailed to their shoulders with spikes.)

The folderol over, old Marshal Boris M. Shaposhnikov, ex-Chief of the

General Staff and ex-Czarist colonel, now assistant commissar for defense, gray-faced and ill-looking, moved to his car. The foreign dignitaries piled into big black Zis, copies of 1932 Buicks. Foreign Commissar Molotov climbed into a limousine with an armored door that clanged shut like a safe. Then all roared off as fast as the cars would go into the city, through streets cleared of people and traffic and lined with heavily armed "blue hats," NKVD infantry.

By 14 August, following day-long conferences, messages going through the Navy code room to the president suggested heavy storm clouds. The farewell state dinner that night would probably be something less than a love feast. It had been learned that during the discussion taking place that same afternoon, Stalin had made a series of caustic remarks that had irritated Churchill. Churchill became so angry that he stood up, growling that he had not come to Moscow to hear his army insulted. Stalin must have realised that he had gone too far, as Churchill broke up the meeting at that juncture, leaving without the usual courteous exchanges.

Although the Kremlin dining hall was big, the available dignitaries taxed its capacity. There were four U.S. generals: Maxwell, Spalding, Faymonville, Bradley (USNA '10), and of course, Admiral William S. Standley, former Chief of Naval Operations, the U.S. ambassador. Special envoy Loy W. Henderson, old Russia hand, had come out from the State Department. Britain's Brigadier G. A. Hill, saturnine old World War I spook, who had been dusted off as coordinator for joint Soviet-British Balkan dirty tricks, viewed these neophytes with amused interest. Below the salt was Captain Jack Harlan Duncan, U. S. naval attaché, an Irishman well endowed with that race's traditional wit, candor, and cunning.

Let us say here that the Russians are a tradition-bound lot when it comes to protocol, with only fragile tolerance for fancied slight. They resent gestures that others might cheerfully pass off as mildly amusing eccentricities, forgivable in those of less-enlightened background—such as American ambassadors refusing to wear knee breeches at Buckingham Palace or African tribal dress at a White House tea. So when Winnie showed up thirty minutes late at the Kremlin banquet wearing his "siren suit," Stalin, in a marshal's full kit, was not amused. The siren suit was a baggy, shapeless coverall that Churchill wore when making long airplane trips or heading for the air raid shelter. His manner was sullen, and his cigar dipped from his mouth. Whether this was a studied affront or a veiled suggestion that he was more than ready to take off at once, one could only guess; to most naval officers, the ways of diplomats are sometimes inscrutable.

As the dinner progressed, the unpredictable Stalin's mood changed; it was apparent to some that he might be trying to make amends to restore Churchill's good humor. The Generalissimus indulged in a series of joking remarks in an endeavor to make Churchill laugh. The endless toasts helped—to this or that hero, the various Allied armed forces, plus, very agreeably to all judging from the response, the most gruesome possible suggestions of what to do to Herr Hitler.

Then, apropos of nothing in particular, obviously feeling the effects of the vodka, wine, and champagne, Stalin hauled himself to his feet to deliver a long dissertation on the benefits of good intelligence. Specifically, he pointed out the dismal, catastrophic failure of the Gallipoli campaign in World War I, due, of course, he explained, to certain gross stupidities in concept and execution, but primarily a failure of intelligence. Gallipoli had been Churchill's baby—a quarter million Australian and New Zealand troops plus a sizeable fleet, that took 120,000 casualities in a vain attempt to open the Turkish straits and the way for military aid to Imperial Russia. Its disastrous end sent Churchill packing from his job as First Lord of the Admiralty.

As the story unrolled, Churchill squirmed and reddened. Then Stalin, clearly well satisfied with having skewered his victim to the amusement of all present, sat down. Next, Jack Duncan rose to his feet. "I am very happy to hear your sentiments regarding intelligence, Marshal Stalin," he said, continuing that he was an intelligence officer himself, but was sorry to have to say that he had been unable to function as such in Moscow because he couldn't get any cooperation. The translation having been got through, Stalin again rose. Looking pointedly at Churchill, with whom he had been conferring since noon, he replied to Duncan with a twinkle in his eye: "Mister Captain, that is the first really honest statement I have heard all day." Then he picked up his glass, and stalked down to where Duncan stood, the latter not precisely sure what was in store for him after a hip shot of such reckless candor.

"*I* will be your intelligence officer," boomed Stalin, clicking glasses with the dumbfounded Duncan. "Let us drink to that!"

When the hours-long affair finally ended, Stalin once more came around to Duncan, taking him by the arm. Then the two strolled out into the great hall together. "The toilet is on the right," said the dictator in a voice loud enough for all to hear.

The memorable evening was over, and one scarcely needs add that Duncan's access to intelligence improved not a whit. But Stalin had made his point, via a deep knife thrust worthy of a Georgian mountaineer into a quondam enemy for whom he still felt only distrust and contempt.*

*The author is indebted to Ambassador Loy Henderson for the above eyewitness account of the Kremlin banquet. The official version, by Harriman, is in Foreign Relations, 1942, vol. 3, p. 623.

Failure to open the Turkish straits in 1915 had been a weighty factor in Imperial Russia's collapse for want of war material and food. Would a delay in the cross-channel invasion be equally disastrous for the hard-pressed Soviets? Would it force them into a withdrawal from the war and a separate peace with Hitler? The hint had been subtly put after the Oriental fashion. There was no doubt about the seriousness of the situation. In Harriman's message to the president, he mentioned that, "Stalin took issue at every point with bluntness almost to the point of insult.*

*Harriman, *Foreign Relations*, p. 619.

4 / *The North*

When Sir Edmund ("Tiny") Ironside, Britain's six-foot-four general became Lord Ironside of Archangel in 1941, it was in recognition of his command of the Allied armies in North Russia during the ill-starred 1918–19 Intervention. If there existed a similar process of ennoblement in the U. S. armed forces, it would be wholly appropriate to follow Samuel Benjamin Frankel's name with, "Of Murmansk and Archangel." *More* appropriate, actually, because unlike the disastrous Intervention, Frankel's efforts were crowned with success. Not only was he awarded the Distinguished Service Medal by the United States, but was commended by Admiral of the Fleet Sir Dudley Pound, First Sea Lord, and even by the top brass of the Soviet government, which normally gave praise to foreigners sparingly.

Frankel started north from Kuibishev in late November 1941 aboard an elderly Soviet four-engined bomber. The shatterproof glass was mostly bad, the panes having become separated from the binding material, but he could still get a fair view of things from his perch in the bombardier's cockpit. Patches of fog became more frequent, so that the pilot was at times barely skimming the treetops to keep contact with the ground. About two hours out of Kuibishev he banked sharply and started circling a small railway station in an attempt to orient himself.

"As we came out of a dense patch of fog," Frankel recalls, "I could see a train about a hundred yards ahead and too damn close to my bottom. The pilot had just time to level off and I to yell, 'Hold tight, boys!' when the undercarriage smacked one of the cars. Then followed an interminable period—probably six seconds—of violent pounding and assorted noises. Someone hit my left thigh with a heavy club and another stabbed me in the back. When we came to rest, the cabin was half full of snow and through the haze I could see Wyburd and Palmer, the former grinning feebly and the latter bleeding about the face. But all were very much alive, including the forward gunner, who was the other occupant of the cockpit. There was very little damage to the other 30 passengers."

"The ship itself was a complete wreck. All four wooden props completely splintered, one wing split, undercarriage and tail surfaces completely gone. The wing had decapitated a telephone pole, which flipped the plane around 180 degrees, so that it skied through the snow tail first for about 300 yards. The bomber's cockpit where we were had several large holes made by bits of the wooden propellers, one of which holes was by my leg and the other at my back, which accounts for the bruised leg and the cut through all my clothing into the left shoulder."

"The local yokels had gathered in a semicircle about a hundred yards away, of the opinion a German bomber had dropped an egg on the railway, then crashed. One brave fellow with a pitchfork approached. 'Who are you?' he demanded. 'One of your people,' replied a Soviet Air Force major general, the senior aboard. 'Maybe so,' said the pitchfork wielder sceptically, 'but show me your documents just the same.' "*

The general, having brought pressure to bear, got the group a special car that was hooked to a Moscow-bound hospital train. Frankel had survived the submarine-infested Atlantic to Archangel, thence an adventuresome train and boat ride to Kuibishev, now an air crash. What next?

On 25 August 1942, Archangel caught its first air raid, a five-hour night affair that started many serious fires, but missed the vital ships and port installations. Of far greater nuisance value were merchant crew troubles, which proliferated in alarming degree. There was wholesale theft of food and lifeboat equipment for illicit sale on the black market ashore. Ships' officers were threatened with mayhem or death. The Soviets were reluctant to take custody of foreigners under those circumstances, but at Frankel's insistence some of the worst offenders were treated to the doubtful pleasures of a Russian jail. "This office may expect repercussions," Frankel reported, "but I am quite prepared to use what might be high-handed methods to protect American property and lives both in port and during the return voyage."† Two men later were removed from the SS *Israel Putnam* for "intimidation of crew members, by threats of violence and death, habitual insolence and abusive language to ship's officers and inciting by threats the crew to rebel against routine discipline."‡ Frankel took a mild crack at his

*From Frankel's 24 December 1941 letter to Roullard; Frankel papers.
†Frankel to CNO, 22 October 1942, Frankel papers.
‡Frankel to CNO, 13 September 1943.

Captain S. B. Frankel, assistant naval attaché and War Shipping Administration representative in charge of U.S. convoy interests in North Russia, with Lieutenant General Andreev, commanding Red Navy Air Forces, in North Russia.

other boss, the War Shipping Administration, by pointing out that some cases were previously reported in Iceland, but with no resultant action.*

When the immensity of the task in the north became apparent, Roullard was sent up to help Frankel, who then could rattle back and forth via rickety railway between Archangel and Murmansk, trouble-shooting.

By July 1942, things looked bleak. The Germans were massing tanks and troops before Murmansk, while their fighters continuously broke through Soviet defenses to bomb the city and airfield.

In mid-July, 11 surviving ships of the 35 that had started out in convoy PQ 17 straggled into Archangel. One, after the disastrous order to the convoy to scatter had been given by the British, anchored off the island of Novaya Zemlya, 700 miles northeast of Archangel. In a panic the crew fled ashore to set up housekeeping, refusing to return aboard their floating explosive dump of TNT and ammunition, a fat target for U-boats believed to be in the vicinity. So Frankel strapped on his 45-Colt and flew over in a Soviet seaplane to successfully supply the necessary pressure to the runaways to get them back aboard and under way.

This was indeed the summer of discontent. Fifteen hundred survivors, merchant seamen and armed guards, roamed the streets or languished in

*Frankel was designated as official representative of the War Shipping Administration in North Russia after a civilian sent for the purpose proved unsuitable.

makeshift hospitals that stank of gangrenous fingers and toes. They had been scooped from the frigid ocean by nimble little rescue ships sent with the convoy for this grim purpose. The Americans proposed to establish recreational clubs to ease the morale problem, but the Soviet reply was a categorical "nyet," and the same to an offer of American books and magazines to the already operating, wholly inadequate International Seamen's Club. Shore activities were curtailed by gross inflation of the rouble, its purchasing power reduced to about one cent when applied to clothing, food, tobacco, vodka, or beer, on the rare occasion when any of these items could be found. (The official rate available to the men was 1 rouble = 22¢.)

In the face of incipient mass mutiny, Frankel took a long chance by calling together the survivors for a pep talk and information session. To assemble a thousand disaffected seamen—rough, undisciplined, some of them already proven to be criminally inclined—was an invitation to an explosion of violence, if not physical danger to himself. The opening moments were precarious; heckling and shouts ominously suggested worse to come. But the stocky, determined, slightly grizzled man in the blue suit soon had them in hand. By the end of the half hour, there was silence. The faces were glum, but the mood was calm. The storm had been weathered; there would be more grumbling but it would be *pianissimo*.

After Frankel left for Murmansk, Roullard, in charge at Archangel, was having troubles with the noble allies as well as the despicable enemy, the latter never seeming to be able to hit any worthwhile target other than McGinnis, who was lightly clipped by a fragment.

Morale problems were important, but the main thing was ships. The Soviets were still endlessly procrastinating in repairing the American SS *Ironclad*, which had been unable to return with her own outbound convoy because of engine trouble. Roullard informed the CNO that judging from past experience, repair equipment available, ice conditions, and the usual prompt Russian way of handling American ships after they had discharged their war cargo, the *Ironclad* would be in Russia another six months. Officer and crew morale was at the breaking point, suggesting repatriation at the first opportunity before general mutiny or loss of life.
Shipping them back was not easy either. Roullard complained to the CNO that in the past he had been forced to humble the office and himself when difficult skippers and union delegates persistently failed to cooperate in emergencies by refusing to take either stranded seamen or Soviet passengers bound for the United Kingdom or the United States. He wanted definite dispatch authority from the War Shipping Administration to knock heads together.

Meanwhile, the only foreign doctor stationed permanently in Archangel, a captain in the British Army Medical Corps, was rendering excessive bills to American skippers for piddling ailments of crew members. Roullard just wanted CNO to know about it. Repercussions were swift, but not in the right quarter; CNO turned the message over to the British Army staff in Washington, who bounced it right back to the British mission in Archangel, including the name of the originator. If Roullard got some croton oil in his next bottle of British cough syrup, he would know why.

The British Ministry of War Transport boys were still giving trouble too—crowding out American cargoes on returning U. S. ships for their own shipments. Roullard thought it lowered American prestige in Soviet eyes; they looked upon the United States as a British pawn.

There still was some moderate grousing amongst the merchant seamen; one Franklin Martin "created extreme discontent among 600 American survivors by wandering in the streets in pyjamas, advising patients to follow his example in order to force the military hospital to return the patients' clothing, which was being disinfected."* Clearly, those survivors were eager to get back into the swing of Archangel night life.

Roullard's message to Frankel at Murmansk reflected the generally held opinion of Vladivostok since the time of Robley Evans:

> "IN CASE YOU DIDN'T GET THE DOPE HAVE BEEN ORDERED VLADIVOSTOK AND LEAVING FEB 21ST X PER ADMIRAL'S ORDERS LEAVING HARSHAW WITH SACK X CONCENTRATION CAMP NEXT†

Murmansk was busy the year around, its Kola Inlet approaches kept clear of ice by the warming Gulf Stream. It was more busy than usual in March 1943 and not because of convoy activities. On the 15th, Frankel reported heavy and continuous night raids plus several daylight raids over the preceding four days. One British ship had been sunk alongside dock, a Soviet ship capsized, incendiaries landed on American ships, and several large buildings were demolished by land mines and incendiaries. There were fairly heavy casualties. To add to the thrill, the Germans were using some delayed-action bombs. Work was at a standstill, with no public utilities functioning. Frankel, a man who rarely lost his aplomb and never his sense of humor, unofficially reported only himself of his team as among the wounded, as he tactfully paraphrased it, "suffering momentary loss of muscular control as well."

*Roullard to CNO, 12 November 1942. Frankel papers.
†Roullard to Murmansk, 1942. Frankel papers.

The bottom line on convoys to the north is that though it was costly, sometimes exasperating, always dangerous, and to a certain degree bumbling, it worked. Conceivably it saved the war. Hundreds of thousands of tons of equipment and war material went out of the ships, into trains that rumbled south, some almost directly to the fighting front so great was the need—others to factories evacuated from the Ukraine to beyond the Urals.

Naturally, there were flaps—some trifling, some potentially serious—all of them wearing on the patience of the small band of Americans working under grim conditions, some of them, like Frankel and Roullard, who both served the full four years of the war in Russia.

The bad things were outnumbered by the good things: sincere, desperate efforts by the Russians to get the job done; kind, generous, cooperative people in most of the ships who were grateful for the help received from those ashore, whether Russian, British, or American, recognizing the difficulties under which they operated. Most shortcomings that did develop clearly were the result of unforeseen conditions in an unforeseen situation. There was a lack of specific authority and regulations to cope with the few bad apples, and with the problems inherent in relations between allies. And lastly, there were those two persistent nettles, the cruel Arctic and the Germans.

For a society as pathologically suspicious of not only foreigners but each other, the influx of Allied military personnel must have been traumatic to the Soviets. Nor did they miss any opportunity to take advantage of the chance of picking up intelligence from foreigners, who although ostensibly on hand with pure hearts to aid in the war effort might also be cooking up some devilish scheme to the detriment of Mother Russia. Their sharp recollections of the 1918–1919 Allied Intervention told them it wouldn't be the first time.

A solid clue to what went on behind the bland exterior surfaced in the form of a carbon copy of a memo produced by the intelligence section of the Northern Fleet. How did it get into our hands? Was it a premeditated act on the part of a dissident in the Soviet naval command at Polyarnoe? Or was it a stupid bungle by some paper-shuffling comrade who somehow let it get into a batch of housekeeping documents that fell into our possession?

Signed by the Chief Liaison Officer, Northern Fleet, it outlined the functions of himself and three principal assistants, the latter covering, respectively, operational matters, supply and management, and personnel.

The chief was the personal organizer for intelligence about the Allies and the enemy, presumably without unfair discrimination. Captain Second Rank Rigerman was a rather pudgy man who perspired a lot. When pressed to speak his rather poor English, his brow dripped. His hand was clammy and limp. There was no doubt that Comrade Rigerman was a harried, worried individual, as well he might have been; the great purges of only five years before suggested that any job requiring contact with foreigners was a high-risk profession.

Material was to be collected from harbor pilots, interpreters, and Soviet naval personnel who had any contact with Allied officers, and from auxiliary organizations dealing with repairs or supplies to Allied ships.

All concerned were directed to study personal characteristics, separating weak and strong sides (courage, education, weaknesses, vanity, susceptibility to material advantages, wine, women, etc.). Also, they were to check place of origin of the foreigners and their connections, if any, with the USSR. They were told to look into technical, tactical, operational preparedness, individual political views, and attitudes toward the USSR. Mutual relations between officers themselves, officers and petty officers, and petty officers versus ratings were to be studied.

A novel and perhaps highly professional aspect of all this was that as far as one could ascertain it was carried out in a passive, nonaggressive manner. There is no doubt that the well-dressed, urbane, pretty young women who made liaisons with foreigners at the ballet and opera in Moscow were operating under the same general instructions. But one was never aware of any pointed action or obtrusiveness on their part. The mere fact that certain of them became habituées while others were abruptly turned away was too transparent a subterfuge to be ignored.

A prime anomaly in this association of fighting allies was the clear indication in the Soviet intelligence directive that they very much wanted Anglo-American operational information, but not being willing to exchange it for similar Soviet experience, would go after it clandestinely. Along with the "exhaustive and deep study of the personnel arriving in our ports, paying special attention to officers, writers, signalmen, cypherers . . ." the Soviet snoopers were also to "ascertain new methods of operational tactical methods of conducting sea and air warfare by the Allies against the Axis . . . what new equipment is used . . . its technical and tactical details . . . especially radio location."*

For more than a year before the United States' formal entry, "Roosevelt's secret war"† had opened the gates to a near full exchange with Britain on tactics, plans, intelligence, new developments (radar) and with some exceptions, cryptology. (With rare prescience, Admiral King took a dim view of British security, amply justified when it turned out that the British Foreign Office was penetrated to the top level by Soviet spies.)

*All quotes from Soviet intelligence memo. Tolley papers.
†*FDR's Undeclared War, 1939–1941* (New York: David MacKay, 1967).

American naval officers rode British warships, observing British tactics and the effect of German ordnance. All this was of great mutual benefit in the common struggle.

Unfortunately, this happy arrangement did not pertain *vis-à-vis* the Soviet Union. U.S. naval attachés in the Soviet Union normally would have been the point of exchange for any such program. But there was no such exchange with the advent of Lend-Lease in mid-1941, nor at any time after the United States actively entered the war.

By 1943, some 5,000 Soviet military personnel and technicians were in the United States, checking material for the USSR as it came through the production lines, or training for taking over such equipment as minesweepers and patrol aircraft. U.S. naval personnel visited Soviet warships in port or building, but only on one occasion did Americans go to sea in a Soviet warship—from Archangel to Murmansk in a Lend-Lease minesweeper, U.S.A. down to the teacups in the wardroom.

A port visit to a Soviet warship was something of a combination of traditional lavish Russian hospitality and a variation of the Potemkin village. On arrival aboard, foreign guests would be led first to a table groaning with delicacies: generally a broad choice of "sakuska," heavy *hors d'oeuvre*, sometimes a full meal. Either would be punctuated by innumerable "doh dnah" (bottoms up) toasts ranging from Stalin and Roosevelt through the whole gamut of admirals, generals, Second Front, everything down to and including the ship's cat. To have refused to carry out the proper procedure would have been considered a mortal insult. Then the inspection would commence, everything a hazy blur.*

*See appendix D for detailed report of a visit to a destroyer.

5 / *Trouble*

Like the good soldier he was, Admiral Standley told us he had come to the USSR determined "to do my damndest," in spite of any disillusion engendered by the Lend-Lease negotiations in the previous autumn. But soon after his permanent return to Moscow, the ominous beginnings of the "Big Bypass" were surfacing. Roosevelt, as his own secretary of state, was dealing directly with Stalin, via the U. S. Navy's communication system and codes.

The ambassador enjoyed the complete loyalty of his staff, including those with dual allegiance and responsibility, the service attachés. The really nettlesome problem was Brigadier General Philip R. Faymonville, a truly complex individual who headed the Lend-Lease Mission. This handsome, silver-haired bachelor had started his love affair with the Soviet Union in January 1922, whence until May 1923 he was "The American Military Observer," accredited to the war minister of the short-lived Far Eastern Republic, Komandarm* (later marshal of the Soviet Union) Vassili Bleucher.†

Faymonville, an indefatigable traveler, crisscrossed eastern Siberia on foot, by river boat, on horseback, and via motorcycle, visiting every town and exploring every river of any consequence.‡ From 1932 to 1934, he had been an aide at the White House, where he became an intimate and trusted adviser to the Roosevelts on Russian matters. Thence, he became military

*Komandarm, Commander Army. Post ranks were replaced by traditional ranks for colonel and below in 1936, for flag and general rank in 1940. "Flagman" was the earlier equivalent for admiral.

†Bleucher had been the mysterious "General Galen," military adviser to then fledgling Nationalist liberator, Chiang Kai-shek, until Chiang broke with the communists in 1927. Bleucher was shot during the 1937 purges, but was posthumously reinstated after Stalin's death.

‡Details in a letter from Faymonville to G. D. Roullard, 13 December 1946.

attaché at Moscow, the sole U. S. service attaché remaining in Moscow after the withdrawal of assistant naval and army air attachés in 1934 in protest to Soviet intransigence over debt solution and the lack of freedom of movement of all diplomatic personnel.

For reasons we shall see later, Army Chief of Staff George Marshall yanked Faymonville out of Moscow in early 1938. Then, in the autumn of 1941 he accompanied the Harriman-Beaverbrook Lend-Lease mission to the USSR, remaining there as director of Lend-Lease. Former Ambassador to the USSR William Bullitt, and Mr. Loy Henderson, assistant chief of the State Department's Division of European Affairs, had both served with Faymonville in Moscow and felt he was too pro-Soviet for the appointment. But Faymonville went directly to old friends Mrs. Roosevelt and Harry Hopkins, who over-rode General Marshall's objections that Faymonville had been almost defiant of regulations in dealing with a Soviet military mission in Washington in July of 1941.

To Admiral Standley's chagrin and disadvantage, Faymonville operated totally independently of the embassy. And it was with Hopkins, not the War Department, that he took up matters connected with promotion or removal of his mission subordinates.*

My awareness of the animosity developing between Faymonville and the embassy came about through a chance remark I dropped at a birthday party for second secretary Llewellyn Thompson.

The party was held at the embassy *dacha*. The place was a late Victorian two-story frame survivor of imperial days of considerable pretentiousness, its principal function to serve as a getaway safe house in case Moscow came under heavy bombardment. The kitchen garden, tended by an elderly grandpa named Voronin, provided welcome fresh vegetables. A stream through the meadow suggested possible escape via boat, so the embassy had provided one. On this late August day the air was as cool and bracing as hard cider.

By 5 P.M. the party had assembled: Generals Bradley and Faymonville, Captain Duncan, Colonel Michela, Majors Park, Boswell, and Cook, diplomat Loy Henderson, and from the ballet, Nina, Olga Dimitrovna, and another, plus a Soviet from Burobin and the famous male dancer Golubin.

There were raw carrots and cauliflower for "sakuska," as we strolled around the estate and gardens drinking the last of the Swedish beer from the evacuation stores. Inside, in the spacious foyer was *real* sakuska: smoked

*The Supply (Lend-Lease) Mission included four civilian clerks and five U. S. Army captains, of the latter, two being former sergeants of previous Ambassador Bullitt's plane crew; one an ex-U. S. Navy chief petty officer; one a reserve; one a U. S. Army medical officer.

fish, caviar, hard boiled eggs, smoked pheasant. Vodka cocktails colored with vermouth came in champagne glasses. Two bottles of whiskey, courtesy of General Faymonville, who never seemed to lack the essentials, were augmented by several other unidentified but highly alcoholic bottles of cheer. Things became chummier and chummier, the girls ganging up on wooden-faced Bradley, even managing to get several drinks into him. (Russians feel generally concerned about a mild drinker and do their best to alleviate his shortcomings.) General Faymonville was at the piano, while I danced the Russian sailor's hornpipe. Then he broke into French ballads, accompanying himself in faultless French. Then Russian. There were some nice presents for "Tommy": a very old goblet, a fine Palekh box, an unusual sterling dipper with a 1730 silver rouble in the bottom. Dick Park was kissed full on the mouth by the Great Male Dancer and rushed for the vodka bottle to disinfect himself. "What a fellow that Faymonville is!" I remarked casually to Bradley. "He would really be something as an ambassador." Then in the chill, blue moonlight we drove back to Moscow, filled to the brim with good feelings toward each other and the world.

Several days later, I was called in by a furious, red-faced Duncan, for him quite out of character. (A few weeks earlier, without a word of admonishment, he had collected our 45-Colt automatics after learning from a terrified news correspondent present that several of us had been shooting at empty champagne bottles at a party in my apartment.

"Young man," said Duncan sternly, I hear you have recommended to General Bradley that General Faymonville replace Admiral Standley as ambassador. What is the meaning of this?" Dumbfounded, I told him the facts. "Well," he said, somewhat mollified, "this stupid story is all over the embassy. Remember you are not in the wardroom of a destroyer here. Mind your tongue!" And that was the end of it.

The end of it as far as I was concerned. What I did not know was the depth of intrigue in progress from that time on by Faymonville to succeed Standley as ambassador. As Ambassador Henderson wrote me on 5 March 1975, "Faymonville was disappointed in the Admiral. He had hoped that he would be the Admiral's chief adviser. When he discovered that the Admiral was more inclined to listen to his Armed Forces attaché and his State Department advisers, Faymonville turned against him and proceeded by intrigue and his connections in the United States to undermine him."

There was far more to it than ambassadorial succession. The Supply Mission vs. embassy affair steadily exacerbated. Harry Hopkins—Washington's Tallyerand or Rasputin, depending on one's politics—along with the Roosevelts was firmly for giving the Soviets anything they asked for. Faymonville, whose communist sympathies were too blatant to be ignored, had a direct pipeline to the chief faucet-opener: Lend-Lease was in

Harry Hopkins's pocket. (Even after Faymonville's eventual departure, the specter lingered on; in 1944, when the Military Mission had absorbed the Supply Mission's functions, its chief, Major General John Deane, once asked Foreign Trade Commissar Anastas Mikoyan for justification of certain orders. Mikoyan replied that he could get anything he wanted, without justification, simply by going directly to Washington.*)

What the Americans chose to provide the Soviets was of no direct concern to Ambassador Standley. What *did* strongly concern him was that the Soviets went directly to friend Faymonville for military information rather than via the proper customary, legitimate agents, the U. S. service attachés. The latter continually and unsuccessfully urged the Soviets to supply them with intelligence on German tactics, enemy order of battle, and captured enemy equipment, all with a view to saving American and British lives. Faymonville asked for and got nothing.

Repeated ambassadorial remonstrances to Faymonville changed matters not one iota. He continued to be his bland, urbane, affable, but wholly insubordinate, self. Finally, in Michela's presence, he was called on the carpet by Standley for an unusually sharp dressing down. Faymonville at last said, "Mr. Ambassador, you are accusing me of treason to my country." Standley answered, "I am glad you understand me, Faymonville!"† The episode was passed to Roosevelt by a reliable party. But nothing changed.

Admiral Standley, Duncan, and Michela, the last two no longer on speaking terms with Faymonville, returned to Washington "for consultation," actually to protest the ambiguous and impossible Supply Mission situation. Duncan and Michela came back to Moscow promoted to rear admiral and brigadier general, respectively.‡ The bone thrown Standley by Washington was a letter directing Faymonville to collaborate with the ambassador, to which Faymonville paid no attention.

The new brigadier and his assistants were accomplishing little but improving their billiard scores. Duncan had more luck, through the Navy's advantageous position in having outposts at Archangel, Murmansk, and Vladivostok. In the former two ports, the inhabitants were far less wary of foreigners than were Muscovites; one could meet and talk with them on an almost normal plane. But as an indication of Russian inscrutability, the Vladivostok consulate general was as isolated as any mid-Pacific islet. Floodlights glaringly illuminated the whole premises at night. Members of the consulate were followed by very evident members of the NKVD. No friendships were allowed with Soviet citizens. The occasional young lady

*From the author's conversation with General Deane.

†Discussed in the Spasso mess, of which I was a member.

‡Duncan, class of 1918, U. S. Naval Academy; Michela, class of 1928, U. S. Military Academy.

picked up in the movies or park who disclosed her naiveté by even speaking with a foreigner was never seen again by the several young bachelors in the establishment. On naval business, Taecker, and later Roullard, met clandestinely with their Soviet opposite number in a hotel room, never the same one twice.

In September 1942, Wendell Willkie, unsuccessful 1940 presidential candidate, now a strong backer of the war effort, came to Moscow with a bang and a flourish as a presidential messenger leaving Standley wondering what, if anything, he was supposed to be doing as envoy.

Willkie's gaucheries affronted, amused, and mystified the Soviets. His inaccurate statements on foreign policy embarrassed the State Department. And his cavalier treatment of Admiral Standley was " . . . so openly deprecatory and hostile . . . " that Willkie was scarcely over the horizon before Standley had requested permission to return to Washington to protest the Willkie affair as having seriously undermined his prestige as ambassador.* Standley's lengthy telegram in part complained that "The embassy did not know whom they saw or by whom they were entertained, whom they talked to or what they said . . . "† and that "He and his party acted completely independently of the embassy . . . did not desire to deal through the embassy."‡ When Willkie called on Stalin, Standley was pointedly not invited to accompany him.

Obviously, the object of the drill was to sharpen one's teeth on one's friends so as to be better prepared for the enemy; while Standley was in Washington, chargé d'affaires Loy Henderson telegraphed Cordell Hull to have Standley acquaint himself with a slight imbroglio concerning our British allies, " . . . the unsatisfactory relations which appear to be developing between Americans and British in North Russia."§ Roullard, in charge at Archangel, had reported that one of the chief causes of differences was British insistence on loading American ships on the return trip with British cargoes, with the result that the Russians were unable to fulfil American cargo commitments.

Roullard, with a staff of four, was coping with large incoming convoys of preponderantly American ships. But his British opposite number, Royal Navy Captain Maund, with a staff ten times larger, was inclined to take a rather paternalistic view of the American activities, although in fairness it must be said that he was always friendly and helpful in personal matters.

*Adm. William H. Standley, *Admiral-Ambassador to Russia*, (New York, Regnery, 1955).

†*Foreign Relations*, 1942, vol. 3, p. 645.

‡Ibid., p. 639.

§*Foreign Relations*, 1942, vol. 3, p. 749.

By Allied agreement, the British were in charge of the Northern convoys as well as responsible for their protection. But they were not too popular with the Russians, whose long memories recalled the British-inspired-and-led Intervention of a mere generation earlier. The British 120-odd staff in North Russia seemed so excessive to the Soviets that they not only refused visas for augmentation, but for replacements for those already long overdue to go home. Liaison officer Captain-Lieutenant Kaminsky, who was aware of the large quantities of booze brought in for the use of the mission, derisively called it "Ginflot," reflecting the partiality of its members for that cheap but cheering liquid. ("Inflot" was the acronym for the Soviet agency that controlled the port.)

Another manifestation of Russian humor directed at the British was the going-away present for the British rear admiral at Murmansk, one who had failed to endear himself to the Soviets. As the old boy prepared to climb into his airplane, the Russians, with considerable ceremony, brought forth the present—a large, live, fully antlered reindeer, just the thing for air baggage. To avoid fracturing protocol, not to mention international relations, the gift could not be refused. A compromise was arrived at. The reindeer, like most of his kind not particularly tame or amenable to suggestion as to which way to go, was finally chivvied aboard a British destroyer bound for Archangel. There, he could be loaded aboard a merchant ship returning to the UK. In due course the destroyer turned up at Archangel and prepared to land the reindeer for transfer. "This reindeer has been outside the territorial waters of the USSR, therefore it is in immigrant status," declared the port officials. "You cannot land it without a *propusk*."* It was scarcely in British naval tradition to keep a cow-sized, thoroughly disgruntled, half-wild beast aboard a destroyer while lengthy diplomatic palavers went on ashore. Unable to get their troublesome passenger into a boat, the squad of sailors that had been unwilling stableboys maneuvered their guest near a spot stripped of railing and shoved mister reindeer overboard. An excellent swimmer, it was no trick to tow him ashore by the antlers, where the spectacle of a large reindeer, digging in its heels every step of the way, being dragged through the streets of Archangel by a posse of straining, swearing British bluejackets was a scene long remembered by the amused residents.

Meanwhile, I had made an independent trip to Archangel, four days by rail, for a change of scene and to scrounge for housekeeping gear and food aboard U. S. ships for our newly opened apartment in Mokovaya, the embassy chancery. Dvina River beaches were crowded with Russians enjoying the brief summer sun. More decorous than their Kuibishev country

*Pass, officially stamped with a *pechat*, or seal.

cousins, who swam nude, the Archangel girls wore their brief panties and well-filled see-through bras. Unfortunately, the river was a military zone, so no photography was allowed. This was a pity, as it was almost too much for the human eye to absorb.

At the International Seamen's Club, crowds of merchant sailors from the convoy ships in port mingled with the local damsels, danced to American tunes, and downed their small quota of vodka. There was little or nothing to buy ashore, but what there was—dolls, wooden carvings, badly cured reindeer hides that stank horribly—were all outrageously expensive at the official rate of exchange of 5.3 roubles for one dollar. Up to June 1942, the Soviets paid bonuses in roubles to foreign ships' companies—1,000 roubles to skippers and lesser amounts to seamen, to use as spending money ashore. The American embassy, meanly ungrateful, informed Washington that it was ". . . tantamount to giving the seamen concerned a cheese sandwich with one glass of vodka a day,"* basing their remarks on the astronomically high prices for food and vodka ashore; there were no prostitutes.

The U.S. Navy armed guard of one officer and some 25 seamen did not receive this bonus, however, Secretary Hull explaining that, ". . . members of the Naval service engaged in convoying of cargo to Murmansk and Archangel have ample reward in the knowledge that their service is of assistance to the Russian armed forces."†

The armed guards also did not receive the double time for sailing in a war zone that merchant seamen were paid, amounting to something like a total of $800 monthly, versus the Navy seaman's pay of less than $50. But for those guardsmen watching port labor gangs of half-starved, haggard political prisoners shambling along in their sorry rags, shepherded like animals by guards with fixed bayonets, one wonders if Mr. Hull's suggested ample "reward" sparked their interest in saving such a system. Perhaps the guardsmen would have opted for that more tangible and palatable cheese sandwich and glass of vodka.

Logistics in the U. S. Foreign Service abroad seems to be largely a matter of living off the land and hoping for the best. When U. S. Navy ships call in out-of-the-way ports, it is not uncommon for U. S. diplomatic personnel to flock on board to take advantage of the ship's store for toiletries and the commissary department for some decent steaks or a few pounds of butter.

In the American embassy at Moscow in 1942 it was U. S. Navy all the

*_Foreign Relations_, 1943, vol. 3, p. 688.
†_Foreign Relations_, 1943, vol. 3, p. 688.

way. Not only did the food that supplemented the miserable diplomatic ration come via the good offices of the U. S. Navy in Archangel and Murmansk, guarded en route by U. S. Navy personnel, but it was eaten with traditional U. S. Navy silverware, although the embassy had before the war provided its own impressive porcelain and glassware bearing the great seal of the United States.

Aside from food, there was antifreeze for both humans and motor transport, oil, spare parts, and toilet paper in a land where this essential commodity was provided only by those parts of *Pravda* and *Izvestia* that did not bear a likeness of the Generalissimus.

A U. S. Navy electrician's mate, whose real mission was to sniff out microphones in the ambassadorial plaster with his little black box, was equally useful in keeping the staff refrigerators, irons, toasters, and hair curlers operating—equipment the like of which a Soviet electrician of that day had never seen. Broadly speaking, the expertise of these comrades was open to question in matters even more minor. On one occasion the Soviet handyman attached to the chancery was sent up on request of an American diplomat to check the voltage in a wall receptacle before plugging in a new radio. Was it 110 volts or 220? The man appeared bearing a screwdriver. "What about a voltmeter?" inquired the American over the house phone to the building superintendent. "He just uses the screwdriver," said the BS, a pragmatic Finnish-American who knew his Soviets. "He sticks it in the receptacle. If it gives him a good jolt it is 110. If it knocks him flat on his ass it is 220."

Such radios as survived the vagaries of the chancery current were kept in order by the U.S. Navy radioman, who also copied news broadcasts and messages for the embassy, No transmitter was permitted.

A Navy medical officer had been assigned to the embassy since its 1941 expansion. With the help of a naval hospital corpsman and a well-stocked dispensary, "Doc" not only watched over the health of the U.S. personnel in a land where cupping was still considered helpful, but extended his expertise to foreign diplomats in need of medical aid.

In 1942, a Navy dental officer was added. Commander Clifford C. Deford and his dental technician worked their way by truck and train from Iran to Moscow, manfully shepherding a dental chair and the cumbersome outfit that goes with it. The $300 worth of gold turned up missing, so that until replacement was made, crowns were fabricated from imperial gold roubles found in commission stores or from spare cuff links. Indeed, such was the ingenuity of the dental technician that he fashioned a wedding band from a gold coin for a young lady betrothed to an American service man, Commander Tolley.

Chief Pay Clerk Timothy Lane, ONI's logistician, was a combination

Commander F. R. Lang, Navy Medical Corps, and I pose in my Mokovaya apartment.

philosopher, second guesser, and dynamo of energy—an institution with U. S. naval attachés worldwide. They depended on him for everything from typewriter ribbons to snowshoes, on a niggardly budget that required a judicious pruning here for some unanticipated expenditure there. Off the top of his head he supplied the original Murmansk/Archangel detachment with the right things to pull them through the preliminaries.

To make sure anyone following would not find himself in darkest Russia unwarned, Commander Frankel sent back a five page memo on living conditions. Reduced to its fundamentals, the Frankel advice was that absolutely *nothing* could be bought locally. The final bit of advice was to pack a few extra sets of half soles and heels, shank's mare being the chief means of transportation.

6 / *Housekeeping*

The Ambassador was still rusticating in Kuibishev with most of his staff in spite of needlings by Stalin when he flew up for an occasional audience or such special affairs as the Churchill conference. This left Spasso largely in the hands of the military, presided over by Captain Duncan with Thompson, second secretary, as the only "diplomat." Duncan and cavalryman McCabe were the only "non-Russian" attachés. Recently promoted "bird" colonel Michela and Majors Park and Boswell all had MAs in Russian studies from Harvard, Park with one from Columbia as well. We had homed in on Moscow from various directions: Boswell from Archangel in the north, Duncan, Michela, and Allen via Africa, and Tolley via Australia. McCabe and Park had had adventurous trips by air from Hongkong to Chungking, Chengtu, Lanchow, Hami, and Alma-Ata, thence rail to Kuibishev—much of it in territory still as old in many respects as when Marco Polo passed that way 600 years earlier. Thus, the conversation at dinner was lively and cosmopolitan. Indeed, there were times when the original masters of Spasso must have looked down in quiet approbation at the degree to which we occasionally brought back the imperial atmosphere with everything but Gypsy music. Such an evening is recorded in my journal for 10 September 1942:

"Called on Zaitsev this afternoon. For the first time in some weeks offered vodka, but Zaitsev laying off with a bad tummy. The atmosphere very chummy, with a lot of material turned over to the Reds. The secretary in after the second vodka and not looking quite as fancy as she did the last time, when it was after *six* vodkas. Off to Olie's [Captain Olson, Supply Mission] en route home, where a pair of real whiskeys & sodas, by which time feeling to the point where having more with Doc and Curly. [Commander F. R. Lang (MC), the embassy physician, and Lieutenant Cram].

Jeff Palmer [lieutenant commander, RN] in to deliver a couple of movie programs and forced him to stay to dinner, wherein began the beatup. Champagne and vodka, with the skipper [Duncan] as head man, and Mike [Michela], Park, Palmer, Doc and Curly. Out with the lights and trotting in those two vast candelabra, making the old music room look perfectly delightful. Banged a few glasses against the walls, undoubtedly for the first time in that vast house in many years. The Royal Air Force boys over after dinner, with iron curtain punch flowing in the passion parlor. Curly playing the piano, but having certain difficulties distinguishing the keys. The place a shambles by midnight, when off to the RAF mess, having sprinkled a fire extinguisher or two over the whole bloody shop, Curly lost his pants, a state of general confusion."

More people were turning up who would have to be fed during the coming winter, some of whom perhaps would enjoy something less exotic than potato pancakes and caviar for breakfast. Two were friends of the ambassador: Commanders John Shaw Young and Victor F. Blakeslee. Young was a promoter of American cultural exchanges, if one may be so charitable as to thus describe the products of Hollywood. The admiral-ambassador was interested in swapping Soviet films for American ones to better get the American scene before Russian eyes. I was never clear as to Blakeslee's function, other than that he was married to the Princess Skariatina, of a family at the very top of Imperial Russian aristocracy. A talented writer, Irina Skariatina was welcomed to the Soviet Union, the only Navy wife ever to see Moscow in wartime other than Soviets who had married Americans there. Blakeslee, class of 1920 USNA, was retired physically in 1924 and recalled to active duty for the Moscow project. A most likeable man, he was approached by British Ambassador Clark-Kerr. "I say, old chap," said Clark-Kerr, a rosy-faced professional who had served in China previously, "when I was in Chungking, I had a very close liaison with your excellent man there, the naval attaché [pronouncing it at*TACH*y, after the British custom]. Chap by the name of McHugh, Marine colonel. We used to exchange a lot of mutually useful information on an informal basis. Much handier than going to your ambassador, don'tcher know!" Blakeslee listened in amazement as Clark-Kerr continued, explaining that items passed "under the rug" did not commit either side to embarrassing decisions, obligations, or even replies. Just feelers, he said. Or clues. "Yes, bloody good clues that would look ruddy awful if picked up in a formal dispatch to London or Washington by the wrong people." Blakeslee was too flabbergasted in his naieveté to ask who were "the wrong people," but one suspects they were the code crackers, both German and Soviet, the politicians in both countries and the leakers, which last included the correspondents. They were loyal all, but none the less in a visceral competition that on several occasions led to bad blood because of the advantages gained by breaking a story first.

Blakeslee, a heavy-set man with the powerful muscles that go with carrying extra ballast, grew especially amiable after a vodka or two. "Why do you hate me?" he would say mischievously, grasping his victim around the waist and near crushing the life out of him. No one was immune to this bonhomie, including Old Stonebottom himself, Commissar of Foreign Affairs Vyacheslav Molotov, as we shall see later.

As for John Shaw Young, his efforts to swap movies predictably got nowhere. His samples were copied and used to titillate the "aristocracy," which is to say, the NKVD-approved government elite. Deanna Durbin, Fred Astaire, and "The Grapes of Wrath" were *grata* for proletarians who sometimes went to an American film half a dozen times, partly to reinforce what they thought they had seen and partly to enjoy some warmth in the barely heated theater in a Moscow winter where one wore gloves inside the house.

While the summer vegetables and augmented diplomatic rations from the Soviets had greatly improved the embassy diet, the coming winter held grim possibilities for a repeat of 1941, when Minister-Counselor Thurston's well-fleshed boxer dog was eyed with considerable envy. How many humans' rations did he consume, one wondered. How would dogburger taste? So it was with considerable glee that the embassy received information that an American ship, the SS *Virginia Dare*, would be in an upcoming convoy, carrying two motor cars for the naval attachés and tons of food.

Like her sisters, the *Virginia Dare* carried a broadly mixed cargo: telephone wire, shoes, leather, airplanes, motorcycles, milling machines, telephones, canned meats, phenol, tinplate, tires, vegetable seed, cloth, barbed wire, and ammunition. The variety stemmed from a necessity to spread the wealth, so that the loss of any ship would not wipe out one category of material. This unfortunately put anything from 400 to 2,000 tons of explosives in each ship, a firm guarantee that a proper hit would obliterate the vessel and crew.

Also aboard *Dare* was Chief Boatswain John Harrison Harshaw, USN, a professional sailor who would have looked perfectly at home and appropriate aboard a cow pony. Lean, tall, tough, he was already an eight-year veteran when he found himself aboard the armored cruiser USS *Pittsburgh*, frozen in Vladivostok's Golden Horn during the 1918–1919 Intervention. Russians were shooting other Russians, Red against White. With fifteen different flags flying over ships in harbor and forces ashore, it was to be expected that some outsiders would be caught in the crossfire, and many were. But although the bullets missed Harshaw, Cupid made a bullseye; he married a Russian.

Rear Admiral Ivan Papanin, Arctic explorer, with Lieutenant John Harshaw, who was in charge of the U.S. Navy office in Archangel, North Russia.

Jack Harshaw retired in June 1941 as a chief yeoman. He had scarcely got used to civvies when the Japanese struck Pearl Harbor, bringing retirees back into uniform.

In a very few months, mid-1942, the volume of Lend-Lease shipments to the USSR had built up to a flood. The Navy was desperately pressed for qualified personnel at the receiving end—Archangel and Murmansk—men who spoke Russian. One might think that in the polyglot USA, language speakers of everything from Ashanti to Urdu would be in good supply. Such was not the case. Youngsters with immigrant parents characteristically demonstrated the normal juvenile herd instinct to ape their peers, including speech. The parents generally were unfitted for the task at hand either educationally or in background. So the punch-card machines clattered through Naval Personnel's stacks, flipping out Harshaw's card as having had some Russian experience. Wearing the broken stripes of a chief boatswain, he was very soon aboard the *Virginia Dare*, headed in convoy for the bleak coast of North Russia.

On 27 July, 27 surviving ships of the original 40 in PQ-18 reached the rapidly chilling waters of the White Sea, the *Virginia Dare* among them, their struggle with the cruel sea and the crueler Heinkels, JU-88s, and U-boats over. Harshaw had been a volunteer gunner. As one Heinkel dropped its fish then wheeled away, exposing its belly, Harshaw's 20mm spat out a burst and down went the Heinkel, into the sea on fire.

The local Russians were pleased with the fact that although 13 ships had been lost, the convoys were still coming. Ashore, many of the 1,300 survivors of PQ-17, fished out of the icy water two weeks earlier, languished in makeshift hospitals. The more fit lounged around dismal log barracks grousing over the wretched food (far better than the Russians were feeding their own), and the nondescript, ill-fitting clothing scrounged ashore and afloat to fend off the increasing chill of approaching winter.

The heroes were recognized. Harshaw's feat of shooting down a Heinkel earned him the Order of the Fatherland War. He was now an "ordenosets," privileged to enter the front door of trams and buses along with pregnant women, cripples, and other wearers of a badge of courage won in defense of *Matyushka Roos*, Mother Russia. That the order also carried a monthly stipend of ten roubles was of no consequence at the moment; ten roubles would not buy so much as a box of matches, even if one were so lucky as to find such.*

In early winter Molotovsk (now Severodvinsk), where the *Virginia Dare* tied up, was a perpetually gloomy, drab place, swimming in mud in the brief thaws or turning to stone when the wind shifted to the north. When the sun shone at all, it was wan and cloud-shrouded, showing above the flat horizon for a few short hours. The port was surrounded by a high wire fence and armed guards, to keep out hungry looters as well as to confine Stalin's political prisoners, who furnished the labor to unload the ships.

The prize was so great in *Dare* that extra special attention was required in the form of a member of the embassy in Moscow. There must be no unfortunate diversion of the goodies because of distraction of Roullard's

*Small books of coupons went with the decorations, redeemable at Soviet government offices during the life of the recipient. American holders continued to collect this rouble stipend in dollars at Soviet consulates in the United States until about 1947, when the lag inherent in any bureaucracy caught up with this leakage in Soviet hard currency in a manner never intended.

outfit being distracted by the tremendous load imposed on them by the survivors and the new convoy.

Communist discipline was sufficiently strict aboard Soviet merchant ships and the penalties for infractions so drastic that their cargoes suffered a minimum of looting compared to the wholesale brigandage too often carried on by the crewmen of other Allied ships. This circumstance ceased at the shoreline. Wartime Russia was simply too desperately hungry and ragged for one to expect some of the less highly motivated individuals to pass up an unguarded case of spam or a bundle of Red Cross sweaters from the Ladies Aid of Kansas. It was not a matter of mere cupidity; it was often a question of human survival.

To carry out Admiral Ambassador William H. Standley's injunction to deliver the booty to Moscow intact, the only firm insurance was a reliable guard sitting on top of the cargo. It would in effect be a small convoy derived from a great one. Its escort, air cover, heavy backup, and screen would be Chief Boatswain John H. Harshaw.

For several days efforts had been made to round up a flat car for the motor vehicles and a box car for the crated goods. Meanwhile, the *Dare*'s cargo spilled out on the dock. Stevedores were swathed in layers of padded winter clothing, men indistinguishable from women. Little knots gathered around dropped crates. Perhaps food? Lard was scooped up and wolfed down by the fistful by these starved wretches. Raw meat scraps or steaming chicken guts thrown out with the ship's galley garbage was seized with fierce eagerness before a guard might interrupt their bloody feast with rifle butt or long bayonet. A body lay on the ice under the slop chute, gradually being covered with new snow, only the shape remaining, where the man (or woman—who could tell?) had been shot by a guard days before while hunting scraps. If there were any communists aboard on arrival, one suspects their politics had suffered a decided swing to the right.

Women did most of the clerical work in the port operation, ran the cranes and yard engines and furnished the liaison personnel, the "trouble shooters," who stood by the ships' gangways to translate or transmit requests. The one assigned the *Dare*, a pert little type named Nina, clomped aboard in felt boots, muffled up in padded khaki jacket, shapeless trousers, a shawl over her head. Obviously she had something big on her mind. "I've got them!" she shouted. "Look! Two cars and a locomotive to tow them." The sighteers on deck gathered around, inviting her down to the mess room to take the chill out of their collective bones and break the good news to Harshaw. She warmed her hands around the coffee mug, then carefully stirred in three or four heaping teaspoons of sugar, something she probably hadn't seen since the war started.

"What a beautiful stove!" she cried, bubbling with excitement. "I've never seen a white one before." She let her shawl slip off her head so that a shock of tousled blonde hair fell around her shoulders.

"That not stove; that refrigerator." said Harshaw, warming up his rusty, highly fractured Russian. "Makes food cold," he explained. (Someone had opened the "fridge" door for more coffee cream. The vapor issuing forth in the hot mess room did indeed look like steam.)

"Ach! Kakaya prelest!" (What a marvel!) sighed Nina. She chirped on in Russian. "We simply set our food out between the inner and outer windows of the barracks. It freezes in a few minutes. That is, when we *have* any food to set out. Mostly we finish off our rations as they give them to us, before even leaving the office."

Jack Harshaw got up from the table and very shortly came back with a little collection of tins of meat, butter, and marmalade. He put them on the table and pushed them gently in front of Nina. "Podarok!" (Present) he said.

"No! No! I don't want them! I have plenty to eat. I am not a prisoner like those working on the docks." She shoved the cans away. Her eyes darted from one to another in confusion and injured pride. The corners of her mouth turned down, like a little child about to cry.

"But Ninochka, you have done us such a great favor. You have gotten us those cars and the locomotive. This is only a very small present to show our gratitude. Please accept it!"

The hurt look slowly vanished and a wide smile appeared. The cans were pushed forward again. Nina took them one by one, examining each carefully, trying to read the labels. Then she tucked them away in various folds and pockets.

"To tell you the truth," she said, "there hasn't been anything but black bread this week. The cabbage and potatoes have frozen, so that even a pig wouldn't eat the soup. Such a terrible smell!"

She drank the last of her coffee, then scraped the sugar from the bottom of the cup and slowly ate it. "I like tea better, really!" she said cheerfully. "Coffee tastes like soup when the cook has burned the beans." She stood up, pulling the shawl back over her head, once more a sexless worker in the human anthill of Molotovsk. Then she patted her pockets to reassure herself that the cans of food really were there.

"I will give a tin of meat to the engine driver," she said. "She can warm it on a coal scoop in the firebox." Then, unexpectedly, she darted over to six-foot Harshaw, stretched up on the toes of her felt boots and kissed him lightly on the cheek. "That is from Nina and from the engine driver," she said, then blushing furiously, she charged headlong for the door.

From Archangel, a badly ballasted, bumpy railway meandered around swamps, through thick forests of evergreen and birch and occasional scruffy farmland, on to Moscow, 650 miles south. Every twenty miles or so, a village of brown log huts straggled along the tracks. In some, an onion-domed church dwarfed the other buildings, its crosses askew, whitewash streaky, and probably now a storage place for the village hay. This was the route of the new convoy.

Harshaw was sitting in something akin to state as he was apprehensively waved goodbye at Molotovsk. Perched in the driver's seat of the sedan, he was smoking a large cigar. On the flat car with the sedan rode the station wagon. Next astern was the box car, four wheels and plenty of locks.

The station wagon was to serve as living quarters for the trip, with mattress, blankets, and a small "stove" made from a slotted gallon can. Firewood in the form of dried sticks was piled in one corner. It could be replenished on the way. Tins of meat, fruit, and vegetables on the front seat stocked what Harshaw would soon discover was the deep freeze.

For five dreary, desperately lonely days, Jack Harshaw watched the bleak Russian countryside crawl by as he alternately froze, then smoked himself to half suffocation over the makeshift stove. He melted snow to make tea and to wash the messkit in which he tried to warm his canned rations. Time came to a standstill, the only guidelines the breaking of the gray dawn and the ending of the day. Winter clouds and gloom at least served one purpose—the German bombers found it too thick to search out the railway.

Then there was a lucky break. During one of the many sidetrackings to clear the way for other trains, Harshaw crawled out of his cocoon of blankets to discover a parked hospital train on an adjoining track. "What a glorious feeling to see and talk to humans again." he said later.

Harshaw was the first American they had ever seen. They crowded around the rumpled, blue-uniformed, unshaven fellow whose documents were impressive enough, but still . . . he *might* be a German spy.

"I have seen Germans during the Imperialist War [1914]. He is no German!" said one. The train guard with his fixed bayonet relaxed his menacing stance.

"Achtung!" screamed a bandaged patient taking the air alongside the train. There was no move from Harshaw. "There! You see? He is no German. We were taught at the front that if you yell 'achtung,' a real German will spring to attention from force of habit." For a moment the bandaged man shared the spotlight with Harshaw. "Hey, tovarishchi!" shouted someone, "That frontovik [front line soldier] knows what its all about." There were murmurs of approbation in the crowd. "Molodyets!" [Smart fellow] they said to one another. "Da! Molodyets!"

"We have heard many things about the United States," said an elderly nurse. (She was the train "brigadier," Harshaw learned later). "We have been told how badly the American workers and negroes are treated, but now since we have become allies, people say that many of the stories we have heard are not true."

The crowd moved in closer—walking wounded, train attendants and nurses, with a sprinkling of country people from the local village.

"How much does a loaf of bread cost in American?" they wanted to know. Harshaw was bombarded with questions. Was Deanna Durbin still alive? Several of her movies had been shown in the USSR, and many had seen them half a dozen times. What salary did he receive? They discovered he had been an enlisted man, risen to officer rank. Had he been beaten and kicked as a sailor? Were negroes allowed to wear shoes? Harshaw was hard put to eat the steaming bowl of borshch he had been given, what with the eager crowd pressing around.

The locomotive whistle shrieked. Harshaw swung himself aboard the lurching flatcar and into his smoky, frosty station wagon. There was always the possibility his precious box car had been shunted off during the train's maneuvers at the sidetrack. He took a quick look astern to reassure himself it was still there. The warm soup in his belly was the only material proof that the whole sequence had not just been a happy dream sandwiched into an all too real nightmare.

For five more solitary , freezing days the train rumbled south, until the squat buildings of a metropolis hove in sight. It was "Moskva," the holy city itself, a trainman assured him. Soon they would be in the marshaling yards, and the accomplishment of a mission unique in naval annals would have been achieved. The goods had been delivered intact, by convoy both great and small.

Awaiting Harshaw at the embassy was not only a much needed bath and shave, but a very interesting piece of paper from the Navy Department. He was now an ensign, U.S. Navy, at just one year short of half a century the oldest ensign on the active rolls, possibly in all naval history.

Harshaw safely launched, I headed at a trot through the marshaling yard to catch the last train for Archangel. A stubble-whiskered individual in nondescript clothing rose up from nowhere, rifle muzzle in my midriff. "Vashi documenti!" (Your documents.) he barked. I pulled out the little red booklet showing my picture, which described in Russian my status as member of a diplomatic mission. The guard scrutinized it carefully from all angles. "You must come with me to my *nachalnik*," (boss) he said sharply, motioning with his rifle. I could see the hours ticking away in a distant sentry box while some lout scarcely more worldly than this one called *his* superior and then he, *his*.

"Take a look at that signature," said I sternly. "Do you think Comrade Stalin would like his name pushed around like a cigarette box?" (The card was signed by some naval functionary in Moscow.) "He trusts people like you to guard your country's safety. He knows he can depend on you to make a good decision and honor his signature," I lectured. "He would be upset to learn you did not trust him by passing the problem to someone else."

The fellow had another look at the booklet, pretending to read it. "Pass, Comrade!" he said briskly, throwing out his chest and saluting. And by the way, did I happen to have a spare cigarette?

A standing joke among foreigners in Moscow was defining the second front. To the Soviet man in the trenches it was said to be his exclamation on the opening of a tin of spam. In Moscow, it was the first row of the ballet, reserved for diplomats and foreign correspondents.

On rare occasions, the correspondents were taken to areas where the front had been some time previously. Or they might pick up some tidbit from a diplomat anxious to keep in their good graces. Otherwise, they were wholly dependent on the Soviet press agency to justify their expensive presence in the USSR. So Henry Cassidy, Associated Press, decided to take direct action. On 3 October 1942 he wrote a letter to Stalin, posting it in the Kremlin gate postbox. To everyone's astonishment, in short order back came a reply from "Uncle Joe," as he was familiarly referred to by the newshawks. The gist of his replies to Cassidy's half dozen questions was that the main consideration was a second front, that " . . . assistance from the Allies to the Soviet Union is meanwhile of little effect . . . "*

Uncle Joe was merely reflecting the attitude of all Russians. I picked up an aviator hitchhiker about that time and he had no more than lighted up one of my cigarettes before launching the question. Like all the rest, he had not heard we were losing ships to German subs at a horrendous rate. When this was mentioned, he said that ships could be built in ten or fifteen days, so what did a few sinkings matter when Russians were dying at the rate of ten thousand a day? (He underestimated; as it turned out, the figure was closer to 13,000.)

Then, on 7 November it happened. The Western Allies landed in North Africa. Once more Cassidy tried on the direct approach and once more he had a great scoop: Stalin was effusive in his approbation. Shortly after that, I wrote a letter to Major Andrew Wylie, USMCR, who had the Russian desk in ONI: "There is no doubt that the people are starting to get more friendly since the North African venture, particularly since the success of their own new offensive all along the eastern front. They

**Foreign Relations*, 1943, vol. 3, p. 461.

apparently are of the opinion that our drawing off of German strength has been partly responsible for this rapid advance. Last night several of us went to see, 'Pikovaya Dama,' and while in the interminable line to park our coats (forbidden to take them to our seats, "*nekulturny*", uncultured, we were much surprised to have a man in army uniform insist we go to the head of the line. He was vigorously supported by the wardrobe man and by the people ahead of us, which is far different from the sentiments voiced when a comrade tries such a stunt. And that old, reliable standby of popularity gauges, salutes, indicates by the large number we are getting that foreigners are OK. All this by no means suggests we are ready to move in and be one of the boys, as official policy regarding handing out information has not changed. However, like many other things here, policy changes overnight; for all we know they might invite us to take a ride on a destroyer tomorrow."

Alas! Not only was there no ride on a destroyer; the surface euphoria was not reflected in deeds. Furthermore, doubts about the future were being seriously entertained. Standley messaged Hull on 12 February 1943 that it was the unanimous opinion of the ambassadors of Afghanistan, Iran, and Turkey that post-war the Russians will follow a Machiavellian policy,* a piece of understatement if there ever was one. British Ambassador Clark-Kerr wasn't even looking that far over the horizon; he was, ". . . quite worried in regard to the situation and not at all optimistic in regard to future British-Soviet relations."† And well he might be. Since the northern convoys started, the British had lost 2 cruisers, 10 destroyers, 6 other warships, 74 merchant ships. Royal Navy officers and men killed exceeded 1,000, plus wounded and prisoners. Five hundred merchant seamen had been killed, wounded over 1,000.‡ The Soviets were doing nothing to help protect the convoys, nor would they allow the British to send air squadrons to North Russia to do it themselves. In early March, the Soviets refused entry of 750 British airmen, but were willing to accept the Hampden bombers they were to fly. More galling, half the British dozen-odd radio stations in North Russia were ordered closed on the technical ground that no official permission had been given by Moscow. This seriously undermined not only intelligence gathering on German activities, but actual control of the convoys themselves.

Admiral Standley got into the act with a real blockbuster. He had commenced one of the usual banal post-front-visit press conferences to hear what the correspondents had seen as to where the front had been two weeks before they saw it. United Press's Eddy Gilmore casually asked how

**Foreign Relations*, 1943, vol. 3, p. 623.
†Ibid., p. 630.
‡Ibid., p. 628.

Lend-Lease negotiations were going. Standley told him that although he had made strenuous efforts to discover any evidence that the Soviets had informed their people of Anglo-American aid, he had found none. "Is that on the record, Mr. Ambassador?" they all shouted at once. His reply sent them racing to the telegraph office: "Yes, boys, you can quote me." he replied.

Under Secretary of State Welles shot over to the White House with the opinion that the ambassador had made a major blunder and must go. But FDR, flashing his generally superior political clairvoyance, demurred. "Let's wait and see." he said. Within 48 hours the American press, less *The Daily Worker*, came out in strong support of Standley's "realistic diplomacy." In less than a week the Soviet press followed with detailed information on Lend-Lease and Red Cross aid. The amateur ambassador had scored heavily. (But poor Clark-Kerr, British ambassador! When he complained to Stalin that he enjoyed nothing like the freedom Soviet Ambassador Maisky did in London, the dictator replied with a grunt.)

In response to polite queries by a now totally mollified Washington, Standley forthrightly declared that, "I do not think that we should sit back and continue to accept the ingratitude of the leaders of this country."*

Actually, Standley fed on success. He was so worked up over this whole affair that the next day he relieved himself of a very long message to the president on the Soviet situation in general, the processes of government, and the injustices perpetrated by Stalin and Company. He wanted to go straight over to Stalin and give him hell. Shape up! But Hull, answering for FDR, in effect said cool it. *Not now*! Stalin was too preoccupied. But there was something tucked in Standley's denouncement that should have made "Kremlin West," as some correspondents called the White House, take notice: "The reluctance to give information [on German methods, weapons, and army] which might result in a saving of many American lives and be of material assistance in our military effort seems to me to be inexcusable."†

With winter coming on, thoughts turned to suitable attire. Temperatures frequently dropped to 20° below zero, occasionally even minus 40°. None of this would trouble a properly dressed North Dakotan, but the U. S. Navy, known to the British as, "Uncle Sam's Yachting Squadron," spent its winters in Guantánamo, Cuba, or on the salubrious West Coast, so that appropriate cold weather gear never had been developed.

For my part, I telegraphed my old Annapolis tailor, Bellis, to make me a blue service uniform of the heaviest material obtainable, the trousers lined with thick wool cloth. This so astonished the old gentleman that the

**Foreign Relations*, 1943, vol. 3, p. 632.

†Ibid., p. 510

Commander Kemp Tolley in fur shapka.

story eventually reached the newspapers, with speculation on everything from polar penetration to high-altitude balloon flights over enemy territory.

Navy caps did nothing for ear protection. British Admiral Miles had solved his problem by devising a black caracul model that expanded in diameter as it rose to a height of about ten inches, a sort of naval busby. Here was a challenge. I would have to have Admiral Duncan's agreement to wholly fracture the Navy's uniform regulations, and certainly not with something like the Mongolian camel herder's ear-flapped version our people were wearing in the north. A little strategy seemed in order. "Have you seen that elegant fur hat Admiral Miles is sporting?" I asked Dunc. "I'll bet it saves his ears, too." Miles was one of Irishman Duncan's pet peeves. He was not amused. "Work something up!" he grumbled. "And not any damned flower pot like His Lordship's." I had already bought two nice caracul pelts from the diplomatic store and had them made up into replicas of the grey *shapki* worn by Soviet general officers. Over the metal Navy cap device on Dunc's were two large silver stars; over mine, a silver oak leaf, indicating my rank of commander. Dunc was not a demonstrative man, but his smile of deep approval was sufficient congratulations on my performance as official hatter. The impressive headpiece brought instant attention.

"*Amerikanski gheneràl*!" small boys would shout to their friends, while military men saluted extra smartly. A broad caracul collar covered my three "sergeant's" stripes; the hat was enough.

Red Square, the huge open space in front of the main Kremlin entrance, is backed by GUM, an abbreviation when stretched into English meaning, "Government Department Store," a building left over from imperial days. In the starlit winter evenings only a few people scurried across the wind-swept expanse in front of the impressive, block-long old building's bronze doors. One evening, on a whim, I climbed into fur shako, full dress aiguillette pinned to my long, Russian Navy style overcoat and took station in front of GUM, arms folded, chin up, eyes front, waiting. An occasional comrade skittered by, some unseeing, with eyes down, others looking this way and that as though expecting something, or someone. "*Boszhe moi*!" I heard several mumble, their steps quickening. "My God! What apparition is that?" their minds clearly read.

The winter of 1942–43 was one of profound change. In November, the Anglo-Americans invaded North Africa. By the end of January Hitler's great Sixth Army had been hacked to pieces at Stalingrad. It was a relatively mild winter, often hovering at the freezing point in Moscow, allowing the Soviets to use their new mobility to keep enormous continuous pressure on the Germans. American trucks, jeeps, and tanks were playing a strong role, which was becoming more widely known in the USSR as a whole. Old up-from-the-ranks Revolutionary era generals had been honorably benched, along with political commissars, all replaced by a new, aggressive, tough lot who brought iron discipline and good leadership to the expanding Soviet armies. Marshal Zhukov, for example, spotted some officers in a motor car passing up several walking wounded. Zhukov had the car stopped, the officers demoted to private on the spot, and the wounded men given a lift. Such news traveled fast and far. Our Navy enlisted men, less closely trailed than officers and with more contacts among the people, came back with much interesting information, such as leaflets originated by German agents describing the Russian army fighting on the German side, entire Soviet divisions captured intact early in the war, now under overall command of former Soviet General Vlasov.

There was the fiction in American minds that a solid front stretched from the Arctic to the Black Sea. Actually, the war in the east was one of points and movement. Wide stretches of Russian countryside far behind the German "lines" never saw a German uniform. In these last great days of horse cavalry, entire cavalry *armies* galloped across the rear of other Soviet armies as they had in the days of the Revolution, to strike unexpectedly as German aviation capabilities declined and observation deteriorated.

We heard stories from the front of the remarkable Russian ability to improvise. The "Katyusha" rockets, little more than gas pipes mounted on trucks, performed the mission of massed artillery. Endless trains of one-horse supply wagons dragged on to the front with ammunition to sustain the massive artillery barrages. The wagon driver became a replacement in a gun crew, the simple wagon broken up for firewood and the horse eaten. There was no necessity to clutter the poor road with return trips. Spare parts and special tools were thrown out of American tanks to make room for more ammunition. If a nut had to be removed, it was done in the proper Russian way, with cold chisel and hammer. American conveniences were gently derided. Why waste pounds to install a toilet convenience in a fighter plane, scoffed a crusty Soviet general. "In combat the pilot is going to piss in his pants anyway."

7 / *Northern Trip*

By the spring of 1943, it looked as though the Soviets might survive. But although Stalingrad was in the Russian bag and the Nazi drive for the Caucasus oilfields had stalled, the lengthening spring days allowed the German bombers and submarines to slash increasingly at the northern convoys, threatening to cut drastically the flow of Lend-Lease supplies that held the thin balance between winning and a stalemate or worse on the eastern front. At the moment, Lend-Lease was the only trump the Anglo-Americans held to counter Stalin's fury at the delay in a second front that posed the specter of his negotiating a separate peace.

To check the status of this vital convoy business, Admiral Duncan decided to see for himself how matters stood in the north—at Archangel with Lieutenant John Harshaw, at Molotovsk with Ensign Joe Richardson, and at Murmansk, with Commander S. B. Frankel.

Each frigid dawn for a week found the party at Moscow's Vnukovo airfield for another false start: Duncan, with assistants Commanders Tolley and Lang—along with the faithful "seeing off" group of half a dozen staff members, carrying out the Russian and embassy tradition that gave appropriate "face" to any official trip. Each night there would be a repeat of the previous evening's farewell party.

Then at last, after the staff's patience and the inspection party's stamina were progressively wearing thinner, it was for real. A DC3 sat on the tarmac surrounded by three MiG fighter escorts, one with eight red stars painted under the cockpit. Its hard-faced pilot saluted stiffly. "Eight Nazi planes shot down," he barked in a parade ground voice.

The DC3 pilot was a millionaire, the liaison officer, newly promoted Captain 3rd Rank "Mike" Kostrinsky said. "But not your capitalist kind," he added with a grin. "It means he has logged a million kilometers."

The only other passenger in the big plane was a Red Navy four-striper thumbing his way to the north. The instant all engines were turning over the planes took off. Gasoline was too precious to waste in any such foolishness as warm-up or taxiing for an upwind takeoff.

The millionaire was justifiably proud of his ship's curtains, rugs, and soft cushions. It was well heated, too, he promised, which was soon to prove a vast understatement.

The escort turned back halfway, leaving the DC3 to wallow on alone, the passengers down to their undershirts in the blistering cabin heat, holding on with both hands, watching the forest whiz by a scant hundred feet below. No point in attracting the attention of any chance Nazi intruder by flying high, explained the millionaire.

Russian introductions are made without the third party, who so often fumbles the names. Two unacquainted people knock their respective heels together, pump each other's hand, and say who they are. In this fashion, we three Americans were greeted by the large welcoming committee of Red Army, Navy, and Foreign Office types who had been stomping their feet for several hours alongside the huge runway in the midst of a forest where the DC3 had landed. Like everything else in the north, the runway was built of wood, possibly even the beer, as a taste test suggested.

Two battered Russian Model A Fords were standing by to carry the party to the railway. The driver of one of these relics had improved his time while waiting by removing the generator and several other vital parts for a quick overhaul. So the admiral and several others rattled off in the one sound car, promising to send it back. Meanwhile, half an hour's frantic efforts on the part of the second car's driver had got it going. So Lang, several others, and I padded the seats with our overcoats, and the Ford ground off through the forest over a trail of mud, snow, and buried logs.

Halfway, we met the other car, which had been sent back. It lay deep in a ditch beside the road. The second driver, pleased with himself at having "repaired" his car, passed by his unfortunate comrade with a cheery wave, remarking it was lucky the fellow was down there, or it would have been a *bol'shoyeh delo* (tough job) to pass him.

It was now clear to all why the car's seat springs were flat. Twenty minutes over what must have qualified as the worst "road" in the USSR brought the Ford to the railway. A two-car train awaited, one a "special," with staterooms and a finely furnished salon in which a meal had already been laid out.

The rough trip in the plane followed by the Model 'A's punishment was not the thing to improve one's appetite. But Russian custom and hospitality dictated that all join in the pickled herring, smoked salmon, cheese, and black bread spread with half an inch of sweet butter. The mountain of food was punctuated at intervals by bottles of greenish vodka, bringing to mind the rumor that several port officials had recently succumbed to vodka of dubious background.

The train lurched over the tracks toward Archangel as the friendly lunch continued, with many mutually complimentary toasts. Nobody brought up the touchy point that the last time an American admiral had visited those parts, 1918–19, relations had run more to shooting.

The party arrived opposite Archangel in an hour, considerably restored and refreshed. There, we transferred to motor cars for the half-mile trip across the river Dvina ice to the city proper.

Archangel was typical of the provincial towns of the north. Everything combined to produce an optimum of unattractiveness. It had neither the majesty of a complete ruin nor the hope of a city that would be reconstructed. It hung somewhere between, swimming in its mud, windows boarded up against the almost nightly bombing, its people in colorless, shapeless bundles of nondescript padding. An occasional battered street car pounded along zigzag tracks, sparks showering from the overhead trolley. Unsmiling people bulged from every opening or hung onto every projection like swarming bees. A few trucks slewed along cobbled streets through the mud and slush of spring, sending sheets of spray in all directions. Pedestrians on the rickety board sidewalks made halfhearted efforts to avoid the splash, cursing softly to themselves, most of them too perpetually hungry to show much enthusiasm, even in anger.

The U.S. Navy was housed in a rambling log bungalow turned over by the famous Arctic explorer Rear Admiral Ivan Papanin. Its windows, doubled to keep out the cold, were all still intact through having been flung open at the first wail of the air alarm throughout the long winter.

The millionaire, having delivered his crew to the tender mercies of the Intourist Hotel, was delighted to accept an invitation to dinner at Navy House. He had been on duty in Archangel, he said, and was happy to stop off for a check on old comrades. The evening air raid delayed his first step in this program—sending the Navy station wagon downtown to pick up an old girl friend. All hands frantically unbuttoned windows, then belly-flopped on the floor. "Those Nazi sons of bitches! They'll break all our plates!" shouted old Anna Pavlovna, the cook, when the house shook from a nearby bomb.

The millionaire was a fascinating man to watch at table. He had no difficulty in simultaneously juggling half a loaf of unsliced bread, a tumbler of neat whiskey, and a large chop harpooned on a fork that he waved about for emphasis during his running fire of conversation. The latter was no doubt enlivened by the two tumblers of whiskey he had tossed off before dinner in the "bottoms up" Russian manner, observing with a gasp that it tasted like vodka in which an old boot had been soaked.

He explained he had been in military aviation. After many heroic adventures, he had been shot down, resulting in a six months tour in hospital. Since then he had been in civil aviation, logging some 1,500,000 kilometers, earning 4,000 roubles a month, and like all Red airmen, living off what little fat of the land yet remained. He wasn't getting any of the 1,000 rouble prize money for shooting down an enemy fighter, he said. Nor 2,000 roubles for an enemy bomber. But he was getting ten times more money than he could conveniently spend in wartime Russia, where consumer goods had all but disappeared. (Note: The diplomatic rate of exchange was 12 roubles for one dollar, the price of one egg.)

Having wolfed two helpings of everything, the millionaire poured out his last tumbler of whiskey, ate two dishes of raspberry jam that he mistook for dessert, then washed it all down with a small glass of gin, a drink he said he had always been curious to compare with vodka. He had one final whiskey before tottering out to the station wagon and the awaiting girl friend.

Navy House was a snug establishment. Ample provisions could be scrounged from U.S. merchant ships. In the attic "deep freeze," hams, bacon, and cuts of meat hung from beams to outwit rats. Barrels of sugar, flour, and powdered milk stocked the pantry. In charge was lanky veteran of World War I, Lieutenant Jack Harshaw, who had arrived that winter as a chief warrant boatswain, personally shooting down a Heinkel bomber with a 20-mm en route aboard SS *Virginia Dare*. Sixty-year-old Anna Pavlovna, the cook, ran the household like any good boatswain's mate, her chief difficulty determining the contents of English-labeled canned food. John McGinnis, chief yeoman, exercised an Irish blarney that had the sometimes dour Soviets eating out of his hand and, to a "sartin extint," even penetrating the crust of His Britannic Majesty's large naval establishment the "GinFlot" mentioned earlier, who viewed the little but highly effective American outfit with characteristic condescension. Lastly, there was Olga, a very comely lass of about twenty-three whose lithe, svelte figure sheathed a set of North Russian muscles that even six-foot McGinnis, a handy man with the ladies, viewed with judicious respect. Olga had many talents. She chauffeured the station wagon, ran errands, served at table, and made reveille for transients by silently leaning over within a few inches of the sleeper's face while beaming powerful magnetic waves, which in short order brought the target to consciousness.

Perhaps born of the conspiratorial nature of the Revolution, and in common with Joe Stalin's habit, it was the Soviet naval custom to operate

American House, Archangel, May 1946, arranged for by Rear Admiral Ivan Papanin, USSRN.

their offices between noon and two in the morning. Duncan called on the Commander White Sea Flotilla at 8 P.M. Admiral Kucherov was much impressed by the recent action of the French in scuttling their fleet at Toulon to avoid Nazi capture. "Just like the Black Sea Fleet, sunk on the orders of Comrade Lenin to block seizure by Allied Interventionists," said the admiral. He proposed a toast to this French maneuver, offering some treasured twenty-year-old port. "In fact," said the admiral, "I like a port or two between vodkas, but I generally follow this with a cognac, to take the sweet taste away." This routine carried on with the admiral and several aides for some forty-five minutes, as a result of which none of us later was in a position to relate the rest of the conversation with any accuracy. We do recall leaving the headquarters in a most amicable atmosphere, mutually determined to whip the Nazis.

Downriver from Archangel the party inspected the port area of Molotovsk, stiff with American merchant ships that had been led through the weakening ice by icebreakers. It was a dismal piece of real estate. Here, as in Archangel, the Russians were doing their best to be friendly to the American seamen. One ship, the SS *Ironclad*, had been left behind the previous autumn, frozen in, with machinery derangements. Her crew had been adopted by the locals, to the point the AgitProp (Agitation and Propaganda) chief ashore concluded for a happy week or so that a mass conversion had taken place; there had been increasing orders for the *Moscow Daily News*, the USSR's only English language newspaper. Then the bubble had burst when he discovered they simply were running out of toilet paper.

Ironclad's skipper failed to share this feeling of international goodwill, having suffered what in modern argot is termed "a bad trip." Inveigled ashore against his better judgment, he was sitting in the local eatery enjoying a vodka or two when the first course bore down on him in the form of a large bowl of fish soup. The waitress, a heavy-handed type probably recruited from the nearest sawmill, tripped over something and poured the soup down the skipper's front. "No problem," the manager declared, bearing his coat off to the kitchen. The waitress, charging back with a reload on the soup, hit the spot of soup on the floor, went into an Immelmann turn and poured the new bowl into the skipper's lap. "Nothing to it," said the manager. They would scrape it off in a jiffy. Taking the old man's pants they wrapped his nether extremities in a tablecloth, whence the meal was completed in fairly good order. By then the pants were back, nicely cleaned, but a trifle stiff. They had overlooked some chocolate bars in the pockets, which the hot iron had welded into the fabric. This was enough. He had had it. Rushing across the street to the supposed sanctuary of the Navy establishment, he opened the vestibule door and met head on over a pool of ice with the maid who was coming out the front door. When they had sorted out the tangled arms and legs and got to their feet again, the skipper, by now close to speechless, got inside just in time to hear a tremendous, sustained crash. It was the cook. She had climbed up on the kitchen table to reach a top shelf. The table had rolled away and Cooky had grabbed at the shelf for support. The shelf detached itself from the wall and it, pots, pans, canned goods, and the cook all tumbled in a shambles to the floor. So the skipper went back aboard, his mix of emotions clearly weighted against socialism in any form.

The men, too, were faced with an occasional paradox. Some of them made friends with the women who worked on the dock: crane operators, checkers, translators. Sometimes they invited the sailors to join them in the three-mile hike through the snow back to town, suggesting they bring along some sandwiches and sugar. A perplexed armed guardsman, back aboard after an excursion to the log quarters of a Russian damsel, approached his lieutenant: "Wot the hell kind of people are they, anyway, sir? They take ya home, eat tha grub ya brought, play tha phonograph awhile, letcha get in bed with 'em. Then ya find out they got on three paira drawers. An' so help me if ya try to get near 'em they get outta bed and set up in a chair all night, freezin' to death. It ain't human!"

There were a number of sawmills scattered along the Dvina, around each of which settlements had grown up out of the ooze and underbrush. No description can adequately paint the drab squalor of these log settlements: dark brown logs, brown mud, and wretched looking, red-eyed, under-nourished people in brown, shapeless padding. The ground was a carpet of brown shavings, sawdust, and strips of bark from the mills. No color but brown, everything as lifeless and inert as a dead leaf in September.

During the party's stay in Archangel, two well-known Soviet artistes, a pianist and a violinist visiting the city, accepted an invitation to dinner with alacrity after several meals at the Intourist Hotel. Lively and cultured, they were a certain contrast to that recent guest, the millionaire. They had studied in Paris and spoke a quaint, attractive brand of English as well as French. Both were married and proudly produced pictures of the children, but like other Russians so far met, were more than vague about what their husbands did. A suggestion was made that the friendship be continued in Moscow, to which there were embarrassed replies that they would be too busy to allow themselves such a pleasure. Alas! The shadow of Beria's secret police reached even unto Archangel.

Five days in Archangel indicated that matters were in good hands. German bombings were more nuisance than handicap. Thousands of tons moved daily out of the ships, onto railway cars, off to the south.

"Have a good bath before you leave," host Jack Harshaw advised. "Not much hot water in Murmansk." While Duncan and company took their turns soaking in the big iron tub, versatile Olga popped in from time to time for a chat, to stoke the "kolonka" that heated the water, and offer to scrub backs.

After the usual several full-dress rehearsals, our party eventually took off for Murmansk. It had to be cloudy enough at the other end to keep the Fritzes away, but not too foggy to find the place. The Americans were ferried over to the island airfield in the Dvina river in a twinkling aboard a sled powered by an aircraft motor and propeller. The warm spell had softened the ice, so the driver had made a dummy run first with sand bags. The sled not having been swallowed up, the sandbags were exchanged for Duncan and friends. "Several trucks go through daily," the chief of staff said. "These country boys are just not quick enough."

We flew over the White Sea, still largely a sheet of ice, then across the snow-covered, rolling land that stretches treeless, vacant, and bleak for hundreds of miles without a sign of human habitation.

At Murmansk's Vaienga airport there was the usual large reception committee, bowing and knocking their heels together.

Duncan had not been able to lay hands on more than a bottle or two of whiskey, so the millionaire was unhappily preparing to settle down to several wasted days in womanless Vaienga. He suggested that the Amer-

Standing by ice sleds to carry U.S. Navy party to mid-river island airfield at Archangel. Left to right: Commander Tolley; Admiral Duncan; Soviet officer; Captain Maund, RN, chief of British naval mission; Soviet officer.

icans would no doubt find the place dull and would want to hurry back to Archangel.

Next step was to land on Kola Island and board an exceptionally neat and well-kept subchaser, having first passed inspection by one of those rare creatures in the USSR, a dog. There are two schools of thought about Russian dogs, or the lack of them: some maintained that no food could be spared for dogs. Others said that all the dogs had been eaten. Some Soviets, perhaps influenced by the shocking behavior of the bloodhounds in their handbook on the American south, *Uncle Tom's Cabin*, felt that dogs were instruments of capitalists and the Gestapo.

At the main Soviet naval base, Polyarnoe, Duncan's party climbed the steep hill to their temporary quarters, the apartment of the absent chief of staff. It was not a bad apartment, considering the front lines were stabilized a mere fifteen miles away. The water ran in the bathroom (cold only), the toilet was very clean, and there was no evidence that anyone had, after the Russian custom, been standing on the seat lately. The living room was a rather bare, fifteen-foot-square space with the inevitable golden oak sideboard against one wall, holding a few miscellaneous dishes and glasses. In the corner was a large and really comfortable davenport convertible into a bed. Its arms, like those of a great many antiques in Norfolk or Charleston, fell off at a touch, but could easily be set back again. A bare board table and four kitchen-style chairs completed the inventory. High overhead, a small bulb glared in the standard Soviet white inverted cone shade.

Each of the two bedrooms had a single, narrow iron bed, a wardrobe, and a small table. The master bedroom in addition had a reading lamp and a telephone with a bell that would have wakened the dead. There were no rugs or curtains. It was clear that the Soviets were not squandering funds on its chief of staff's wartime apartment in Polyarnoe.

Dinner was provided at once, the cocktails in the form of undiluted alcohol from kits assembled for downed aviators. (If not completely down already, this would do it.) The cold ride in the subchaser had whet appetites. All hands did full justice to the smoked salmon, salad, caviar, cutlet, potatoes, fruit, cheese, and tea—the traditional Russian hospitality to foreigners in a sea of want. The liaison officer, who had been in and out several times to the telephone, interrupted the final glass of tea to say that Duncan was expected at the CinC's headquarters in a few minutes (10 P.M.).

All tottered over to the big staff building and up to Vice Admiral Golovko's reception room, full to bursting and feeling very pleased with the success of the trip so far.

Golovko met us at the door. The whole atmosphere of this place and of the man Golovko himself were superior to anything we had so far encoun-

At Polyarnoe, Kola Inlet, North Russia. Left to right: "Ivan Ivan'ich"; Vice Admiral Arseni Golovko, CinC Northern Fleet; Captain Rigerman, Intelligence; Captain Lieutenant Krivoschekov, liaison officer.

tered in the Red Navy. The building inside was impressive and well kept. There were many excellent and appropriate paintings on the walls, including by far the best one of Joe Stalin we had ever seen, splendidly lighted, in the "altar" at the end of the reception room. There was none of the musty smell one almost invariably meets in a Russian house in winter, the combined aroma of boiled cabbage, boots, old clothes, and damp mold.

On the table, dwarfing everything by comparison, was a tremendous spread of smoked salmon, salad, caviar, fruit, and cheese.

Golovko was frank and to the point. His answers were factual and precise. He spoke clearly and without hesitation, exhibiting a keen sense of humor. Undoubtedly his time in Spain during the 1937 Revolution had been a broadening influence. He was short and stocky, stalking around rubbing his hands together, making no purposeless move, like a cat.

Golovko explained in detail what sort of opposition he had found fifteen miles away what the Reds had accomplished with their modest naval forces. He was of the opinion that without his subs and aircraft, the Germans would have been able to cut off Murmansk, meaning the loss of a vital entrance for Lend-Lease goods. It had cost eleven Red subs, two hundred aircraft, and one destroyer. Twenty subs remained to harry Nazi shipping and lay mines in Norwegian fjords.

It was a custom, Golovko said, for returning submarines to fire one gun for every ship sunk. For each shot, the people ashore would butcher one priceless pig in preparation for a banquet for the crew. There was plenty of volatile Murmansk vodka to go with it. While the Americans listened to Golovko explain the custom, a submarine arrived and fired one gun.

Murmansk port area was a perfect picture of ruin. Like a movie set, one expected to see the partly submerged ship alongside the dock turn out to be a painted backdrop, or the twisted piles of rubble that once had been warehouses really made of papier maché and laths. On the burnt out hillsides stood hundreds of chimneys, lone sentinels remaining of the city's residential area.

The city had developed a camaraderie one generally finds in conditions of extreme and constant danger. The sentries were friendly and cooperative. Anyone offered a lift in Sam Frankel's jeep hopped aboard without hesitation and cheerfully started a conversation. What a contrast it was to grim Vladivostok, where the naval representative, Lieutenant Commander G. D. Roullard, was shunned like the devil himself and his house surrounded by floodlights. What an amazing people to show such contrasts.

Even in April the sun shone in Murmansk for only a few hours each day. The nights, in complete blackout, made progress through the city a problem for the uninitiated. The evenings were long, so the travelers gladly accepted an invitation to dinner in the Red Navy Club to escape the gruesome nightmare of the town. The contrast, passing from black desolation to the bright interior of the club was tremendous. Outside, a tomb of darkness and ruin; just on the other side of one of those blank walls left standing, people, lights, music, food, vodka.

A half-dozen lieutenants were having a noisy game of pool, the balls as big as grapefruit and no tips on the cues. Every officer wore a sidearm dangling from two straps at his rear; big revolvers, small revolvers, automatics.

The dining room was the center of activity, brightly lighted by well-arranged indirect fixtures. Around the polished dance floor were ranks of small round tables with white tablecloths. Everything looked well painted and clean. Each table was occupied by a group of Red Navy officers, crouched over plates of hors d'oeuvre or meat and potatoes, a decanter of vodka within easy reach. A phonograph loudspeaker right overhead blared continuously at double proper speed and with sufficient volume to rattle the dishes on the table. There were several women scattered about the room, not too young nor too attractive, dressed in badly fitting prints, run-over heels and shoddy stockings. The great war effort left little for mere beautification. One pair was whirling around the dance floor to a waltz going at the speed of a fox trot. Beads of sweat popped out on the forehead of the fat little captain, a head shorter than his partner. His gun was flying out in a wide arc behind him. Friends were offering shouted encouragement from the sidelines. Several very young officers at the next table who had had too many vodkas and were starting to get careless with the glassware were hustled out with speed and precision, their protests hardly audible above the thunder of the music.

A day was spent viewing the ruins of Murmansk, checking Lend-Lease, hoping meanwhile that Jerry would put on a show. But the weather had been too cloudy for them to accommodate. Not too cloudy though for the millionaire and Golovko to speed the party on its way, each with his private reasons.

Admiral Golovko had been very apprehensive over an American admiral's staying overnight in Murmansk. Admiral Duncan replied that as a junior officer he had always observed with mixed feelings the passing of older officers. Sorry to see them go, naturally, but helpful to the flow of promotion.

The liaison officer, Lieutenant Vladimir ("Volodya") Krivoschekov, rode out with me to the airfield, half an hour over a hard, winding road. The fatalistic Red Navy driver clearly operated on the theory that he was expected to closely follow the lead car carrying the admiral, regardless of what manner of interference developed between—wagons, trucks, country Russians with the indecision of chickens, rocks, and what not. The Fatalist cut in and out among them to the accompaniment of a spirited exchange of comments with the liaison officer on the character of the driving. It was an instructive lesson in Red Navy command performance on the field grade level.

In lulls between arguments with the driver, the liaison officer enlarged on the history of his life. He was a Siberian, of an "old" family, no doubt Czarist exiles. They had come to view the antlike, humdrum existence in the big cities such as Moscow with the disdain a Texas cowboy looks on New York. He lived in a small town, buried in snow in winter, surrounded by a sea of multicolored wild flowers and pleasant woodland in the short summer. In school and later in the university in Moscow he had concentrated on English, history, and psychology, with the intention of becoming a professor. (It was clear the brand of psychology he had learned was not the type useful to influence chauffeurs.)

As he had grown up he had traveled considerably in the Caucasus and the Black Sea region. When his time for army service arrived, he was offered the opportunity of a commission in the Navy, which he accepted rather than go in the ranks as a soldier. That was six years earlier. Now, he was a captain-lieutenant, roughly equivalent to a lieutenant commander, outspoken, undiplomatic, gangling, yellow-haired, and pink-cheeked—but extremely charming and thoughtful of his charges. A typical remark to a British officer, a breed not too popular with the Russians in the North: "You know, I didn't see one attractive girl the whole three months I was in England. They all have flat chests and their bones stick out." About their own Navy supply department: "The thing is full of Jews, Armenians, and the like. You can't get the damned fellows to go anywhere there is any danger of getting hurt."

The "inspectors" left Murmansk's dank twilight with no regrets, nor envy for Sam Frankel and his half dozen assistants who were doing a magnificent job under the most dreary, dangerous conditions. Frankel, and Jack Harshaw in Archangel, were the northern bearings on which the enormous Lend-Lease machine turned, their powerful contributions to the war effort recognized by high American and Soviet decorations.

Duncan would be able to report to Admiral-Ambassador Standley that the Soviets were fortunate in having such a man as Golovko commanding in the north. In my pocket was a reminder. During the conversation at the meeting, Duncan had commented on the pleasant unconventionality of the "front" versus the stifling bureaucracy of Moscow. Such a piddling request as mine, for example, for a cap ribbon for a souvenir—no reply in weeks. Golovko turned his head to the door. "Ei! Ivan Ivan'ich!" he called to his orderly. "Come here!" The smart looking young sailor came over, clicked his heels and saluted. "Give me your hat," said Golovko. He pulled off the cap ribbon. "Here is your souvenir, Mister Commander.* We do business more directly here than in Moscow!"

Indeed it would not be like that in the Moscow where the three Americans were headed, hedge-hopping and sweating in the millionaire's luxury craft.

*The Soviets precede rank with "Tovarishch," (comrade) for their own people, "Gospodin," (mister) for foreigners. Only Admiral Papanin, a widely respected and loved man in his own country, ever addressed Americans as "tovarishch."

8 / *Baku*

The many plants in and around Moscow turning out war material were out of bounds to foreign attachés, so when Duncan had exhausted the repertoire available locally: chocolate factory, military hospital, graveyard, he requested and surprisingly got permission to visit the Red Naval Academy, which had been transferred from besieged Leningrad to Baku.

At the northwest corner of the Caspian Sea, Baku was close to the great Caucasus oilfields, their presence made evident by an overlying odor of petroleum. The wells extended out over the sea, connected by a maze of catwalks. In July the semitropical city was blistering hot. Dark-skinned, hawk-faced Azerbaidjanis outnumbered Russians on the streets.

The Soviets had reason to be proud of their Naval Academy; its cadets were handsome, sturdy, intelligent-looking lads. The whole atmosphere of the place was a good cut above anything we had seen so far. The superintendent, Rear Admiral Ramishvili, was a Georgian, as was his second in command, Captain First Rank Sukhiashvili.* They are a people who smile more easily than most (even "Uncle Joe" did), and who like their liquor straight, often, and preferably in water glasses. Hospitable to a fault, Georgians nonetheless enjoy an occasional bit of blood letting, no better race alive for instilling the martial spirit.

The faculty must have been a picked lot: elderly, cultured professors, a few old ex-Czarist officers, one of whom was a sort of ex-officio dean beloved of the students, and a sprinkling of sons of former Czarist officers with well-known names. The uniformed members all had on brand new, straight-from-the-tailor white service blouses to go with navy blue trousers, shoes spit-shined. Hats were the right size. The small talk at table was

*Ramishvili's U. S. tour in 1945 ended disastrously for him. Possibly his freewheeling Georgian nature was too much for the NKVD, who took him back to the USSR under arrest.

At Baku, summer of 1943. At left, Rear Admiral Jack H. Duncan, in an earlier form of détente, hams it up in a Soviet rear admiral's jacket and cap, the owner of which is on the right, wearing my uniform.

spontaneous, cosmopolitan, and wide-ranging, without the normal requirement of a string of quick toasts to get things off dead center. Nobody picked his teeth or drank more vodka than was good for him.

We had been twice to Murmansk, now to Baku, in the course of which we had been, in effect, bedfellows with several dozen assorted Soviet naval officers—admirals to midshipmen. The Baku group had in no way altered our opinion as to Red Navy accomplishments with vodka, but they did help to make us realize that there was more to them than just a rubber lining to their stomachs. There were three basic types in the Red Navy: the Bright Boys of the new generation, from which came the most prepossessing, including flag officers, some of whom were under forty; the Broken Down Boys, ex-Czarist officers who had the necessary know-how, such as Admirals Haller and Stepanov, but who were old and being phased out;* the Hopeless Boys, old pitch-thumpers risen from boatswain's mate to lieutenant. And there they stuck, with frayed collars, run-over shoes, baggy pants, looking greasy enough to boil up for soup stock.

This was my first opportunity to be alone with "Mike" Kostrinsky, who had accompanied Duncan and me as liaison officer. He had been working with me for some weeks on an English-Russian joint signal code book, sponsored by the British and was becoming a good and close friend. But in Moscow there was always the cloud of the NKVD. The two of us worked together in a small Mokovaya office abutting Moscow University, the common wall an obvious place to expect a bug to be implanted, which we both realized. On one occasion, after working late, Mike rather hesitatingly agreed to drop by my apartment to share dinner. During the meal, the phone rang. "It is for you, Comrade Kostrinsky," the maid called in. The color drained from Mike's face as he rushed out to the phone. "I must leave immediately," he said. We took an occasional ride in the U.S. Navy motor car, having got permission from Mike's boss, Zaitsev, on some pretext or another for him to go along. But with one or two other Americans in the car, his conversation was obviously guarded, suggesting the typical Russian distrust of the "troika," the third man.

Mike was in his element with the Baku Naval Academy group. His three years in London as assistant naval attaché had broadened him well beyond his earthy boss Zaitsev, whose appreciation of the finer things ran more to chasing Metropole Hotel chambermaids. Now in Baku, we could stroll the seawall promenade, or sit on a park bench, while Duncan, who as senior took the brunt of the toasts at evening affairs, slept late. (Translators such as Mike and myself were never pushed to drink too much, all well aware that our unclouded efforts were essential to the enterprise.)

"Why are you sweating in that blue blouse instead of wearing a white one?" I asked Mike. "Dammit! Because I haven't *got* one!" he replied testily, exhibiting for him a rare petulance, not to mention more frankness than usual in a Russian.

But frankness had become the order of the day with Mike. He was a dedicated Stalinist, like the majority of Russians at that time. "Without strong and ruthless leadership, we Russians would be running off in all directions," Mike explained. "Without Stalin the whole edifice would have collapsed. The Germans would have met the Japanese at the Urals. *Then* where would you and those precious British be?"

*Haller, former CinC Baltic Fleet; Stepanov, Deputy Navy Commissar.

"You are always making mild cracks about the British, Mike. You don't like them?" I asked.

Like all Russians given a horse to ride, Mike let go the reins. "The English foundation of imperial greatness was erected on the fragile base of superior seamanship," he said, "and their superb ability to create situations where the criterion is, 'lets you and him fight.' In other words, a magnificent display of the ability to manage the balance of power. They always inject a bit of their own military into the picture, to give the thing an air of genuine participation. But they never suffer the losses others do. Their own power has metamorphosed into an imperial arrogance and an infuriating condescension toward their colonials, many of whom were writing beautiful poetry when the Britons were in blue paint."

"Furthermore," said Mike, warming up to his subject, "they enjoy the safety of an island redoubt, which gives them a feeling of security we Russians have never known."

"But Mike," I interjected, "they have done a great lot to bring order to parts of the world that never knew it, and even though belatedly perhaps, also came up with some beautiful poetry."

"Sure they did," said Mike. "But like in Imperial Russia it was done on the backs of slaves. The money accumulated in both England and Russia in the nineteenth century allowed and encouraged a flowering of thought, literature, and drama that rivaled ancient Greece, where also it was possible through use of captured enemies as slaves. It simply takes a leisure class and money to do these things. We have no leisure class in the Soviet Union, so our arts are sterile. But so are yours in America, where everybody is so busy making money there is no time for reflection or original thought."

I asked Mike about the Jews and their influence, recalling a remark by Krivoschekov in the north, which reflected on their ambition to fight in the front lines. "I am a Jew myself," he replied. "But notice that I am blond and blue-eyed. Most Jews in the Soviet Union are not Jews at all, but Khazars, descended from an Asiatic tribe living right here north of Baku seven or eight hundred years ago. They are round-headed, with black, curly hair, short, stubby fingers, and black or brown eyes. They had an animistic religion, worshipping trees, lightning, evil spirits—junk like that. But their king felt it should be replaced by a monotheistic religion he could associate himself personally with, to better control the people. So after checking around, he opted for Judaism, rather than for other possible choices such as Byzantine Christianity or the Arabs' prophet Mohammed. Both of these were practiced by strong temporal powers, the Princedom of Kiev and the Caliphate of Baghdad. They would swallow him. But the Jews, like Stalin remarked of the Pope, had no divisions. When the Mongols swept in at the time of Genghis Khan, the Khazars were scattered.

Many went to Hungary, the rest to the Ukraine. The Khazars were always traders; living between the Arabs south of the Caucasus and the Russians, they controlled the trade via the Volga, taking 10 percent. They have been traders by choice ever since, rather than military men. But we do have several Jewish generals."

Mike assured me that there was no anti-Semitism except self-imagined. "The thought never struck me until you mentioned it," he said. "We depended heavily on the Jews in the beginning because they hated the Czar and were reliable; because they were the few we had who could read and write. That is why so many were political commissars; the Red Army commanders were in many cases illiterate. But in the reorganization [Mike so referred to the bloody 1936–37 purges in which millions died], it was felt that a better balance should be struck between the people in control as to national origin."

"But Mike," I said. "What do you mean by 'national origin?' You are all Russians—or excuse me, Soviets—are you not? One nation?" A less intelligent Soviet would have countered by, "Well, what about the negro problem in the United States?" Mike pointed out that each country has its cleavages. In Britain, the Scots held themselves separate from the English. The Irish and Welsh felt distinctly apart from either each other or the Scots and English. In France, it was even worse, Mike thought, with the difference in dialects not unlike the situation in the USSR. Italy was worse. And Spain! Those Basques, Catalans, Andalusians were as different as Ukrainians and Muscovites. "And as for you Americans," continued Mike, "your Catholics, Jews, Protestants, secret societies, and criminal groups are politely at each others' throats."

Here again, as in the far north, we found the Russians unsullied by the cautions and precautions of Moscow against telling anything more than the time of day to a foreigner. The "fleet" officers were full of interesting matters concerning the brackish little sea on which they floated. The Caspian was slowly but surely dying, drying up, they said. Its level then was 90 feet below the Black Sea, dropping three inches annually. In the days of Xenophon, he and his ten thousand Greeks, homeward bound, had come to the Caspian, thence down the Mainych Kanal, now a dry, winding valley, to the Sea of Azov, thence to the Black Sea.

The Kara Bugach, an appendix-like bay on the Caspian's east side, has an entrance several hundred yards wide through which flows a heavy current, water which will evaporate in the basin's hot, desert climate. Close it off? Then what about the thousands of tons of Glauber's salts bulldozed up along the shores for use in metallurgy? There was the possibility of opening up the Mainych Kanal so that the Black Sea would return some of the water it had received in ages past. But then, the Black Sea waters where the depth is greater than four feet are inimical to fish. This poisonous Black Sea water would then be sucked into the Sea of Azov, wiping out its enormously rich seafood industry. Another idea was to divert one or more of the great north-flowing rivers to turn their flow to the south, as had been the case when ice dammed the north 10,000 years ago. This would augment the Volga River, the Caspian's chief but dwindling source of water.

It was of course interesting to us to learn more of the vagaries of their private sea, but even more was it enlightening on the broad interests of the Soviet naval officer, not just in ships and their operation, but in the geophysical questions relating to the *use* of those ships—the canal system, for example, which made it possible to transfer small vessels between the various Russian operating areas, the Black, Baltic, and Barents seas. With our own freedom of access to all the world's oceans, we perhaps do not realise the extent to which Soviet naval thought, strategy, even basic mentality, are conditioned by their almost total constriction of free movement by the Dardanelles, La Pérouse Strait, the Kattegat, and the relatively narrow passage between Norway and Greenland. Our conversations in Baku made this very clear.

Admiral Duncan did not wear his aiguillette as naval attaché. Perhaps his having been aide to Admiral Standley for many years when the ambassador had been on active duty had dimmed its glamor for him. Perhaps he felt it impinged on his dignity as a senior in his own right, a dignity he was not above defending. Rear Admiral Miles, Chief of the British Naval Mission in Moscow, had on occasion been the subject of comment by Irishman Duncan on the imperious ways of the lordly Britisher. One evening the phone rang. "Its for you, sir," I told Duncan, "Admiral Miles." Putting down his glass, Duncan picked up the phone. "This is the admiral speaking!" came the lilting Dartmouth voice at the other end. "*What* admiral?" inquired Duncan in a most innocent tone, a pixyish grin on his face.

Following Duncan's example, the assistant naval attachés had not worn their aiguillettes either. But on the adventure into virgin territory that was less engaged in active hostilities than the embattled north, Duncan directed me to pin on not just the undress four-strander, but the full-dress version—a heavy, braided, gold rope looping from shoulder point to lapel, with two gold pendants resembling miniature fire hoses said to have metamorphosed from writing implements when in earlier days staff officers were battlefield dispatch writers.

Starved for knowledge of the world outside and what its people looked like, our conspicuous presence in the once-royal box at the opera, accompanied dignitaries from the city and Naval Academy, drew enormous interest from the audience, packed as always. An Azerbaidjani cast performed an ancient national drama, singing, dancing, and banging cymbals, manfully doing their best to bring down the rafters, but it was clear that the focal point of interest was the two visitors from outer space, one wearing accoutrements seen only on the stage or in history books that portrayed the bad old days of imperial finery. "They think you are the admiral and I am the sideboy," Duncan whispered to me with a grin.

"We would appreciate it if you would allow us to put in a few passengers with you on the way back to Moscow," asked the Russians, who had provided a DC-3 for the trip. The big plane sat on a packed dirt runway, haphazardly being loaded with an assortment of bales, bundles and boxes. Inside, a soldier casually lolled comfortably back on what today would be called a water bed, but in this case was an inflatable fabric fuel tank full of gasoline. He was smoking a cigarette.

"You had better give me more time to stow this baggage properly, or you'll never get the tail up!" a man back aft called to the pilot. "The hell with it!" said the pilot. "I don't want to get stuck at Stalingrad for the night. Get cracking!"

Loaded up, with the usual thirty-second engine warm-up, we started rolling along the bumpy runway, faster and faster. Then the plane lurched to a halt at the very edge of the field. The cockpit door opened and the pilot stuck his head out. "You're right, Ivan Mihai'ich," he shouted. "I can't get the tail up. Shift some of that cargo forward!"

9 / *Komsomolsk*

Happy to be back in Moscow's relatively salubrious climate, "Dunc" soon dropped into the old routine of semiweekly visits to friend Zaitsev, the liaison officer, taking me along as interpreter. Zaitsev's secretary, a pert young lady in Red Navy skirt and sailor's blouse, skittered about, bringing tea, which nobody ever drank, and vodka, which all did, including the secretary. Exceedingly good Russian chocolate or a plate of smoked herring and black bread provided bites between bottoms-up of the thimble-sized glasses of vodka.

Prior to Duncan's arrival on the Moscow scene, all Lend-Lease transactions including Navy had been in the hands of General Faymonville's mission. There were no naval people on his staff, so Duncan was doing his best to stem Faymonville's "give-'em-anything-they-want-no-questions-asked" approach, sort out orders, and justify requirements. There was this matter of stern posts for cruisers, said Duncan on one of our visits. These things were large, expensive, complicated castings, he told Zaitsev. They were in tight supply due to our own huge construction program. Perhaps if we could visit one of their shipyards and inspect the vessels requiring the stern posts we could better coordinate the whole program. Zaitsev, a basically stupid man, by this time lightly primed with vodka, didn't even consider the matter. "We have no navy yards in operation now," he said brightly. "They have all either been occupied or cut off by those damned Nazis." Dunc's face broke into a pleased smile. "In that case you of course won't want those stern posts," he said. Zaitsev's jaw dropped, his face paled. Close to speechless, he stood up and offered his hand as an indication the session was over. With the vodka bottle still half full, this clearly had to be a crisis situation.

The next day we were called to the liaison office. A businesslike Zaitsev grasped our hands and led us in. "Which navy yard would you like to visit," said Zaitsev, without even awaiting the secretary and bottle. "Molotovsk or Komsomolsk?"

Molotovsk, Duncan well knew, was just outside Archangel. Komsomolsk was in far Siberia, within striking distance of Vladivostok. It was the USSR's brand new industrial city in the wilderness that very few foreigners had ever seen. His bland face as inscrutable as in any poker game, Duncan pretended to ponder a minute. "Well, I guess Komsomolsk would be just fine," he drawled, in the same tone he might have announced four of a kind. Indeed, if such a visit were allowed, he would consider holding in abeyance that cancellation of the stern posts already written up.

In a week, arrangements had been completed, Trans-Siberian Railway tickets delivered, courtesy of the Red Navy. Duncan and I would be squired by Captain-Lieutenant Stepan Tarasov.

The usual seeing-off party was on hand at the station while Duncan and a month's rations for three were installed in one elegant *wagon-lits* coupe, while Steve Tarasov and I, primus stove, pans and coffee pot, and more food were in another adjoining, with a small washroom between. Steve, a gangling, somewhat cadaverous, blond, blue-eyed six-footer had staggered down the platform under the Russian version of a Chinese yo-yo pole—the type village girls use to carry water from the well. From each end dangled a square, five gallon tin with a screw cap. This was Steve's contribution to the common larder, one which on first thought might have seemed a trifle bizarre: five gallons of sweetened condensed milk in one, five gallons of neat grain alcohol in the other. Those tins were in effect a thick pack of traveler's checks. Across the endless rolling plains of Russia, the Urals' worn hills, and the flower-studded steppes of Siberia, that condensed milk and alcohol, doled out in tiny dollops at the innumerable whistle stops along the way, could be traded for the roast chicken parts, hard-boiled eggs, potatoes, forest nuts and berries, cabbage, and beets, that peasants had brought to swap for whatever the train's forehanded passengers and crew had to offer—bits of cloth, soap, old newspapers, tobacco, pins, matches, or even better, condensed milk and the double-strength makings of vodka.

Steve Tarasov truly was one of nature's noblemen. He had just been invalided out of Black Sea submarines with a bad stomach, which in no respect had diminished his outgoing good disposition. Russians by nature are predisposed to kindness and hospitality to strangers, especially foreigners, in spite of the manner in which they have been put upon by almost all outsiders who over the ages have ravaged their land and people. Traveling twenty-five days, most of which was spent in the narrow confines of a railway coupe, would scrape raw the nerves of most pairs so confined. But at the end of that extraordinary month, Steve was as close to us as any dear relative. No effort was too great for him in rounding up delicacies "ashore" during the sometimes 20- to 30-minute stops at stations to water the locomotive, let the "hard" class passengers swarm to the *kipyatok* (boiling water) tap to fill their tea pots, or carry on the barter game with locals. On cooler mornings I would awake to find Steve's overcoat tossed on top of my thin blanket. I was not especially cultured from Steve's point of view, so to exercise my Russian and inculcate in me an appreciation of Russian literature, Steve read aloud to me for hours. I was exposed to considerable quantities of Chekhov—over whom Steve would come close to rolling in the aisle at some of the humor an American sometimes finds obscure.

Often when Duncan was not snoozing away from the monotony of the passing scene, he would join us in our coupe for a chat, and of course at mealtime, where he gave sage advice on the cooking from his experience as a country boy in Indian country.

Each car carried an elderly *babushka* who inhabited a cubicle at the end of the coach. She swept up, made the bunks, and provided endless glasses of tea from the samovar that bubbled away constantly in her tiny box of a room. One day she brought a copy of *Pravda* to Duncan, a rare prize that could be used for many things other than enlightenment. I thanked her on Dunc's behalf, adding that unfortunately, the Admiral couldn't read Russian. "Oh! The poor old sookin-sin (son-of-a-bitch)," she commiserated in Russian. "Illiterate, eh?"

Khabarovsk was the transfer point for Komsomolsk, which lay on the new northern branch of the Trans-Sib 300 miles above the touchy Manchurian border. The other branch of the railway continued the 400 miles to Vladivostok. Duncan had, of course, wanted to go there, too, for a visit with Lieutenant Commander George Roullard, our assistant naval attaché in mufti, pretending to be a consular clerk. But the Japanese situation was far too delicate to have a U. S. rear admiral rattling around that vital military area. It was probably embarrassing enough to have one stuck in Khabarovsk. And stuck he was. Duncan had developed a severe cold en route and on arrival in Khabarovsk, ten days out of Moscow, he was hospitalized rather than whisked across to the Komsomolsk train.

The unexpected, unplanned stopover was a mixed blessing—tough on the boss, but giving me four days to case that important center, plus a chance to socialize with counterparts of the Amur River Flotilla. As an old Yangtze sailor I found much in common with the Soviet "River Rats," which we on the Yangtze called ourselves. Their gunboats were very like ours—flat bottoms, shallow draft, plenty of power, and an ample battery of medium artillery plus small automatic weapons. Problems were the same too: unpredictable navigation over rapids and shoals, channels ever changing, swapping shots with bandits ashore on the Manchurian side. Also, the same camaraderie aboard, born of isolation in squalid river towns or patrolling long stretches of riverine grandeur, through mountain passes and serpentine valleys.

Duncan would very much have liked to have met the Patrol's commander, a vice admiral. But he was "out of town," as any tyro on the Russian scene could have predicted. Our stopover being unexpected, Soviet officers who were available obviously had not been briefed or otherwise warned what to say and what not. So Steve and I enjoyed several uninhibited evening bull sessions with opposite numbers in age and rank over vodka and sakuski. Vastly more open than any we had met before, they freely discussed the shipbuilding problems at Komsomolsk: how the ships were launched in the shallow river, then floated half-completed to one of the several Far East ports for arming and outfitting. Again, as on the Caspian, we were reminded of the Soviet Navy's preoccupation with its semiprison walls, its narrow gates to the open sea.

A foreign uniform had not been seen on the local streets since the Intervention's end in 1922. Out for a morning promenade, flanked by Steve Tarasov in uniform and the city's mayor, I was spotted in my Australian horse pants and khaki by a small boy of about eight, who grabbed his mother's skirt in consternation. "Boje moi!" he cried out. "Mamma! Vot poshol Fritz!" ("Good God, Mamma! There goes a Kraut!")

As we sat in a park, watching people stroll by, the inevitable gaggle of urchins gathered around. "Ei! Your shoulder marks are not nearly so pretty as ours!" one said, referring to my modest cloth shoulder straps. "Look! Our Soviet ones are gold," he added, pointing out Steve's resplendent shoulder boards. But they had good things to say about Americans. "Some of our people tried to get across to Alaska," one volunteered, "but they were shot." Another said that *everybody* would like to go to the United States, but they weren't allowed. "Get away from here, you little devils!" barked the mayor, his face crimson. Stever smiled indulgently and said nothing.

Steve knew quite well what America was like, having spent a year there as a language student in the mid-thirties. He undoubtedly silently agreed with the boys, although he had several reasons to entertain mixed feelings. While Steve was driving the $40 vehicle he had purchased on a second-hand car lot, a yokel policeman had picked him up one time in a speed trap. His bumbling English didn't help matters when it came to the constabulary's dealing with "them durn furriners." It was about the same era that an Iranian diplomat had been similarly nabbed, wherein his protest that he was the Iranian minister elicited the comment from his captor that a minister of the gospel should be ashamed of himself for so flagrantly breaking the law. Thus were diplomatic passports viewed by the township of East Bumwad, Eastern Shore. The main consideration was that they were worth fifteen bucks apiece to the town's treasury. So both minister plenipotentiary and language student Steve spent an uncomfortable night in the village slammer. The Iranians broke off diplomatic relations; Steve was bailed out by his embassy.

When it came time to return to the USSR, Steve left in mid-month, his ogress of a boardinghouse keeper refusing to return a prorata share of the rent. "I must tell you honestly," Steve said, between sessions of Chekhov, "that those of your bourgeoisie are too tinged with avarice. The proletariat is kinder, because they know what it is to suffer. The rich don't seem to care much one way or another. Their feelings are superficial."

Duncan was mended by four days of thoughtful, hovering attention on the part of a bevy of doctors, cheerful, robust-looking, plump nurses to whom all patients were infants, and Dunc's own desire to get on with it. At the end of a swaying ride via a new railway built on land exposed to great extremes of temperature, we were introduced to the debatable pleasures of Komsomolsk.

Widely publicized at the time of its almost instantaneous construction as being the work of volunteer Young Komsomols, the city was row on row of identical three- or four-story log and masonry barrack-like apartments strung along very wide mud streets bordered by wood plank sidewalks. Even though it was only mid-September, the chill of a coming harsh winter hung in the air. And as always, hospitality was overwhelming. In the raw board hotel, Soviet planning had really enjoyed a field day. The light switches were behind the door as one entered the rooms. Mirrors hung not over the lavatory (no stoppers) but on the opposite wall. Nor was one likely to linger in contemplation in the toilet down the hall without a gas mask. Nevertheless, the whole conception and operation was certainly a challenge that greatly credits the nation and people whom nature and geography have forced to such extremes of effort, ingenuity, and determination. That it can but rob the souls involved of so much that is precious in human life strikes outsiders such as ourselves with an overwhelming sadness that fellow humans should have to exist in such hardship, without a shred of beauty, no control over their private destiny—in effect, human manure that will hopefully fertilize and improve the lives of succeeding generations.

The *raison d'etre* for Komsomolsk was to establish some heavy industry in eastern Siberia out of easy range of Japanese aircraft, principally a shipyard. The Amur, a near-Mississippi-sized river at Komsomolsk, which with its tributaries formed a thousand miles of the Sino-Soviet border, turned left into Siberia at Khabarovsk, then meandered northeast 350 miles to Komsomolsk, thence another 450 miles to the Straits of Tartary, the narrow, shallow passage between Siberia and Sakhalin Island, the lower half of which was Japanese. This was the tortuous route by which ships launched at Komsomolsk were towed half-completed to Vladivostok, Sovietskaya Gavan, or elsewhere for fitting out and arming.

The shipyard was an enormous, roofed structure, all building ways under cover. Windows were blacked out as a precaution against ever possible Japanese surprise attack, so that the eerie gloom inside gave an unreal aspect to the shadowy bulks of a cruiser, three destroyers, and numerous smaller craft, illuminated here and there by dim bulbs or the flickering blue-white lightning of welding torches.

The light cruiser *Kaganovich*, 8,500 tons, nine 7.1-inch guns in three turrets, sat on the ways three-quarters completed. She would draw a minimum of 17 feet, so although turret guns already were mounted, much would have to be done later if she were to be skidded over the Amur's fifteen-foot spots en route the sea.

For a welcome change there was no preliminary vodka and sakuska before the inspection. I was therefore able to produce a long intelligence report, noting particularly the general substitution of riveting for the welding then standard in American construction. Manifesting the versatility prized in Russian shipbuilding for generations, she was fitted not only for guns, but mines, torpedo tubes, and depth charges. Approximately three inches of belt and gun-house armor provided more than the usual protection for such a ship. If she could go fast and far with what we could see, she promised to be a damn good cruiser.

Ruefully concluding the report was the statement that: "It must be mentioned that the Soviets are in a class by themselves when it comes to secretiveness. They are eternally suspicious of motives of foreigners and consider that any such inspection of building facilities and ships as we made at Komsomolsk is solely in the nature of legalized espionage which can only hurt and certainly not help the USSR. Any attempt to ask detailed questions of military features of ships or of anything they consider beyond the bounds of the stated mission (in this case, to check lend-lease material use) results in an immediate and complete freeze-up. The taking of notes or making of sketches is not considered cricket, which Soviet officers will make no bones over pointing out. If the above bits of information seem meagre results of an inspection of a shipbuilding yard, it is because everything is from memory, covering only those items which can be recalled without doubt as to reasonable accuracy." (The report covered most of ten 8 by 13½-inch pages, single spaced.)

We left Komsomolsk delighted to have come, but with no regrets at leaving. Already the days were getting shorter and colder. I had left Moscow with six shirts, changing to a clean one at decent intervals. On the way back, the clean shirt simply went on top of the other one, until arrival at Moscow found me with three or four layers of shirts, one over the other.

On the train the Chekhov sessions had tapered off into long discussions of life, marriage, children, and the war, eschewing politics. The center of Steve's life was his seven-year-old daughter, Nina. It was for her he was hoping things would be easier. He and his wife were tough, he explained; they would survive under any circumstances. But Nina! Yes, Nina had stars in her eyes when she talked about the Fatherland and went on Young Pioneer picnics with her red scarf framing a radiant face. "Would you ever think of getting her to America?" I asked. "What!" replied Steve, aghast. "Tear a wild flower from the forest and transplant it to a garden? Or vice versa?" Steve was fond of allegory, sometimes only vaguely apropos. Or even more, proverbs. Russian is rich in proverbs, there being very few situations for which an appropriate one cannot be quoted. "*Poslovitsa yest*!" they say, holding up an admonitory index finger for attention. "Proverb is!" Then follows the line of wisdom from Russian antiquity.

"You are not married at thirty-four. Why?" Steve wanted to know. I explained that as an only child I had always been a sort of loner, independent. Besides, in the Navy ships moved about so much that liaisons ashore never had time to firm up. But it was clear that one got more discriminating and less attractive as the years passed. "Why don't you marry a Russian?" said Steve, his comment on forest flower Nina obviously forgotten. "I found American girls—now please forgive me if I speak frankly—I found American girls were inclined to be not sincere. One never knew where one stood under that veneer of sophistication and coquettishness. Russian girls are more open. They give and they take according to established principles of equality. It is a game of chess. All the players are in sight. It is up to the player to select winning moves. American romance is a game of cards. One cannot see what is in the hands. There is too much bluff. Sometimes even cheating. One cannot cheat at chess, which one might say is our national indoor sport." I had to interject that until recently at any rate, a Soviet divorce meant merely an exchange of postcards between contending parties, and that there was a good bit of it, so perhaps the chess theory bore closer examination. "Indeed you are right," admitted Steve, "but what is better? A twenty kopek postcard or some lawyer who spends a year arriving at the same end? As for chess, it is true that some subterfuge is to be expected. One must plan one's moves far ahead, so that the move of the moment may not give a clue to the trap that is being set."

Steve had a good sense of humor and bore chiding well. "You are not talking about romance now, Steve," I said. You are talking about the way your diplomats work."

"You mean the way *British* diplomats work," he said with a wry grin. "We had to start with absolutely nothing in 1918, with idealists instead of professionals such as the British had been developing since before Queen

Victoria. Besides, English is ambiguous. Without amplification one is never sure what is being proposed. You can say in Russian, 'I hired a servant,' which provides the gender both of the hired and the hirer, and if the hiring is temporary or permanent. The safest thing for us to say is, 'Nyet!' then try to find out exactly what is wanted."

Thus did the days go pleasantly by. On arrival at Moscow the tins of condensed milk and alcohol were near bottom. The remaining cans of spam, beans, tomatoes, and corn were passed on to Steve. "Nina has never tasted such things before," said Steve gratefully. "And certainly I never will forget you both." We parted after affectionate bear-hug embraces in the Russian fashion, with the mutual sad but solid expectation we would never meet again.

Zaitsev was glad to see us back, relaxing to the point of accompanying Duncan and me back to Mokovaya for a spur-of-the-moment party in Duncan's new apartment to celebrate our return. Mike Kostrinsky came along too.

During the warming up period, Ronnie Allen had gone out several times to answer the telephone. Then, while Ronnie was in the kitchen struggling with a champagne cork, the phone rang again. I answered it, to hear a dulcet female voice suggest that she and two friends join us. They could see the light and hear the music, she said. Yes, they knew the telephone number because the apartment had been the temporary digs for transient couriers in from Vladivostok or Teheran before Dunc's and Allen's occupancy. They had dropped in on occasion in the past to check on the welfare of the couriers.

Zaitsev, as Russians often do, had insisted that the men dance together. He had already swung Kostrinsky around the floor several times. Now he was at it with Dunc, who with obvious distress on his usually bland face, was not following very well. It seemed like an act of mercy to promote some more appropriate partners. Dunc would thank me. "By all means, come on up!" I said.

The three damsels, who in short order knocked on the door, burst in like a summer storm. Aside from thick eyebrows which met in the middle, the leader of the little pack was a well-dressed, rather attractive looking girl. The next, for want of any announced name, we called "The Turk." Her tight black curls, jet eyes, arched nose, olive skin with high coloring suggested she well might have been from the Caucasus—a fierce, independent world of passionate love, sharp knives, and tall fur hats. Bringing up the rear was Tamara. Demure, large curls hanging to her shoulders, with the big round eyes of a startled rabbit, she sank into the corner of a divan in open-mouthed silence. At fourteen years old, as we discovered later, it was

Tamara Gilmore and Eddie Yorke. Her husband, Eddy, was the UP correspondent in Moscow.

no pose.* Not so Miss Eyebrows. She charged into the kitchen where Ronnie was still battling the champagne cork. "*Dai mnye booteelku*!" she barked. (Gimme thuh bottle!) Grabbing a towel, she wrapped it around the bottle's neck, then bashed it across a gas pipe. Strained champagne cascaded through the towel, minus the shards, whence the real party commenced.

*A year later, Tamara married 37-year old Eddy Gilmore, Moscow United Press chief, author of a number of books, including, *Me and My Russian Wife* (1954), describing his successful life, romance, and four children.

10 / The Watch Changes

Will Durant said of Voltaire that by telling the truth he offended everybody. Perhaps Admiral-Ambassador Standley was too truthful. He told the world that the Soviet people were not being informed of the extent of Allied help, and he told President Roosevelt he didn't like being bypassed either by General Faymonville or special messengers from Washington.

In the beginning, there was no doubt Standley was making an honest effort to excuse and understand the Soviets. The Germans had betrayed them. How could they trust *anybody*? We in the mess admired and liked the old gentleman. He had a sort of elfin charm about him. Short, with a good head of wavy, steel-gray hair, gold-rimmed spectacles, merry eyes, he enjoyed sound health, an occasional scotch, and a game of doubles tennis. Reserved in manner, scarcely what one would call jocular, he had an appreciation of country wit that probably had drawn to him such low-key humorists as Jack Duncan, who had been his aide for so many years. Once a slightly bawdy story at the mess table drew such a stern look from the old fellow that the message instantly was got across as to his views along those lines. But he could bend a little. George Hickman, embassy chief radioman, recalls a Standley tale. Hickman was part-time chicken custodian. Eggs were the equivalent of 60 dollars a dozen. So Standley, well known for his parsimony, had got himself a white leghorn rooster and two hens.

One day the admiral received a visit from the British ambassador and his lady, to whom the admiral wished to show off his chickens. Hickman was told to herd them out into the yard where they could be observed, so he opened the coop and spread some corn around.

A hen emerged first, closely followed by the rooster, his neck stretched out as long as a boathook. There could be no doubt as to his intentions. But whilst in hot pursuit, he suddenly diverted his attention to the corn and began pecking away at the grains. Whereupon the admiral remarked to Lady Clark-Kerr, "I hope I never get that hungry!"*

Since Admiral Standley's arrival in the USSR, a parade of important people had passed through the Soviet capital, some with special projects, others with private messages to Stalin from a president who liked to carry on personal diplomacy. Most galling of the latter type had been Wendell Willkie, erstwhile Republican candidate for president, whose visit is earlier described.

We watched in concerned sympathy in this case as the ambassador sat in a rage in the mess room discussing with the seniors what he should do.

Interestingly enough, Standley's opposite number in Washington, Soviet Ambassador Maxim Litvinov, complained to Secretary Hull that he was disgusted with being bypassed as ambassador and was going back to Moscow to try to convince Stalin of the necessity of recognizing the force of U. S. public opinion. We all thought it rather a good joke.

While Standley was in the United States protesting the Willkie fiasco, another rambunctious, but far more personable, messenger of the Washington gods, Patrick J. Hurley, appeared on the scene, also with a message for Stalin—its supposed urgency reinforcing a large curiosity on Hurley's part as to what was going on in the USSR. This handsome, dashing two-star political Army Reserve from Oklahoma had been President Hoover's Secretary of War. Standing six feet tall in highly polished cavalry boots and impeccable, wasp-waisted uniform, pink cheeks set off by a white mane of hair and flowing mustache, he was a recruiting poster model of a modern major general.

Nevertheless, all this plus his recent employment as ambassador to New Zealand cut no ice with the Generalissimus, who kept Hurley cooling his spurred heels in the ambassadorial suite for almost a month awaiting an audience. Was it possible, we speculated in the mess over Hurley's scotch whiskey, that after Willkie, perhaps the wily Georgian was trying to tell FDR something? At any rate, Hurley improved his time by a visit to the front, the *real* front. Bullets whistled and shells burst over the command dugout, where Hurley popped the eyeballs of Soviet generals with his Comanche warwhoop.

Then at last Hurley got to shake the hand that held Russia in its palm. Fortified by Stalin's promise of impartiality between communist Mao Tse-tung and Nationalist Chiang Kai-shek, Hurley went on via the back door to China as ambassador, there to feud bitterly with his staff, taking a fighting corner in the war-within-a-war, the fierce power struggle between

*By kind permission of Hickman and the editor of *Shipmate*, Captain Roy C. Smith III.

the American factions in China—Generals Chennault and Stilwell, the OSS, and Rear Admiral M. E. Miles, USN, deputy under China's secret police chief Tai Li of SACO, the Sino-American Cooperative Organization. And indeed, Stalin kept his promise—until VJ Day.

Snatched off as chargé de'affaires during Standley's absence was one of the State Department's most experienced Russian experts, Loy Henderson, innocently passing through on an inspection tour for State's housekeeping department. One strongly suspects it was a clever move on State's part to surreptitiously get a real Russian expert of senior rank into the Moscow picture without the messy procedures on both ends involved in a formal investiture. I had known Henderson in Riga, as one of the pre–World War II professionals whose duty at the Baltic listening post had removed any delusions a sensible individual would have entertained about the basic Soviet motives and modus operandi. Henderson's forthright *ad interim* views on the Moscow scene instantly identified him to the White House as far too dangerous a man either to remain in the USSR or to have rattling around the Sate Department just next door to the White House, thinking dangerous thoughts. So he was banished to a "safe" spot—minister to Iraq. There I stayed with him in May 1944 for several days, filling him in on Moscow developments, while with his characteristic acumen he informed me of his ferreting out the Soviets' Byzantine plans to support a Jewish homeland in Palestine, knowing that the United States and Britain would be forced by internal politics to support it and thus alienate the Arab world. Henderson's urgent warnings, ignored by Washington, are available now for all to read.

Willkie was merely a blustery prelude, Standley's trip of protest to Washington obviously an exercise in futility. In April 1943, General James Burns, executive director of Lend-Lease, who had been nominated as ambassador to the USSR until it became more expedient to appoint Standley, arrived for six weeks of negotiations, and often disappeared into the countryside without informing the ambassador when or where he was going, or when he returned, what he had seen.

Burns's constant companion was Faymonville. Standley once again called him on the mat for engaging in independent intelligence activities and reminded him of his subordinate position as had been certified to Standley in his previous Washington visit. The ambassador was dumbfounded at Faymonville's reply. He was, he said, operating under a highly secret letter of instruction that he could not show the ambassador.

What Standley did not know was that Faymonville enjoyed a close to sancrosanct position, starting in January 1938, when Roosevelt directed his ambassador to the USSR, Joseph E. Davies ". . . to explore the possibility of securing a liaison between the military and naval authorities of the United States and the Soviet Union with a view to the interchange of information as to the facts with reference to the military and naval situation of the United States and the Soviet Union vis-à-vis Japan."*

Davies proposed that the information be known to "*only four men*: the president, secretary and under secretary of state, and the liaison officer—*Lieutenant Colonel Philip R. Faymonville*." (Italics supplied.) The suggestion was most favorably received by both Stalin and Molotov. The latter, Davies reported, spoke very highly of the proposed liaison officer. But Chief of Army Staff George Marshall got wind of it and temporarily clipped Faymonville's wings by recalling him to duty in the United States in 1939, where he was known among his contemporaries as "the Bolshevik."

Overlapping Burns's visit was one by this same Davies, as "Special Representative of the President," with ambassadorial rank and aiguilletted aide. He bore a letter to Stalin, the contents not shown to Standley, who was not allowed to be present when the letter was delivered. Under these circumstances, it would be difficult to imagine a man, who once had held the highest position in the U.S. Navy, humiliated to this extent yet still retaining his civility and decorum. But Standley did—seething underneath, composed and in command of himself.

Davies had written a "best seller," *Mission to Moscow*, a saccharine account of his Moscow ambassadorship, made into a movie highly favorable to the Soviet Union. Who knows what is in a man's heart? Davies's assessment could indeed have been a typical manifestation of the fine old American missionary spirit that all people are inherently good, needing only the impetus of American enterprise to put them on the right road. It scarcely could have been financially motivated, as Davies was an immensely wealthy man. But he worked hard to push "Mission" publicity. With him were prints of the film that he hoped would one day be shown all across the broad Russian land in every village meeting hall. Admiral Standley, as CNO and in his post-retirement experience probably had acquired a better understanding of the mechanics of the market place than most officers. He expressed the view that the whole thing reeked of crass commercialism combined with an inflated ego.

Alas for poor Davies! At Stalin's banquet in his honor, *Mission To Moscow* was the finale. The lights were turned off and the film boomed to a glorious end of super *detente*. It roundly condemned "unfair attacks" on the USSR, such as a cartoon copied from an American publication showing Stalin as a bloodthirsty ogre. When the lights went on again, Stalin's chair

*State Dept. file 800.51 W 89 USSR/247 dated 17 January 1939.

was empty. He had left in the darkness without a word of farewell to Davies or the other guests. The concensus was that he was angered that attacks on him should be shown in the Soviet Union even though dubbed "unfair."

Davies retired to his bed in the sumptuous guest house the Soviets had provided and was in so foul a mood for days that relations with Standley deteriorated even further. If we in the admiral's mess rejoiced in another's adversity, perhaps we can be forgiven.

Davies's visit was the culminating blow. Almost as an anticlimax came the announcement of another special envoy, Captain Eddie Rickenbacker, World War I ace. And yet two more: *New York Times* scion Arthur Sulzberger, under Red Cross cover, aided by James Reston, top-flight correspondent.

Standley was almost 71. Another Moscow winter was approaching, a season that had given pause even to such raunchy youngsters as Napoleon

Casual group in Mokovaya courtyard. Left to right: Captain Lieutenant Laurier; Captain 3rd Rank M. Kostrinsky; Commander F. R. Lang; Rear Admiral J. H. Duncan; Arthur Sulzberger; kneeling, Commander Tolley.

and Hitler. This, plus Washington's short-circuiting and Moscow's obfuscation had got in their fatal licks. On 3 May 1943, the admiral-ambassador submitted his resignation. And like an earlier resignation in protest as CNO, the president amiably pressed him to stay on, in the safe assumption he would not change his mind. On 18 September he left Moscow for the last time.

Averell Harriman, possibly the only available man personally powerful enough to demand his own terms, succeeded Admiral Standley. The terms were a clean sweep. Faymonville, Michela, and Duncan went home, their spot star ranks relinquished, the feuding ended. Duncan took command of the cruiser USS *Phoenix* in the Far East. (She was later to sink off the Falklands in 1982 as the Argentine cruiser *General Belgrano*.) Michela served in the Office of Military Intelligence, while Faymonville was relegated to an obscure ordnance depot, and was eventually involved in postwar legal hassles over alleged communist connections.

With Harriman came a new deal, a military mission under a Marshall favorite, former American secretary to the Combined Chiefs of Staff Major General John R. Deane. In his maiden speech to the fifty-odd Army and Navy officers and men, Deane paraphrased Marshall's instructions: "Our mission is solely to help the Russians win the war. Intelligence-gathering and bargaining are not a part of it and will be scrupulously avoided. I want to be able to invite Soviet officers into our code room to read anything they want." We old-timers sat back aghast.

Deane was a handsome man of trim, athletic, medium build with a sort of Dick Tracy cut of the jaw. He looked as though he might have a bulldog tenacity about him, in strong contrast to Faymonville's urbane affability and Michela's Buddha-like impassiveness. Obviously the U. S. Army bred all kinds.

We Navy types, feeling put upon at losing our attaché status and even more so at the supposed indignity of serving under the direct command of an Army officer, were instantly on the defensive. Deane or no Deane, if any Soviet officer wanted to get into the Navy code room, it would be over our dead bodies. Curly Cram and I, the plank owners, decided we would comply but not obey. The others were different. Ronnie Allen revolved in his own little orbit—the ballet, keeping the books as special disbursing agent for the Navy office, and adjudicating the use of the Navy's little fleet of two sedans and a motorcycle. Lieutenant "Joe" Chase, a recently arrived reserve, was wedded to his coding machine. "Eddie" Yorke, reserve lieutenant commander, not interested in office politics had come over to check on the end use of the extraordinary number of diesel engines the Soviets were demanding. The rest of the Navy was in the field, primarily up north, Roullard in Vladi. None of them were either involved or much affected by

Major General John Deane, chief of the U.S. Military Mission that replaced the naval attachés and Supply Mission.

what went on at headquarters. Of keen interest to all, however, was what Duncan's relief would be like.

Commodore Clarence E. ("Oley") Olsen, called "Swede" at the Naval Academy, was the first live specimen of that recently reinstated rank I had ever seen. His was a Navy family all the way. Papa had come from Norway in a sailing ship to sign up with the U. S. Navy, rising to lieutenant. There were six sons and a daughter. One son died going back into a burning dorm to save his roommate. Another was killed in World War II. Two were selected for flag rank. The daughter married a naval officer. Oley stood 35th among the 546 in his 1921 USNA class, this high mental capacity matched by sound common sense. Six feet tall, imposing, with a ready smile, Oley could be stern when the situation demanded, but he had a compassionate understanding of honest error and a keen interest in the welfare of his subordinates. It was an interesting exercise in character analysis to compare Olsen and Duncan. Oley, it turned out, accomplished his ends versus the Soviets by force of character and good judgment as to how they should be handled; Duncan achieved equal success through Irish canniness and a master poker player's acumen. So by the time poor old Zaitsev (appropriately meaning "hare") might have got a handle on Dunc's mental jiujitsu, along came a new player, a fast, heavy-hitting, ball-carrying quarterback.

The new ambassador, W. Averell Harriman, was my first exposure to an Ivy Leaguer other than FDR in his fireside chats. Most Navy encounters

Rear Admiral Olsen dancing with actress Zoya Feodorova.

with what was felt to be the social elite of that genus might have been some chance brushes at a Newport function during a midshipmen's cruise. The Ivy League colleges, which we never met in athletics, remained a remote, in our eyes rather effete, outfit, something like the Eloi of H. G. Wells's, *The Time Machine*.

Harriman, as might have been expected, was socially adept, charming, engaging enough in conversation, though seeming to be a bit detached, chatting away while giving the impression that perhaps his thoughts were elsewhere. He was a strikingly handsome fellow, quite tall and possibly as a result of it, slightly stooped as though about to duck under a low doorway.

The new ambassador came with top credentials. He well understood the president's quirks and desires, having long been one of his intimate and confidential advisers. A leading role in several high-level conferences involving the Combined Chiefs of Staff, Churchill, the Soviet Lend-Lease program, and Stalin gave him a unique insight into the manifold problems facing the oddly assorted coalition against the Nazis. On learning he was to be the new ambassador, Harriman had invited Deane in September 1943 to head the military mission that would be under his supervision. Aside from all these attributes, "Meester Garriman" was well known to the Soviet people through his efforts at establishing the Soviet Lend-Lease program and to the Kremlin as a man close to friend Roosevelt.

The new deal was a vast step up for the service representatives. The attachés had had two masters: the ambassador and their respective Washington offices, ONI and MID. In dealing with the Soviets they were operating through and under the ambassador, who had been discredited in Soviet estimation by Washington's having so blatantly bypassed him. In any case, Faymonville was a quicker, surer pipeline to a compliant White House.

The Military Mission was an entirely new ball game. While operating in close collaboration with Ambassador Harriman, *Deane was a direct representative of the Joint Chiefs of Staff*, bypassing not just a piddling MID but the whole War Department, speaking authoritatively with the voice of the most powerful instrument in the United States next to the president himself. It made a vast difference in the level one reached in a hugely rank-conscious Soviet Union. Duncan dealt with a messenger boy, Zaitsev. Deane met with General A. E. Antonov, Deputy Chief of Staff of the Red Army. (Chief of Staff Marshal A.M. Vasilevsky was constantly on the go in the field.) The talks Deane held were not about visits to some soap factory or an obsolete destroyer, but about air coordination, communications, choice of supreme Allied commander, intelligence exchanges, invasion support, war against Japan, joint operations, junction of forces, the Poltava and

Siberian air bases, strategic air force operations, and many other super-level subjects of a nature never dreamed of in the Standley days.

Harriman was more given to panoply and the refinements of diplomatic representation than Standley. When the latter called on Soviet bigwigs, he usually limited his train to a secretary-interpreter. When Harriman went to present his credentials to President of the Soviet Presidium Kalinin, three or four Navy and Army "missionaries" were included. It was my first Kremlin experience—the grandeur of long interior stretches of red carpet leading to vast marble stairways at an easy slope. In the grand reception hall stood Old Bolshevik Mikhail Kalinin, President of the Presidium of the Supreme Soviet, a benign grandpa in steel spectacles and billygoat beard. Towered over by Harriman, Kalinin shook hands all around, smiling and exchanging *vdrastvuityes* (hello's). I managed to fight off an almost irresistible impulse to brush the cloud of dandruff off his dark coat collar. It was hard to imagine that this affable little gnome, once a peasant blacksmith, had been active in the communist cause since 1898, had taken part in the 1905 Revolution, had been arrested by the Czar's police sixteen times before 1916, and had spent a lot of time in Siberia; yet somehow he had managed to live through even the mid-nineteen thirties' purges, which left very few of the founding fathers alive. If he had survived all that, perhaps he would survive the dandruff as well. Such were my random thoughts on this solemn occasion.

Roosevelt, who took a personal interest in the USSR, often exchanging messages with Stalin on what appeared to be trivial things, learned that Olsen was a commodore. Boost him to rear admiral at once, he ordered, even though reinstitution of the obsolete rank of commodore had been one of his pet projects. Was he by any chance reading some of my intelligence reports harping on the importance of rank? I knew they were being routed to the White House, and I was the only naval officer writing intelligence reports from the USSR. And did Deane's directive stop me? Not bloody likely! Olsen too was "complying but not obeying," God bless him, in his encouragement. In fact, Olsen had been in the saddle only a short time when he decided to fare forth on an intelligence-gathering expedition of his own.

11 / We Meet the People

Anyone wanting to meet citizens of the USSR should by all odds choose the train. Passengers climb into lounging pajamas and let their literal and figurative hair down. They drink your whiskey with a wry face while offering you their vodka, with a mutual sharing of snacks of tinned meat, smoked herring, cheese and bread, which are considered no less essential for train travel than toothbrush and razor.

Although four days was the norm for the 600 miles from Moscow to Archangel, Rear Admiral Olsen, with his party of Commanders Lang and Tolley, and Lieutenant Commander Yorke, felt the train preferable to the indeterminate wait and daily dawn standby trip to the airfield until Russia's capricious winter weather provided proper flying conditions: clear enough to see the ground at 500 feet, too cloudy for Jerry to have fighters in the air.

Olsen, four days' rations, an ample supply of booze, and a Sterno stove occupied one coupe, "the cabin." The rest of us shared its neighbor, with a "lavabo" between.

The Soviets we met on this two-week junket, totaling 25, represented a good cross section of the "ruling class." The action started at once. A group in a nearby coupe was eager for our opinion on an article in the current *Pravda*, entitled, "Willkie Muddies The Water." This was based on a story in the *New York Times* of about 31 December 1943, headlined, "Don't Stir Up Distrust of Russia!"

The disputants, as we later discovered, were a mixed bag:

1. An ex-naval political commissar with former rank equivalent to captain; graduate of the General Staff College, present activity a dark secret.

2. A director of a fishing enterprise in Archangel, formerly in the Far East. Member of the Party and a very well informed individual. His father was a merchant mariner in the Atlantic trade. He himself was formerly in

the merchant service, with a salary over the last fifteen years averaging a respectable 1,200 monthly, as indicated on his party ticket.

3. A foreman in the Molotovsk shipbuilding plant.

4. A Red Army medical major, commandant of the Army hospital at Archangel. Very drunk and very talkative.

5. A political officer (major) accompanying the above as his watchdog.

6. An engineer recently returned from a trip to the United States.

7. The "provodnik," (porter) of the car, a woman of about 35.

These "grazhdani" ("citizens," frequently used in place of "tovarishch,") were all unable to understand what they considered utterances treasonable to the Allies' cause by one whom they considered practically an official mouthpiece of the American government, and that they were OK'd by the government itself since a newspaper printed it. (Anything printed in *Pravda*, which means "truth," was—and still is—accepted in the Soviet Union as holy writ.)

All were anxious to have an American's explanation of what Willkie was up to in even mentioning in passing that, "Americans were worrying about the fate of Finland, Poland, the Balkans and the Baltic States." These matters, *Pravda* declared, were none of Mr. Willkie's damn business, particularly the Baltic States, which were a part of the Soviet Union. *Pravda* was of the opinion that the whole affair was simply a sample of dirty American politics, with Willkie trading on popular susceptibilities and raking up anti-Soviet feeling purely to gain votes in the coming election. The debaters were all with *Pravda*, the general concensus being that American newspapers are provocative and dangerous, although not as subversive as were the World War II French papers.

The discussion then wandered around to the French, who were looked upon with esteem and a certain degree of pity in that they were occupied by the hated Germans. The French Normandie Air Squadron fighting on the Soviet front had got its full share of publicity and looked particularly good to the average Russian, who knew of no other Allied force "fighting shoulder to shoulder" with them, as they liked to put it. Why the others were not doing this they attributed to the Allied governments, as they had read in a vituperative *Pravda* article. Had we told them that Stalin would not even let a British hospital detachment ashore in Murmansk to care for their frostbitten merchant seamen rescued from sunken ships, they would have scoffed.

The medical major, suffering from a first-class Moscow hangover, aided and abetted by several quick ones that morning, had looked in at our compartment, flicking a second finger under his chin in the old Russian sign meaning that a drink would not be refused. Through the next ten hours and an assortment of gin, whiskey, and vodka, the major, in spite of our efforts to pass him out, became progressively more lively and less coherent, literally begging on his knees for another drink, not excluding the alcohol for our cookstove. He was a fellow earthy in the extreme, a dirty, stubble-whiskered, battered Russian version of W. C. Fields in his lowest comedy role. Oculist by profession, born and raised in Siberia, he had been inducted into the forces and was probably fighting a lovely war with the Archangel hospital's medical alcohol, a hospital we made hearty promises to ourselves to steer shy of if ever in need of medical treatment.

A piece of shrapnel had taken a sizable chunk out of the major's hand, which in no way affected his grip on a glass. The splinter that had sliced through his rump had likewise left no lasting handicap other than heeling him over a bit when sitting. All this had broadened the old boy: the war, meeting foreign seamen in his hospital (God help them!), and hearing about our materiel assistance. He was willing to accept capitalists in the conversation and respectfully saluted Admiral Olsen every few minutes, confusing him from time to time with Commander Lang as we changed places in the compartment. "There will never be a true alliance and friendship between your country and mine until you have your proletarian revolution," gasped the major, reaching for a graham cracker after downing 200 grams of neat vodka. "When can we expect it?" The fisherman, as a Party man, was beginning to view the situation with a troubled eye, matters further deteriorating when the major upset and spilled a box of sugar in one of his sweeping gestures of how to mow down Germans.

In the afternoon, the political watchdog in a major's line officer shoulder boards appeared, announced by the medical major as his "politicheskiy nachal'nik" (political boss). This individual was simply a caricature of a foreigner's idea of a political commissar, a little, hatchet-faced man whose conversation consisted almost wholly of shouted catch-phrases from a primer on rabble-rousing, waving his arms for emphasis. His arrival had an electric effect on W. C. Fields, who went to such extremes of propriety as to refuse a drink. The political major apologized for the unofficerlike conduct of the medical major, which he had heard about through the providnik, who with tears in her eyes had swept up the spilled sugar and carted it off for her own purposes.

The political major evidently never had been warned against the solid effects to be expected from whiskey, which he evidently mistook for another form of tea; two half tumblers drunk in the usual Russian bottoms-up manner soon had him in a state close to that of his intended charge.

Through some sort of magic, no doubt connected with a Party ticket, the fisherman got the pair of them out of the compartment and locked the door.

Until 2 A.M., without the inhibiting influence of fellow Russians, the fisherman talked freely and confidentially on a number of subjects. In the thirties, he had gone to Liverpool to take delivery of a ship. In the process, he had developed a hearty dislike for the British as individuals, in addition to the usual centuries-old Russian distrust of the British Empire. His father's ship had visited Boston recently for repairs, where the old man had got his preconceived ideas of Americans considerable altered. His worst experience was with souvenir and autograph hunters who swarmed aboard their first Soviet ship in a frenzy of looting for souvenirs. He was impressed by the efficiency everywhere, but taken somewhat aback by the abrupt treatment by various U. S. officials.

On leaving for the night at last, the fisherman collected several packs of cigarettes, some copies of *Popular Mechanics*, and would have got away with the rest of the bottle of whiskey and the pack of cards if he hadn't been intercepted.

Our reception by the Soviet naval officers at Archangel was hearty, almost a home-coming for Tolley and Lang, who had made previous visits. Every possible effort was made by old friend Vice Admiral Kucherov,

The naval attaché, Rear Admiral C. E. Olsen, chats with Soviet naval officers in wartime Archangel. Our navy maintained representatives in Archangel, Murmansk, and Vladivostok to help expedite the millions of tons of Lend-Lease cargo and to assist American ships. A working knowledge of the Russian language was a prime asset.

Commander White Sea Flotilla, to provide scarce transportation and accede to Admiral Olsen's every request. This included permission to visit the Molotovsk shipbuilding yard, which Admiral Duncan had been told in Moscow the previous year did not exist. Even more intriguing was his permission for us to ride aboard a Soviet warship from Molotovsk to Polyarnoe (naval port at the entrance to the Kola Inlet leading to Murmansk). The granting of either of these privileges a few months earlier would have been out of the question.

The night before departure was celebrated in the quarters of our representative on the spot in Molotovsk, Lieutenant (jg) Philip Worchel, USNR, who, along with the usual stock of rations scavenged from U.S. merchant ships, had wangled a case of gin. In the light of sober reflection it seems beyond reasonable belief how in the span of some eight hours, five Americans and an equal number of Soviets managed to knock back that case of gin less the one bottle Worchel had accounted for earlier. Rear Admiral Vasyunin, commanding at Molotovsk, was sick and lost his false teeth in the snow outside, but they were eventually retrieved. It has been said that the best way to stop a Russian army was to plant a barrel of vodka at every milepost. Judging from our send-off, one barrel per milepost would never do it. Indeed, if the general staffs of the two countries could arrange such a get-together, it might at least guarantee they would not feel enthusiastic about going to war the next day.

The bracing wind felt good as we watched from topside in a grey dawn while the U.S.-built trawler *AM-114* wrenched herself free from the ice alongside dock. Captain third rank Debelov, a 230-pounder with a voice like a soprano fog horn, had no need for electronic amplification, and when he pulled out a cigarette, there were at least three people jumping with a match to light it.

Breakfast, immediately after getting under way, was just the thing for a queasy stomach: heaping plates of very greasy fried ham and potatoes, a sherbet glass of neat vodka at every American place.

These were the same officers who had trained and taken over *AM-114* in the United States several months before, where they had picked up some naive and bizarre ideas of life under capitalism. The Russian is a gregarious type, loving discussion like no other race on earth, engaging in endless chatter over frequently abstract subjects: art, literature, life, human character. Wardroom conversations reflected this, but with modifications. When there was only one Soviet officer present, he was always talkative and without reserve over the endless glasses of tea, more or less freely giving his opinion on anything but such taboo subjects as Soviet politics—even to passing out items of intelligence concerning the Red Navy. With two officers present, the picture changed. At best, the conversation became noncontroversial, an exchange of platitudes. At worst, an effort would be made by individuals to show the rest of the Soviets present that they were "red hot" and full of zeal for whatever it was the party line had been chasing down lately.

The entire U.S. political picture bewildered them. What was the point in scrabbling for political office, from sheriff to president, at a time when only a dictator in every category could possibly maintain the necessary discipline in wartime? They noted with surprise that the service given Soviet sailors in railway dining cars was not nearly so good as that given officers, because the officers had money for tips while the sailors did not. The fact we had a Communist party in the U.S. was well known to them, but they were incredulous when told "The Party" participated without restriction in any and all elections, but never had polled more than a few thousand votes. American military discipline was pretty lousy, they thought: orders casually obeyed, even sniffing, rather hypocritically, I thought, at American weekend drunks with hangovers lasting until Tuesday.

In round-table after-dinner wardroom discussions, all mess members including the skipper were intensely interested in any explanation or discourse I had to offer on any political subject other than Soviet, particularly the viewpoint of an average American toward the USSR's future policy. They were quick to refute any suggestion that the USSR might have any claims outside her May 1941 boundary. And the merest hint that the status of the Baltic States might still be a matter of postwar adjudication brought down a storm of protest. The ultimate fate of Finland was another matter. *Pravda* had said the Finns must be classed with the Germans and beaten to a pulp, and that was that.

One of several supercargoes was an officer of distinctly Jewish appearance, wearing the shoulder boards of a captain second rank and thus senior to the ship's skipper, who concurrently was also division commander of three ships. This elderly man, a political officer with no executive function, rode each of the three ships in turn. In the wardroom he rarely entered the conversation. On the bridge, with no other Soviet near, he answered questions hesitatingly, but sufficiently to indicate he was a roving troubleshooter in an advisory capacity apparently directly under that part of the Northern Fleet staff engaged in political education. The old prewar system of coequal status between commanding officer and "politruk," (politicheskiy rukovoditel', or political director) had been discarded as hopelessly unwieldy in making quick decisions.

Some of the American officers who had helped train these Soviet minesweeper crews rode the ships to North Russia, the 7,500-mile voyage providing a fine opportunity to observe the Red Navy in action. Off North

Cape, a three-day running battle with Nazi submarines had kept all hands at battle stations, with one British destroyer sunk.

Our people found that the Russian sailorman can be a complex fellow. By nature slovenly, they kept their ordnance, engineering, and most mechanical equipment clean, plentifully greased, and operative. Not energetic, they were physically capable of great hardship. They were "heavy-handed" in the operating, maintaining, and repairing of equipment; wasteful of spare parts, tools, and supplies. Their mechanical sense was crude, jumping to child-like conclusions that they knew it all, to the hazard of the inanimate gear they were working on. But discipline was high, there was cheerful compliance with all orders, even though some were irrational, occasionally stupid, and meaningless.

Attack doctrines, although promulgated before departure from the U.S., were either forgotten or ignored; it was every ship for herself. The extremely successful "creeping attack" developed by British Captain Walker, well-known anti-sub specialist, had been seriously received by the Soviet division commander, but no attempt had been made to incorporate it into ship's doctrine. (Shortly after the Soviet ships had developed two strong contacts north of the Azores, Captain Walker searched that area and made three sure kills, with one more "possible.")

Station keeping was only fair, the stadimeter an object of curiosity, seldom or never used. Ship handling, towing, and refueling of subchasers was invariably hit-or-miss, American opinion of their seamanship low.

Perhaps their belief in the great God above was sketchy, but not so with demons; they flatly refused to sail on Friday or Monday, when these malevolent creatures are most active. Hit the Soviets at 1330, was the final recommendation, that being between noon meal and 3 P.M., during which all hands off watch enjoy a long siesta in port and at sea.

Much of the wisdom above was reflected in our three-day experience aboard *AM-114*. Several submarine alerts en route had all hands racing to battle stations in considerable confusion, with Captain, or rather Commodore, Debelov's large bulk and the shrill vibrancy of his powerful voice dominating the bridge.

Admiral Golovko was again our charmingly active, impressive, and able host at Polyarnoe, where instead of allowing the visiting American admiral to confine his activities to bestowing decorations on Soviet heroes, as had been the case with Duncan, he took us on a personally escorted tour of the underground headquarters bunker for a detailed description of the fighting front only 15 miles away.

It is interesting to compare this trip, January 1944, with the picture presented in July 1942 and the intervening period. The situation then was black, with Germans advancing in Russia and Africa and the Japanese doing so well that an evacuation of Moscow embassy personnel eastward held no more promise than north or south. Kids on the street were piping up with "Vtoroi front!" (Second Front!) at foreigners. The grown-ups were beginning to recall the panicky days of the winter of 1941, when Germans were under Moscow's walls. Refugees from the north, from Leningrad and the Ukraine, were apathetic, without hope. It seemed there was no end to suffering, the people not reluctant to voice their opinions. Foreign military representatives sat in Moscow week in and week out, drinking their monthly four liters of vodka, wondering whether or if ever they would get within striking distance of the front. Newspapers were bare of any kind word about the Anglo-American war effort, either on the home or war fronts. "Spam" was known to Soviet troops as "second front." "Second front" was on every Russian's lips whenever a foreigner was within hearing distance. It was a cry of distress and of ridicule in one.

Then came Stalingrad—a huge Nazi army destroyed—then North Africa. Then the blast from Admiral Standley that forced the Soviet press to print the story of colossal Allied materiel assistance to the USSR and to the gradual turning of the tide in North Africa. Kids no longer tagged after foreigners, derisively calling, "vtoroi front." The people and the military immediately began to reflect the change in official attitude.

In our exchanges with the Red Navy, even in the transaction of ordinary housekeeping business, one originally got the impression they habitually procrastinated or attempted to avoid giving information by putting it off until one's patience was so exhausted that one gave up. Actually, many indications and my experience over a period of two years gave me the feeling that the blame lay in plain bureaucracy and delay inherent in Russian makeup: intricate plans and protocol that must be followed at all costs, even if rarely fulfilled; the wide dispersal of the various departments of the Soviet Navy Commissariat over the Soviet Union. And it must not be forgotten in making too harsh a judgment of the Soviets, that in many cases, answers to *their* questions had not always been forthcoming in record time from the United States. This point they not infrequently brought up in a polite way when too strongly pressed on delays of theirs.

So now in North Russia the stops were all out. We made a long visit aboard the destroyer *Razumny* and the submarine *K-21*, which had an impressive record of German kills along the Norwegian coast. In both cases mess tables groaned with a great assortment of sakuski, punctuated by many bottles of vodka, to be accompanied by endless toasts and complimentary speeches. An adroitness in minimizing vodka intake perfected in the past two years of such engagements is reflected in my intelligence report.*

The New Look was in all over; everybody was cordial in the extreme. The Second Front was touched on only perfunctorily by the Russians, they having come around by then to the belief that like prosperity, it was inevitably just around the corner.

The Soviet families, as was almost uniformly the case, did not enter the social picture, partly perhaps due to a profound inferiority complex, partly to language difficulties, and partly to the fact that a Soviet never seemed able to divorce business from pleasure. Light dinner conversation came hard to most Soviet naval officers, even harder for the wife, who usually was squirming around being generally uncomfortable. One can scarcely appreciate the influence a political system can have on a people until one compares the social accomplishments of a Soviet with those of a White Russian émigré, from whom a great many Americans have formed their impressions.

At Murmansk, Engineer Major General Dubrovin entertained our party at dinner.† An official of his staff, Lieutenant Colonel Ioffre, was the most outspoken Soviet so far met concerning the Japanese. He traced their provocatory attitude toward Russia during the course of the last fifty years, concluding that the only way to end this annoyance and continuous threat once and for all was to drive the Japs back to their islands and put them to growing flowers and pulling rickshaws again.

Having revealed how an admiral and entourage fare on a soviet train, the adventures of a more modest traveler, a junior grade U. S. Navy lieutenant en route to Murmansk, will be recounted in lieu of our return trip. He was in a "soft" coupe, two uppers, two lowers, along with the wife and daughter of a Red Army colonel, a discharged sailor, a commercial photographer in real life, and a minor official of the Trans-Siberian Railway headed home on leave.

The first night was very quiet, occupied mostly in conversations with the colonel's eight-year-old daughter, who was not sure what her father did, but "it was very important." Mama was equally uninformative.

At Vologda, the leisurely pace of Russian railway travel was manifested in the one-hour stop. Mama and daughter disembarked, at what must have been a major military base as about 120 Red Army officers and men also detrained. Meanwhile, the discharged sailor improved his time by borrowing our man's canteen and canteen cup, filling them with vodka

*See appendix D.

†Naval staff officers, such as medical, engineer, aviation, and engineering used military titles of rank.

"ashore," somewhere in the depot. This process, which considerably enlivened the group that had formed around the coupe, was repeated during successive stops for the rest of the journey. The Trans-Sib man, who had come to be known as "Dyedyushka" (grandfather), appeared somewhat later with three slices of bread smeared with red caviar. Later variations included dill pickles, sausages, smoked fish, and raw cranberries. Once, he brought milk. For the American's part, he shared his sausages, K-rations, and the greater part of three quarts of whiskey he was carrying to Archangel as presents.

During the course of the journey, a countless stream of visitors dropped into the compartment for a chat and a drink. These included a Hero of the Soviet Union, who said almost nothing; a chief engineer who said a great deal; an Army captain with an accordion, and two female conductors, who came offering hot water and stayed for a shot of whatever was being served at the moment. They giggled incessantly and uncontrollably.

The Trans-Sib man talked a lot about cathedrals and the deplorable state they were in, pointing out the monastery at Yaroslavl at various points along the route, although they had passed it the night before. He also sang the entire Easter Mass, and had begun it a second time before he went to sleep. Nowhere had there been any talk of railroads.

The discharged sailor was interested in the U.S. Navy and in American movies. The Red Navy was superior to the U.S. Navy, he thought, because in the Red Navy officers were not permitted to strike sailors as the fancy took them. Furthermore, there was a sensible division of labor in the Soviet Navy. For example, they had people regularly assigned to prepare meals, whereas in the U.S. Navy, each man went to the galley when he got hungry and fixed himself a sandwich and a cup of coffee. Soviet sailors slept in their clothes, making them instantly ready for combat. American sailors slept in pyjamas.

He was enlightened on other points as well. He preferred the American films, he said, as they were simple and full of pretty girls. Films about the Red Army were boring. The best film he had ever seen was "Blood and Sand," having sat through it seven times. Other favorites were "The Great Waltz," and all the Deanna Durbin pictures. (Deanna, the darling of Soviet moviegoers, was almost as well known as Stalin.)

The strong, silent man, Hero of the Soviet Union, produced only two observations during th entire trip, to the effect he liked Americans and disliked British, and whether or not it was true Deanna Durbin was dead. Later in the afternoon, he was seen through the window at one of the stops demanding "cucumbers for the American comrade."

The "chief engineer" was en route to Archangel on an assignment, which, he hinted darkly, was of a "very important nature." He had been in charge of a group of German prisoners in Moscow. They worked more slowly than Russians, but more thoroughly. And well they might, as they received decent quarters and better food than Russians doing the same job. He was pleased with their work, he said. He had worked with American engineers in Leningrad, and although he respected their ability and knowledge, he considered Russian engineers superior, since their knowledge was not so highly specialized. A Russian engineer, he said, knows how to build apartments, construct dams, streets, parks, industrial plants, and be a practical doctor. Some even could fly airplanes.

The "chief" had a small German pistol, a "Braunik," as he called it, of which he was obviously very proud. (All Russians seemed to be armed.) When no one appeared to be showing the amount of interest in it he had expected, he demonstrated its merits by firing it twice through the coupe door. At the next station, a militiaman (policeman) examined the damage, took the names and addresses of two witnesses, remarked casually that somebody might have got shot, accepted a drink and left, taking the engineer with him.

The captain with the accordion was interested primarily in learning new American songs. He could play, "The Beer Barrel Polka," and "Somewhere Over the Rainbow." In the background, the Trans-Sib man was continuing the Easter Mass, uninterrupted.

From Archangel to Murmansk, over a roadbed about as smooth as a palmetto-log corduroy in the Florida swamps, the American had been demoted to accommodations more appropriate to a close approach to the front, a noncompartmented "hard" car. Fellow passengers were members of the Northern Fleet jazz band and a group of dancers on their way to perform at the Polyarnoe Naval Base.

No mattresses were furnished, but this is not as important as it may sound. Members of the band practiced constantly and on different pieces of music at the same time, so that sleep would have been impossible in any event.

It also developed that it was impossible to eat. The sailors were furnished with rations of black bread and Lend-Lease lard, which was cut in quarter-inch slices for a spread. Whenever the American showed any inclination to dip into his own store of provisions, the sailors insisted that he share their food or offend them mortally. Pleading indigestion, our man managed to abstain the 40 hours it took to make Murmansk.

In the general chaos, there was one event that bears chronicling. The vocalist, first accordionist, and a chief petty officer, whose function appeared to be that of political watchdog, spent several hours in the dining car consuming vodka and herring. At the end of it all, they discovered that their bill amounted to 300 roubles more than they had between them. About eleven o'clock that night, the chief returned and borrowed the 300 roubles from the American. Deeply upset, he said he knew of no other on the train from whom such a sum could be borrowed, lamenting that it would be laughed about among the Americans when they heard of it. During the entire second day, the chief was uneasy about talking, and on the third day paid up in full. The same day, the American discovered a carton of cigarettes had unaccountably disappeared.

One can imagine by this time that anything that could have happened on our man's return trip to Moscow would have been an anticlimax. Actually, it was prosaic. During the entire four days, his coupe mates were a woman doctor who spoke with such a strong lisp as to be almost unintelligible, plus her two sons, aged five and three. Early in the proceedings, the doctor obviously had conceived the notion that the American was a spy, watching him closely whenever he looked out the window or stood in the corridor. War between the USA and the USSR was inevitable in her opinion. She didn't want it, nor did the Soviet government, but if the United States persisted in its present anti-Soviet policy, it could lead nowhere except to war.

The children were somewhat more bearable, although they stomped on the American's feet, kicked his shins, and vomited on the floor whenever he began to eat.

Yes, ride the train, meet the people, be patient, go well armed with eatables, drinkables, trade goods, and good humor. It will all be repaid in kind.

12 / *The Transition*

The winter of 1942–1943 might have been called the Winter of Discontent. Deep schisms between the Standley-Duncan-Michela triumvirate and Faymonville left the mid-level people such as myself in a sort of limbo. I liked Faymonville's crew personally: Captains John Cook, Clinton Olson, and John Waldron, the Mission's medical officer. Waldron, more used to giving shots than taking them, had been on the receiving end of one—a 45-caliber Colt automatic slug in the thigh, courtesy of a fellow Supply Mission member, motive unclear, the gunman an Army captain risen from former Navy chief petty officer. Narrowly missing the main leg artery, from which he would have quickly bled to death, "the compassionate bullet," as Waldron later remarked of it, had reminded him of how sweet life can be. It broadened his own already considerable sympathy for sufferers to include Russians needing help. One of these he spotted on the street, a young Soviet girl of perhaps twenty, the beauty of whose classic features was not wholly obscured by sunken eyes, sallow cheeks, and pale lips. Under a regular regimen of vitamins, proper food, and what has come to be known as TLC, tender loving care, Tania blossomed into the golden-haired beauty she was meant to be, then became Mrs. John Waldron, one of the earliest Soviet war brides.

An even earlier war bride, married in 1940 to Joseph E. Vargo, the embassy's electrical expert on loan from the Navy and since returned to the USA, had a sister remaining in the USSR. Byron Uskievich, a Navy chief storekeeper delivered a package that had come via diplomatic pouch from Vargo for his wife's family. Uskievich met younger sister, who in due course became *his* war bride. Thus did Cupid sling his made-in-America arrows at Russian damsels, some with glancing blows, others with firm hits that provided the Soviet bureaucracy with problems hitherto unplanned for.

Major John "Doc" Waldron, (MC) USA, and Olga.

To get back to Faymonville. Treasonable though it might appear in Dunc's eyes, I liked the man, although feeling he was too pro-Soviet. One could not help but be appreciative of his thoughtful personal kindnesses, while fully aware that below that bland, affable exterior lay a steely determination to be his own man, ambassador be damned.

The April visits of General Burns and "Ambassador" Davies had of course put the whole establishment in turmoil, drawing the Spasso-Mokovaya-Washington battle lines into even stronger relief. All of it was for me an extraordinary lesson in high-level diplomacy as the public rarely imagines it. Aside from that, my own thoughts and activities were pleasantly diverted by the burgeoning opportunities to get around the country, from Murmansk to Baku to Archangel to Komsomolsk, trips that would be Duncan's last hurrah.

The advent of the Military Mission and its many additional Army

At Father Braun's apartment. Left to right: Rear Admiral C. E. Olsen; Tolley; Commander F. R. Lang (MC); Captain Denys W. Knoll; Lieutenant (jg) Lexow; Lieutenant W. W. "Curly" Cram; Lieutenant Commander Eddie Yorke; Lieutenant Miekeljohn; and Lieutenant Joe Chase.

people split the Army-Navy down the middle as it had not been before. Old regulars Boswell, Park, and McCabe still remained stalwart friends, but the close bonds of the Spasso mess no longer prevailed. We had been weaned to our own devices, cooking and partying in our own little households in Mokovaya. Our only link with former opulence remained the loan of embassy glassware beautifully etched with the eagle emblem, apprehensively passed on by Tommy Thompson. No toasts to the Queen, please, or any others that inspired smashing glasses into the fireplace; they cost six bucks a copy.

As for our new boss, Major General John Russell Deane was not a warm man personally, making no particular effort to cosy up to the working naval members of his team by get-together cocktails, dinners, or coffee breaks. Clearly he had been brought up in a Washington atmosphere where one's rapt gaze was upward. Early in the game we discovered where we stood; at a party of six or so of us in my apartment, we had worn our undress aiguillettes, four blue-and-gold rings around the arm at the shoulder. Deane got wind of it somehow, passing the word through Admiral Olsen that there would be no more aiguillettes worn in Moscow, informally or otherwise. Naval attachés were an extinct breed.

"Russ" Deane might have been able to clip our sartorial wings, but he was in fast company when he tangled with old newspaperman Curly Cram. By pure chance we discovered what power we held in our hands. Or more accurately, in our bathtub plug. Under the tub there was a hole in the tile floor into which water from the tub or water that splashed out was supposed to run into the waste line. The Commissariat of Bathtubs clearly must have had a very shaky liaison with the Commissariat of Drain Lines, as the hole in the floor was too small to accommodate the flow from the tub when the plug was pulled unless one cocked the plug or held a heel lightly over the drain hole. Lacking these precautions, the floor flooded, inevitably leaking to who knows where. In this case, as anyone who has ever tried to trace a roof leak is well aware, the water followed a highly unpredictable course, which we had discovered only accidentally. It went two apartments across and one down, to a spot directly over Deane's bunk. "Let's give old Russ a thrill!" Curly might propose, after returning late from a party. The results from unplugging the drain were entirely predictable. In reports from the Army's next morning staff meeting, to which the lesser Navy types mercifully never were invited, Deane would be in a foul mood, having enjoyed a wet night.

It is not improbable that had Deane been told later of our water-cure peccadillos, he would have had a good laugh at himself, as his excellent book on those Moscow experiences gives every indication he had a sharp sense of humor. I met him in Washington at a cocktail party shortly after the end of the war, remarking that I had heard he was writing the book. "What do you have in mind for a title?" I asked. "I'd *like* to call it, *Two Years With The Bastards*," he said with a wry grin, "but it will be, *The Strange Alliance*."* Indeed, things had come a long way since that maiden speech.

The new mission was all hustle and bustle, no better exemplified than in the person of Brigadier General Sidney P. Spalding, class of 1912, USMA, head of the Lend-Lease section. A key member from the Soviet point of view, he was immediately tendered a large formal lunch at the National Hotel. Obviously nobody had clued in Sidney P. as to what would be on the agenda. The zakuska part went off swimmingly, many cold dishes washed down with toasts following innumerable laudatory speeches from both sides. Then, as the wreckage from the zakuska was being cleared up, Spalding bounced to his feet, said he had enormously enjoyed the lunch and the manifestations of good feeling, but that it was time to get back to the office and to work. There was a war to win. The Russians, awaiting a translation, were not aware of what was up. "For God's sake, man!" cried out a nearby American, grabbing Spalding's arm as he was pushing his chair aside, preparing to depart. "Lunch has just started. There is soup, fish, meat, dessert, coffee and cognac yet to go." Spalding sank into his chair with a look of dumb amazement on his face. Yes, he was going to win that Distinguished Service Medal for a sterling Moscow performance by the time it was all over, but judging from the kickoff, it was not going to be easy.

Obviously Harriman and General Marshall meant to turn things around in Moscow. Aside from such top-flight people as Deane, Olsen, and Spalding, Brigadier General Hoyt S. Vandenberg was sent over for six months to shake down some sort of cooperative air enterprise. He would eventually become Air Force Chief of Staff, then SACEUR (Supreme Allied Commander, Europe). It was distinctly an "A" team.

Senior man W. (for William) Averell Harriman, Yale '13, was 52 on arrival at Moscow. Top railroad executive, banker, diplomatic troubleshooter, he gave the appearance of youth and vitality, someone with whom it was easier for a "youngster" of 35 to identify. Standley had been a father image; Harriman was more like an elder brother. As we got to know him better, we liked him, not realizing then that his apparent naiveté vis-à-vis the Soviets was of course largely a good, snappy, "Ay! Ay! Sir!" to the boss at 1600 Pennsylvania Avenue, a man who still was laboring under the impression he could charm "good old Joe" out of those Russian birch trees as deftly as he had won over so many tens of millions Americans.

Harriman's hostess was daughter Kathleen, lithe, tall, very pretty, in

*New York: Viking Press, 1947.

Kathleen Harriman, daughter of the U.S. ambassador, at my apartment.

her twenties. Would she fit in with the Slavic overtones of our informal parties? Her father's companion in sports, helper and adviser in domestic affairs, perhaps she would find us boring if not juvenile. Suppose we told her of our latest "scientific" caper? Would she laugh hilariously or smile enigmatically?

Since the breakup of the Spasso cocktail and dinner colloquies on Soviet mores, our less prestigious debaters at informal apartment gatherings went in for more catholic areas of discussion. What, for example, is the normal human reaction when suddenly faced with a panic situation? The elevator and stairwell of Mokovaya divided the building into two parts, apartments on each side, two opening onto each landing. Half a dozen scientific investigators—some might say conspirators—carefully laid newspapers on the floor just outside an apartment door. A Russian girl then lay down, closed her eyes in feigned unconsciousness, trying desperately to keep from laughing as others poured streaks of catsup on the paper near her head. Then we rang the doorbell, immediately beating a hasty retreat to cover behind the stairwell banisters where we could see but not be easily spotted. It was well after midnight.

In due course the door creaked open. "Doc" Lang, half asleep, reacted instinctively as might be expected of a trained medical officer; he knelt down, swiftly but calmly seeking her pulse. "What did you think, Doc?" we asked as with one voice. "Oh, I knew all along it was a joke," he said, looking sheepish and not very convincing.

Reinforced by Doc Lang we next tried Joe Chase. The door opened and Joe's round face peered out, totally expressionless. Then he turned and went back inside. In a few seconds he was back with a pitcher of water. "Where did you go, Joe?" we asked. "To get some water and my bedroom slippers, of course!" he said indignantly. "That concrete is cold on the bare feet." We stopped him before he tossed the pitcher of water in the sleeping Venus's face.

Freddie Barghoorn was an embassy secretary, a benign, scholarly fellow with a dry wit, unmarked by any naval conditioning. He appeared at the door in knee-length nightshirt and quizzical expression that in a sort of slow motion transmuted into a picture of total, deep-frozen horror, arms spead out like a slightly wilted scarecrow. In a few seconds another victim appeared in the door, Praskovia D'mitrovna, the cook. Her wrinkled old face, lace nightcap askew, peered out from under Freddy's arm to complete a tableau of *statues vivantes*.

It seemed hilarious at the time. I'm not sure it does now, in hindsight. And we didn't try it out for laughs on our new ambassadorial hostess. Was she the madcap type who would have lain on the floor surrounded with catsup? Dear Kathleen, I suppose we shall never know. At any rate, she attended several parties—soft-spoken, reserved, smiling, a good dancer. Several French pilots, members of the Normandie Squadron fighting on the eastern front, asked me as host for permission to dance with Kathy. "Why do you ask permission?" I inquired. "Mon Dieu! Elle est la jeune fille de Monsieur *l'Ambassadeur*!" they replied all together, obviously astonished at my peasant's innocence.

Harriman came to my parties, too, where I followed the Russian custom of inviting so very senior a fellow only when Admiral Olsen also was a guest. Obviously he enjoyed dancing with movie star Zoya Feodorova, darling of the Soviet masses, whose shock of blonde hair hit towering Harriman about the second vest button. Zoya's soft, well-rounded body and low soprano voice, full lips, large grey-blue eyes, and saucy pug nose often embellished our parties. Along with her came a new set—no more Vasyas and Zenas and their black underwear. Czech correspondent's daughter Liuba Vashek was a sinuous, handsome young lady of about twenty. Chinese minister Liu's half-Polish daughter Anya was more Soviet than anything in her no-nonsense straightforwardness. There was our own interpreter and some of her Moscow University former schoolmates, plus

Ambassador Harriman chatting with Zoya Feodorova.

several Soviet officers' wives who had served abroad, one from my old bailiwick, Riga. Members of the *corps de ballet* had been visitors to foreign apartments early on, concentrating in the Supply Mission where Faymonville took a genuine interest in the arts and his assistants in the bodies. I personally found them a rather sterile lot, self-centered with narrow interests and most un-Russian bosoms—two brown-pink buttons on a hard, flat expanse, their general musculature a pack of rubber bands under strong tension.

To those who have read this far, the impression might be gained that all was hilarity and night life, a poor man's replica of what one imagines the imperial orgies as depicted by Hollywood to have been like. Actually, the informal parties served a wholly useful and necessary function—that of gathering, pooling, and checking intelligence on the developments, mood, temper, and direction in a country where normal sources did not exist. In such a society, informal, sometimes wholly unexpected, sources turned up tiny clues, which when fitted in with other pieces of the jigsaw, produced a recognizable picture that was supposed to help fashion intelligent responses or countermeasures. That they often did not accomplish this response is not so much a measure of the value or validity of the information as it is to a lack of appreciation by the authorities who were in a position to act on it.

As Harriman's regime continued, it is now obvious in the now-available State Department records* that he and his team, in the bluntest terms, clearly divined the increasing intransigence of the Soviets as they saw victory more and more certain, a victory in which they would be in a position to call the shots. By what means Roosevelt himself was converted remains to be developed, but by the time of his death he was indeed disabused of Soviet sincerity. But one can hardly doubt that intelligence and opinion derived from the Moscow embassy had to be a major factor.

Harriman had barely got his seat warm when the most stupendous social event so far gave a clear indication of the Soviets' burgeoning confidence. This was the celebration on 7 November 1943 of the 26th anniversary of the Bolshevik Revolution. Spiridonovka, a huge, sprawling pre-Revolutionary private mansion had been turned into a center for official entertainment, a fairyland of lights from hundreds of chandeliers and sconces. Intricate parquet floors, paneled walls, paintings in massive gilt frames, sculptures on marble pedestals, and brocade hangings gave one the impression that only an emperor of all the Russias could have conjured up such an extravaganza. And indeed, so he had. The czar, now called "Generalissimus," was in a special room closeted with specially favored ambassadors and top government officials.

Foreign military had been requested to wear dress uniforms, which in our case translated into workaday blue or khaki. Those who remember the epic film, "Anna Karenina," perhaps recall villain Karenin, a high state official dressed in a sweeping uniform frock coat and epaulettes of rank. The huge imperial state bureaucracy all wore such uniforms. The Soviets had thrown out all this folderol indicating the pecking order. All would be equal under the Sickle and Hammer. But gradually the pendulum had swung back, with ranks of admiral and general reestablished; there were

*_Foreign Relations_, 1943, vol. 3; 1944, vol. 3; 1945, vol. 5.

A party at my apartment with two Free French aviators (Normandie Escadrille), Curly Cram under flag, and at lower right, the Mexican military attaché, McCabe on his right.

also Cossacks in red capes and tall fur hats, even the orange and black ribbon of the imperial St. George's Cross now circled the hats of elite Red Navy Guards units. Now another facet of the old order was back: diplomatic uniforms. No sweeping tails, to be sure, but a smart, ash-grey double-breasted military-type affair with gold buttons and shoulder boards denoting rank equivalent to marshal on down. The wheel had come almost full turn. Only grand dukes and princes yet remained to be recognized.

The guest list of five hundred easily fitted into the huge ballrooms, moving about, chatting, taking glasses of champagne and morsels of zakuska from the dozens of smartly dressed waiters circulating with trays. Even the Japanese were on hand, keeping a low profile. There were no baggy Russian military tunics here. Brilliant dress uniforms in blue, olive, and gold, chests covered with medals, black boots glistening—this was the new breed.

For years I had seen pictures of such legendary characters as Marshal of the Soviet Union Klimenti Voroshilov, Revolutionary days crony of Stalin, and another equally famous marshal, Semeon Budenny, veteran of the Russo-Japanese War, sergeant in World War I, then at the head of a huge cavalry army that galloped up to the gates of Warsaw in August 1920. It seemed almost unreal to see them both here in the flesh—Voroshilov's round, bullet head, close-cropped, Budenny's sweeping mustachios, still black-haired at sixty. Below their collars hung the *marshalskaya zvyezda* (marshal's star), gold, with a two-carat diamond at each of the five notches.

Foreign minister Vyacheslav Molotov himself finally appeared, splendidly arrayed in ash-gray uniform with the gold shoulderboards of a marshal. He was carrying a large tray of brimming glasses of champagne, going up to guests at random to offer a drink from the ministerial hand and exchange toasts. Wooden-faced, expressionless, his pince-nez glinting, he raised his own glass again and again: "To victory! To victory! To victory! To victory!" with each in turn. Next to me, the Swedish ambassador waited expectantly. Just days before he had conveyed to Molotov a German offer of negotiated peace. Would Molotov gratefully remember his service? Molotov drew near, walked toward the Swede, then sharply turned on his heel with his back to the stricken man. "Weeee donnn't liiike *neutrals*!" the minister rasped loudly in Russian.

Budenny, stalking around like a peacock, had been approached by several American plane pilots who were in town on a ferry trip. I noticed that matters seemed to be going poorly, so joined the small group to help. "What the hell's wrong with this guy?" asked an American major petulantly, he and his buddies giving the suggestion that they had had more champagne than was good for them. Trailing to the floor in one American's hand was a strip of stuck-together banknotes, twenty or so pieces from many countries known in the jargon of the day as "short snorter" notes. They represented countries visited, each signed by whatever notables the owner managed to dragoon. Budenny, the most gloriously attired individual in sight, stood out as a superior candidate for signing. But he obviously was a suspicious one. I disabused him of the idea they were offering him a tip for the party, explaining that the object of the drill was to add his signature to the ten-rouble note at the tail end. "What? Deface Soviet currency?" growled the marshal scornfully, his handlebar mustache quivering in agitation as he stalked away. The situation had been defused, but the peace dove's feathers had been ruffled.

What does a "foreign imperialist" mid-level naval officer say to a living national legend, a sort of J. E. B. Stuart, Rough-Rider Roosevelt, and George Patton combined? I had never really given it much thought before, nor prepared a fitting speech. But even after a jolly cocktail party, some merciful human mechanism straightens out one's thoughts at a serious confrontation. So after quite a few vodkas and champagnes did my mind clear. There was no flip, "Zdravstvuite, Tovarishch Marshal Sovietskovo Soyuza!" No, "Hello, Comrade Marshal Voroshilov!" Relieving me of the necessity for initiative in the greeting, Voroshilov gave me a firm handshake, a tight-lipped but friendly smile on his cherubic round face with toothbrush mustache. "How do you like Moscow?" he inquired pleasantly. In a flashback, the thought struck me that almost exactly a decade ago, an even more junior American, Captain David Nimmer, USMC, assistant naval attaché about to leave Moscow as protest, had chatted for some time with this same man, then commissar for war. Though relations were strained, they parted friends. "I am glad we are back," I said. "The U. S. Navy has not been here in a long time. (Of course I didn't mention Nimmer. How could he have remembered?) The Red Navy has been very hospitable to us. We are hoping for more professional exchanges. We want to go to sea in Soviet warships so that we can have a real brotherhood." (I said, "tovarishchestvo," comradeship.) "Why not?" he replied rather noncommittally, smiled, bowed slightly, shook hands again, and moved off.

Admiral Olsen was having difficulty communicating with some top Soviet naval officers. I had no sooner joined them to translate when Kathy Harriman breathlessly rushed up, not even noticing Red Navy boss Admiral of the Fleet Kuznetsov. "Admiral Olsen, quick! Come help." she said. "Daddy is ill!" Clearly, Yale in 1913 had not included a course in the finesse of vodka drinking *a la Russe*. But to the Russians' credit one must cheerfully admit they set the pace. Only shortly after Olsen had got off on his rescue errand, a knot of some dozen people appeared from the direction of the sanctum sanctorum, looking much like bees at swarming time. Clustered around were a dozen NKVD officers in uniform and others in plain clothes. In the middle was Molotov. Clinging to him like a drowning man was someone in a blue suit who surfaced once or twice long enough for me to identify him as none other than our own Commander Victor Blakeslee. Had I been a lip reader there is no doubt his words would have registered as, "Why do you hate me?" while holding Comrade Molotov in a rib-crushing bear hug. I dashed over to help and was rewarded by a stiff jab in the midriff that took the breath out of me, courtesy of a very mean looking Mongol in NKVD uniform. One blue-suited three-striper no doubt was felt to be enough in his estimation. They would take care of matters themselves, he said sharply. Meanwhile, the group struggled off, with Molotov grey-faced and ill-looking. Victor disappeared in the melee, all headed for the main entrance in a scene reminiscent of a football scrimmage an instant after the ball is fumbled.

Such cocktail parties were something for the history books. Indeed, it was reported in detail by the ambassador, who described it in his dispatch to Washington as, "a brilliant affair," pointing out the appearance of the new diplomatic uniforms and the cool treatment of the Japanese,* but delicately abstaining from comment on the more personal aspects.

**Foreign Relations*, 1943, vol. 3, p. 595.

Vlada Tolley.

Shortly after the Spiridonovka extravaganza, there was, on 15 November 1943 eighteen months after my arrival, a far more modest social event: my marriage. Indeed, the old padre who had blessed me at the age of one in the Philippines had been right when he told my father that no one could determine life's path—design, fate, or accident. The steps between then and now appeared partly by design, but certainly some of the more recent ones had hung on a thread so flimsy that other elements must have entered the equation. Perhaps that first introduction to Russians on a club bandstand in the Philippines at age six had inevitably aimed me at Kuibishev. At any rate, there I was, in May 1942, picking my way in Australian cavalry uniform down its cobbled street with fellow attaché George Roullard. A block distant, one could scarcely miss noticing a red, red sweater approaching. As its extremely attractive occupant drew abeam, it was a pleasant and unexpected denouement when George stopped to chat, the young lady speaking in flawless English, peach-pink cheeks glowing, dark brown hair flying loose. Walking on, George filled me in. When the Harriman-Beaverbrook Lend-Lease Mission came to Moscow in the autumn of 1941, the Soviets plucked two translators from the student body of Moscow University's Foreign Language Institute. Both had developed their accentless English in London as youngsters, where their parents were on government assignment. They had been inherited by Faymonville, who had come with the Lend-Lease group and remained to form the Military Mission. In October 1941 when the government and foreign diplomats were evacuated to Kuibishev, Vlada rode high overhead in the baggage rack of a jammed train compartment. Her colleague had stuck with the Mission, while she went to the Navy.

Over the following year and more, our friendship ripened over Russian lessons, walks in the park, evenings at the ballet, and picnics on country weekends. For a decade, I had been the reluctant dragon matrimonially, always sailing away over the horizon just as each romance seemed approaching the inevitable. However, I could appreciate that I was getting less attractive and more discriminating every day. But, for a quick, final decision on our part we are indebted to an organization blissfully unaware of the possible consequences, and badly shaken when they came to pass: the NKVD. Directed by them to give notice, Vlada dejectedly had been allowed to come in to collect small personal items before saying goodby, to which under these circumstances one could confidently append "forever." We decided to get married.

Would ZAKS, acronym for the Soviet bureau that was a full-service station for registering Soviets from cradle to grave—births, marriages, deaths—allow us to sign the book? As backup, we quickly contacted Father Braun, American rector of the only foreign-operated church in Moscow, avoiding, of course, the use of the telephone. "In case they refuse, I'll make you both Catholics in 15 minutes," said Father Braun. "Then I'll perform the rites and supply the documents."

At ZAKS there was no hitch, the lady taking a foreign client with total equanimity and a faint smile. We came back to the apartment in such a state of relieved anxiety that I cannot recall whether or not the bride was carried over the threshold. Not forgotten, however, was a much more important ritual: throwing a plate at the ceiling. It broke, prophesying a successful marriage. To Katya, the maid, her stainless steel teeth alternately flashing and hidden as she smiled or grimaced, it was a mixed blessing; one of our four dinner plates had been sacrificed to the gods.

Vlada, of course, continued her office routine. The NKVD, unable to substitute a more compliant replacement, was upset. It was one more indication of the hamhandedness of those worthies at the working level. (They had only belatedly closed off, for example, our visiting the extensive photo archives of TASS, the news agency, to order dozens of copies of Soviet warship photographs.)

Clearly, the influence of the NKVD did not sway the attitudes of Soviet Navy contacts, who offered obviously sincere congratulations. After

Our wedding reception. Left to right: Lieutenant Commander "Eddie" Yorke; Vlada; Rear Admiral Olsen; Lieutenants "Curly" Cram and Joe Chase.

I had left Russia and had jokingly written Vlada for her opinion on whether I should come back to the USSR to stay, she mentioned this to a mutual Soviet Navy friend. "What! Has he gone crazy?" the friend wanted to know in the greatest astonishment.

Admiral Olsen was mightily surprised, but wholly understanding, sympathetic, and helpful, allowing me to overstay my tour by six months hoping for Vlada's exit visa so she could accompany me. Several years later in Norfolk, it was Admiral Olsen's personal, active intervention that greatly speeded up and eased Vlada's quick naturalization. Even the Soviets relented, to the extent of passing an act in the Supreme Soviet divesting her of Soviet citizenship, so that she since has been free to visit and travel in the USSR on numerous occasions for lengthy stays.

13 / *The New Order*

The real and dramatic turnaround was the conference at Teheran on 1 December 1943. There, FDR at last came face to face with "Uncle Joe," not only at the long, sometimes acidulous sessions in the conference room, but as Stalin's house guest at the Soviet embassy. The U. S. embassy across town was said to be too great a security risk in spy-riddled Teheran for the president to be traveling to and fro. It also was a golden opportunity for Roosevelt to try on his snake-charming act without Churchill peering over his shoulder. Would he become a sort of latter-day Talleyrand, saving the wartime alliance of convenience for peace in our time by taming Russian intransigence through winning Stalin's confidence, if not love?

Harriman and Deane came back jubilant. Threshed out to mutual satisfaction had been the general date for the long-delayed cross-channel invasion of *Festung Europa*, code-named "Overlord," with plans for coordinated Soviet operations in support. For the first time, the Anglo-Americans were furnished figures on Soviet troop strength and dispositions. A preliminary agreement on shuttle bombing was set up, the Soviet terminal at historic Poltava, where Napoleon (called "Bonapartay" by the Russians) had met his come-uppance. All Germany would then be within range of Anglo-American heavy bombers. This would force the Germans to spread their AA defenses as well as lose a *manufacturing sanctuary*, heretofor unreachable from Britain or Italy. Big formations of heavy bombers, 350 B-17s and B-24s, would take off from Italy or Britain, fly to Poltava and the other two fields, Mirgorod and Pysyatin, bombing enemy territory en route. Then operating from the Russian fields for a few days, they could hit some targets on the eastern front in support of the Soviets. Bombed up again, they would return home as the weather dictated, dropping their loads en route. The operation was code-named, "Frantic," one that turned out to be highly appropriate.

Meanwhile, General Deane, pleased at Soviet "cooperation," was looking for some break in the vodka-sakuska routine. The physical fitness crowd had discovered the skiing ground at the gentle slopes of the Sparrow Hills. (They had been renamed, "Lenin Hills," but like "Cape Kennedy," it had never taken with the locals.) Cram, Chase, Yorke, and I used to flounder down the hills to the amusement of the urchins, who short-changed like everything and everybody else in the war-short USSR, were scooting down on one ski each. "When did you start skiing, Uncle?" inquired one. "Last week," we replied. "You had better forget it," volunteered an old grandma out watching the fun. "You have to start at three years old." This piece of advice should have been taken seriously by Russ Deane, who broke an ankle and was on crutches for weeks.

One of the stalwarts of the Moscow foreign colony was that remarkable fellow, Father Leopold Braun, SJ. He had come to Moscow from the United States in 1934 as part of the Roosevelt-Litvinov negotiations that guaranteed freedom of worship. There, he had taken over the Church of St. Louis of France, the only Roman Catholic church in Moscow, and had not been out of the USSR since that time, fearing that if he left on leave, he would never be allowed back in. Most of his parishoners were members of the foreign diplomatic delegations, but there were a few elderly faithful among the Russians who listened to his carefully noninflammatory sermons in Russian. He was particularly partial to the Navy contingent, although few of us were among his official flock. We reciprocated his frequent hospitality in his gloomy, but rather opulently furnished, flat by passing on to him various goodies in from the north.

Intrigued early on by the small black bag "Padre" Braun invariably carried, we once asked him in a jocular way if the Soviets were not suspicious of his always toting that case of burglar's tools. "That's for carrying the holy oil," he said with a grin. And then a little more grimly: "If I leave it unattended at home, what with the scarcity of fats, it's likely to be pinched for cooking." Close to egg-bald, jerky in movement and speech, the good padre was an incongruous sight in his long black gown on the streets of Moscow. This shortage of cooking oil was reflected in the National Hotel's cuisine, which sustained a good many of the transient Americans. They used linseed oil for frying, a favorite method of preparing meat. Because of the many foreigners who used the hotel, the menu was written in English as well as Russian. The spelling sometimes was picturesquely contrived. On one occasion it included the item, "catlets." "My God!" exclaimed a horrified U. S. general. "Now they're eating cats!" It is probable that neither his appetite nor his credulity was restored on hearing that "cutlet" is anything from a hamburger to a chicken breast, and that the wrong key had gone up for some amateur typist.

The on-again-off-again attitude of the Soviets toward foreigners was "on" during the winter of 1943–44, one particular case under rather startling circumstances. In our box at the theatre we had got into conversation with a fellow occupant, a Soviet major, who expressed a willingness to drop by our apartment after the show. The five or six of us who occupied the box, plus our new friend, drove back to Mokovaya, where we were able to take him through the gate in the motor car. (On foot he would have been denied entrance by the uniformed NKVD watchdog.) Soon, the victrola and its American records, vodka and good fellowship were all in high gear. The major, who had the usual revolver slung from his Sam Browne-style belt, was a real *frontovik*, a front-line fighter, obviously an eager Hun killer. As the evening wore on, a sort of Jekyll-Hyde syndrome surfaced. With each vodka tossed off, the former amiable fellow now increasingly suggested a tendency toward viewing *all* foreigners—not just the hated Nazis—*all* non-Russians as sinister. He took out his revolver and twirled the loaded cylinder. "You see this gun?" he growled ominously. "This is my only real friend. That is true of all Russians. Their only real friends are their guns. Now I want to get out of this place!" Capitalists, Nazis, Englishmen, Americans, all appeared to be assuming an equally unpleasant aspect to this earthy son of the Russian people, all of whom who can turn from joviality to black anger in an instant.

With Curly Cram as chauffeur, Chase and I and the major, the latter with me in the back seat, set out in the Navy Ford in the total blackout for parts unknown. Our guest wanted to go to his sister's house, to which he gave wholly befuddled directions. Turn this way, turn that way—no, the other way! Oh! How we sighed for that NKVD car that so often trailed us. Pulling out his gun, the major held it to the back of Curly's head. He was leading him astray, the major shouted. Take him straight to his sister's or else! A half hour of this mini-nightmare and Curly let out a cry of triumph. "We've found it!" he said jubilantly. "Here it is!" He ground to a stop. We bundled the major out and Curly roared off as fast as the Ford would go, zig-zagging as we went. "How the hell did you know where his sister lived?" we asked with one voice. "I didn't." replied the man with an ex-newspaperman's quick wit. "It just looked like a good spot for a change of pace."

One might think we would have been less than eager for a repeat of what could have been a very real session of Russian roulette, but with *all* the chambers loaded. In our next case it was again a fellow boxmate at the ballet, a pink-cheeked young Air Force cadet, probably 22 years old. We had early, and of course secretly, named him, "*Mejdu Prochim*," (by the way), an expression he used in the same profligate and wholly unconnected manner as one now hears, "*You* know." Also smuggled in via motor car, he continually expressed wonder at the "luxuriousness" of our apartment, which actually was rather modest by any American standards. His was the wide-eyed wonder of youth. We knew that in his innocence it unfortunately and inevitably would become known to the authorities that he had exposed himself to the perils of foreign association. So we carefully refrained from prompting him into replies on military subjects, in view of any third degree he might be subjected to later.

Mejdu Prochim was more respectful of the solid effects of vodka than had been our late guest the major, so that on departing, our cadet was filled with (to him) exotic food and good fellowship, but totally in control of himself. As a parting gesture indicating the depths of his feeling, he had pulled out his wallet and presented me with a small passport photo of himself in uniform as a memento of an evening he would "never forget the rest of my life." About a week later, we received a telephone call from our cadet. He was on his way over with a small present for us, he said. I was torn by qualms, various thoughts flashing through my mind as I chatted on the phone, which we knew, of course, was bugged by the NKVD. Should we agree to a meeting place, so that I could pick him up in the car? No. (The NKVD later would run him down like a rabbit. Let nature and the system take its course, painful though it might be.) As we fully expected, the young man failed to show up—either intercepted at the gate or earlier. We hoped fervently that our solution had softened the blow he would unquestionably suffer for his naivete in proposing his visit. Not only the lad himself, but his father, an Air Force colonel, whose precepts and adequacy of indoctrination of his son the NKVD would find wanting. Yes, indeed it probably *had* been an evening he would "never forget the rest of my life."

Russians enjoying the use of motor vehicles as drivers often used them for personal gain. Truck drivers picked up hitchhikers, expecting a token of something useful other than roubles, with which little could be bought. Official limousines acted clandestinely as taxis when the comrade boss was absent. Hence, after depositing Curly and date at the theatre one stormy night, while still at the curb, I was not surprised when a citizen opened the door to ask my destination. "Mokovaya Square," I said. "Fine!" he replied. "That's just where I want to go; Moscow Hotel." He jumped in without a "by your leave" and settled back alongside me, a dapper young fellow obviously out for a night on the town. What was I short of, he wanted to know. Cigarettes? Razor blades? A pack of fish hooks? Small pair of scissors? Vodka? "Let me think it over," I said. In due course we arrived at the Moscow Hotel. "Wait here for just a few minutes," he said. "I have to pick up someone." Breaking into a stiff foreign accent, I explained that I was awfully sorry not to be able to wait, but had to get back to the embassy. Just consider his ride so far as a gift from the American Navy. Had I been

Mephisto himself, suddenly materializing in the winter darkness, the reaction could not have been more satisfactory. "*Boje moi!*" (My God!) he gasped, and was off like a shot, my career as a Moscow taxi driver expired aborning.

Moscow was a fertile playground for practical jokers of the telephone variety. There was no directory. Lack of such minor amenities as a pencil or piece of paper to write down numbers produced many wrong ones. "Is Olga there?" one might ask. "Sorry, citizen, but Olga is not here." "Where did she go?" "Well, she left about fifteen minutes ago with Pavel." "Pavel? Who the hell is Pavel?" "Oh! A six footer in a black leather coat (mark of a commissar or plant manager). Heard her say something about the Aragvi." (Most expensive restaurant in town.) Explosive sounds at other end.

Motor cars generated keen interest in another group of our Soviet associates, the watchmen at Mokovaya's arched gate. Dressed in "militia" (Soviet word for "police") uniforms, they were of course NKVD. Were they allergic to American Fords, thus causing them to sneeze as one went by? Or was it the thought of an American naval officer venturing forth into the many perils of Moscow that evoked a sentimental throb in the throat that brought tears to their eyes? Whatever the underlying cause, the passing out of the Navy Ford generally (though not always) brought forth the militiaman's handkerchief to be applied rather flamboyantly to his nose. At this signal, the Russian model A Ford parked a block away would belch out a burst of blue smoke as its 30-octane fuel took fire. Then, at a discreet distance Ford B would follow Ford A. It was the lack of predictability in this routine that was the hallmark of all Soviet dealings with foreigners. We assessed various combinations: was the car being driven by chauffeur Olaf, or by one of us? If one of us, how did they react to our attire? Sometimes we wore uniform, sometimes formal civilian, other times à la Russe, with pullover sweater. We never were followed to meetings with the Red Navy liaison officer, which suggested the liaison was not only with us but also with those ubiquitous gentlemen in the blue hats. Occasionally we were trailed walking on the street, but not when we were taking the old familiar track from Mokovaya to Spasso House.

As for plain old bugging, here indeed we were in fast company. As an example, Harriman sent a dispatch to Washington reporting that Stalin had bluntly stated that his military did not trust Lieutenant General M. B. Burrows, chief of the British Supply Mission in Moscow, explaining that this was personal in respect to Burrows and not the British in general.* Well might Stalin's men have so felt. I was making a routine call on some piddling business at the British Mission when on barely entering the

**Foreign Relations*, 1944, vol 4, p. 966.

building I could hear blasphemous shouts emanating from general's country, so joined the half-dozen people converging to see what the flap was all about. There stood Burrows, purple-faced, dancing around like a man who has just inadvertently sat on an ant hill. In his hand, held high overhead was a bunch of what looked like cocktail carrots. Out of the confusion the story came at last into focus. The old boy had stumbled onto a microphone under his desk. Following the wire like a beagle on a hot game trail, he had come on one microphone after another, until he had racked up about a dozen. From my own experience with the British in Russia, I can attest that their views on their hosts were not always laudatory, and the Soviets undoubtedly had got a good earful of Burrows's uninhibited comments in the supposed sanctity of his office.

Not long after that, Burrows was relieved by Lieutenant General G. LeQ. Martel, a peppery, dignified little man who stalked around in a pair of highly polished boots, twitching his military mustache, uttering the choked monosyllables commonly affected by the professional Sandhurster. He was in marked contrast to that other resident Britisher, Brigadier George A. Hill, an easygoing, cherubic oldster who had carried off some hair-raising stunts in World War I Russia—an outstandingly brave man who operated a team of spies behind enemy lines, transported the Romanian crown jewels through five battlefronts from Moscow to Jassy, then finally wound up as Trotsky's air adviser. Now he was a liaison man between British intelligence and the Soviets for agents in enemy territory. Hill understood the Russians, playing the British hand with a finesse never even remotely approached by such neophytes as Martel and Deane. I enjoyed nothing more than an evening in "Pop" Hill's beautifully appointed mess, along with his half-dozen or so wholly unaffected fellow spooks, a fascinating slice of time wholly out of the ordinary.

World War II had brought about a vast expansion in the American intelligence effort, including the world-targeting Office of Strategic Services (OSS). The latter's director, Major General William ("Wild Bill") Donovan, came to Moscow to open negotiations with the Soviets' dread NKVD, which not only terrorized its own citizens, but operated worldwide as an espionage apparatus par excellence. The proposal was to have the OSS and the NKVD represented each with an agency in the other's capital, purportedly to coordinate dirty tricks against the Germans. Deane pushed the arrangements on the Soviet end after Donovan left, expecting the usual obfuscation and delay. Astoundingly, the reverse proved true. Deane's contacts, Lieutenant General P.M. Fitin, head of the External Intelligence Service, and Major General A. P. Ossipov, head of the section conducting subversive activities in enemy countries, proved friendly, cooperative, and ready to give instant answers. Ossipov, a Boris Karlov type who spoke faultless English, expedited mutual communication. It was apparent that the NKVD operated in a super stratum, where decisions could be made directly without reference to higher authority. But when the road seemed all clear, detailed arrangements on paper and the plan laid before Roosevelt, there was a strange reversal of the usual procedure. It was not the Soviets, but FDR who said, "Nyet!" In an election year, explained FDR, no chances could be taken on having a Communist secret police establishment in the nation's capital. If the public got onto it, there would be hell to pay. And that was the end of it.

Meanwhile, the new responsibilities falling Deane's way called for more help. From a beginning of about 20 people when the Military Mission was first constituted, it grew swiftly to about 135, most of them Army, a great many of them enlisted clerks, supply people, or other housekeepers. Airplane loads of swabs, desks, typewriters, and filing cabinets filled the available housing to bursting, pushing personnel into makeshift quarters in converted hotels. Even Deane himself, who had visited a Soviet division in the field, came back expressing chagrin at the size of his organization and

Wartime people-to-people in the USSR. Moscow girls and U.S. Military Mission personnel picnic in the country.

the population explosion, ruefully remarking that the entire staff of the Soviet division totaled 15 men. They had neither post exchange, doughnut wagons, or much of a logistic tail, depending for morale on the fierce desire of the Russian soldier to avenge himself against the tyrannous invader. Most hideous thought of all, there was not a single typewriter in the Soviet division headquarters.

Now having become "missionaries," no longer attachés, the Navy carried on in the north. Frankel received a second spot promotion, to captain, to enhance his prestige and as a reward for work well done. The American dental officer in Moscow, Commander Clifford C. deFord, went up to inspect teeth, the frigid landscape, and the physical situation confronting several American seaman prisoners in Soviet jails. One was a psychiatric case. A Soviet psychiatrist took Cliff in to interview the man. The psychiatrist, a rather wild-eyed fellow, was anxious to prove that the patient was indeed off the rails, to which end he began asking him questions, explaining his conclusions from the answers received. As matters continued along this vein, Cliff noticed a developing tendency on the Soviet's part to ask *him* the questions, then explain the replies to the patient. "Time to get out of here!" said Cliff to himself, "before they lock *me* up and let the nut go."

The Ukrainian air bases meanwhile were humming along, with some 2,000 American personnel expected. Some already had arrived, making sightseeing expeditions to Moscow.

This burgeoning Army influence by weight of numbers increasingly overshadowed the Navy in the Mission, which was logical enough when one compares the modest operations and power of the Red Navy compared to the vast spread of those of the Red Army. The division of U. S. forces was not because of personalities, but simply a reflection of the century of apartheid that had existed between the two services, which worldwide had served us badly in every theatre of military enterprise. This is particularly true in the Far East, where "divided we fell," in the early phase of the war.

Then it became apparent that in some areas of endeavor, such as weather forecasting, the Navy not only had the expertise, but the desperate need for it, to carry on the offensive against the Japanese. Weather flows from west to east. What would soon happen in the seas off Japan could be foretold by what was being generated on the Siberian steppes. General "Hap" Arnold, Army Air Force chief, was deeply interested too, in connection with the plan to base large numbers of bombers in Siberia to raid Japan. So he characteristically pounded his desk and demanded that a weather service be set up in Russia. The ball was passed to Admiral Olsen, who very shortly was reinforced by the arrival of Captain Denys W. Knoll, '30, USNA, who was in some respects a man after my own heart. He had gone in for "weather" early in his career as I had for Russian, in a day when weather came mostly from the *Farmers' Almanac* and "Russian" was a type of salad dressing. Caught on besieged Corregidor, he was classified as property valuable enough to be evacuated by submarine. With an outgoing disposition, giving the impression of knowing what he was talking about, this big, hearty, voluble fellow, who really knew an enormous lot about weather, was the ideal man to browbeat, cajole, or otherwise bring the Soviets into the American orbit weatherwise.

"Give 'em ten millions worth of equipment," said Hap Arnold, on the good old American premise that money solves everything. With the Russians, only to a certain extent is that valid. Security is a major consideration. The dire results personally of a miscalculation on the part of decision makers all along the line inhibit quick anwers that can be relied on. In the case of the weather question, as usual, a compromise was arrived at. The Soviets would welcome the equipment but not the operators. Again, as we found in the case of the lack of communication between the theoretical Commissar of Bathtubs and the Commissar of Drain Lines with reference to our malfunctioning Mokovaya bathroom, the weather people and the communication people, without which the former could not operate, were in dire need of coordination so that the combination operated harmoniously. In a few words, the end results were spotty. If we were to carry out our expectations and hopes in setting up vast bomber bases in Siberia to hit Japan, obviously we would need something far better. Alas! The results of agonizingly slow and sometimes acrimonious discussions ended up so late as to be of no use in the war. The weather equipment arrived in mid-1945 and was reported operational by the Soviets as of 27 August, 10 days after VJ-day. It had been given very low priority by the Soviet expediters of Lend-Lease equipment in the USA.

As for the weather in the Tolley apartment, one might say it generally was fair. The parties partly reflected a legacy from the gala days of the Far East and partly a requirement to fulfil properly the duties of intelligence officer. The air was becoming more international. There had long been crossed flags over the *takhta*, the traditional Russian deep settee, made of a rug-covered mattress with another rug hung on the wall behind it, pillows all over, a reminder of the oriental inside every Russian. One of the flags was the Stars & Stripes, the other, a Soviet naval ensign: big red star and hammer & sickle, with a broad blue stripe at bottom, all on a white field. Mike Kostrinsky, who in spite of his latent antipathies for the British, remembering no doubt the brighter aspects of his years in London as assistant naval attaché, suggested that in the interests of wartime amity, the British flag be added. So we had pinned up the colors of our most frequent and hospitable hosts, the Royal Air Force.

Czechoslovakian officer, Lieutenant General Nijborski, CinC Czech Forces, England, and Soviet movie actress Zoya Feodorova. The former executed; the latter sent to Siberia for eight years. (Mysteriously shot 13 December 1981.)

A genial Londoner, Air Commodore D. M. Roberts, was over often. So were Canadian Brigadier Hercule Lefebvre, Chinese Major General Kuo Teh-chuan, and Mexican Colonel Ruben Calderon. For the more Slavicly tinted jousts, those where the guests' tastes ran more to vodka than scotch, we called in the Czechs, who had set up a respectable fighting force drawn from Czechs captured from the Germans and happy to turn coats. Two of their top officers, Lieutenant General Nijborsky and Brigadier General Heliodor Pika, much enjoyed an opportunity to dance with movie star Zoya Feodorova, and having her pose wearing their tall fur shakos.

All these parties were enlivened by the addition of several British cypherettes (now that women were trickling back), apparently selected for pulchritude as well as agility with the code machines, and by several ambassadorial daughters: the American, the Iranian, and the two winsomely strapping Jugoslavs, plus some of wife Vlada's more reckless former

*Both generals subsequently were executed in "liberated" Czechoslovakia by the pro-Soviet puppet government. Zoya was found in her Moscow apartment in December 1981, shot in the back of the head. She had several times telephoned her daughter, living in Connecticut, fathered by then naval attaché Captain Jackson Tate, that she was intending to start a big publicity campaign over her being denied a Soviet exit visa to visit the United States, where several times previously she had been allowed to go.

schoolmates. The earlier, frontier-style bashes, with roughhouse and even gunplay, had been tempered by the steadying news from the fronts, quite a change from the black days of late 1941, when the mood, especially for one just in from the disaster area of Southeast Asia, was eat it, drink it, shoot it up, because tomorrow we and/or it might no longer be there.

The trickle back of women to combatant embassies did not include the American embassy, with the exception of Kathy Harriman, although Commander Victor Blakeslee's wife, the former Princess Skariatina, had popped in and out to do a magazine article for a prestigious American weekly. But one enterprising wife did it on the sly, slipping in from Teheran for a quick visit to her Military Mission husband, to stay until the very next outbound plane bounced her back. It brought about one of those little contretemps that sometimes occur in even the best-regulated embassies. At a very large and jolly party that night—newshawks, military,

Left to right: "Curly" Cram, Eddie Yorke holding Liuba, and Denys Knoll; Standing: C. J. Zondorak, Cliff deFord, Johnny Ahy, and Vlada; Seated, clockwise: Leila, Joe Chase, Olga, and Dr. Fred Lang (glasses)

ballet, diplomats, and so forth—the husband, like any middle-aged dog, was slow to catch onto new tricks. The party near over, he picked up his long-time ballet friend and went home with her, forgetting completely his newly arrived spouse. Somewhere during the ensuing interim, the connubial pair got reunited. Both showed up for breakfast next morning with eyes black beyond the rims of dark glasses, the husband with what suggested the marks of a high heel here and there about the head.

Entertainment of a different sort faced the American airmen visiting Moscow from the new bomber bases in the Ukraine. They came with tales indicating mixed emotions over their new assignment. It was a totally different world from their life in staid England, where the amenities came by shipload. Here, they had built a control tower out of aircraft engine boxes and five telephone poles. Women soldiers were everywhere, working on the runways, as truck drivers, engineers, mechanics, antiaircraft gunners, clerks, and sentries. The Americans weren't kept away from the Russian people at all, although the women soldiers had instructions not to mix except in line of duty. Punishment for disobedience was immediate shipment to the front. The commanding officer had explained this, and as one airman put it, "They were such swell janes that we didn't want to get them in trouble." But they dated civilian girls, and plenty of them. There had been rumors that registered prostitutes were available to Soviet troops holding an appropriate "ration card," a total falsehood, the Americans thought.

The Russians were all business. If a Soviet officer noted that some individuals in a work detail were leaning on their shovels, the next detail would be reduced by that number. One American reported having been invited to a Soviet recreation hall, where he soon found the "recreation" not wholly his bag. It was flinging around a 23 kilogram iron ball.

Soviet discipline was tough. Privates saluted corporals and so on up, sometimes following it with a handshake. There was no fraternizing off the job between officers and men.

Each U. S. crew chief was assigned three Soviet helpers, all of whom had seen plenty of front line action. "We tried to teach them about Forts," said one, "and after two days they were asking questions that we crew chiefs couldn't answer."

The Americans followed the Russian work hours: sunup to sundown, after which they were glad to find their bunks. These turned out to be considerably better than what they called their "aching-back" British sacks: good mattresses, pillow, pillowcases, and two Russian camel-hair blankets.

The airmen visitors to Moscow were the usual wide-eyed sightseers, royally treated by the resident Americans. They were taken to their choice of opera or circus, visited art galleries, parks, and museums, winding up as guests at the embassy of Ambassador Harriman and daughter Kathy, ever the thoughtful and kind individual.* An official dinner was about to begin at the embassy. The tourists looked in long enough to shake hands with Molotov, Marshal Rokossovsky, and Chinese and British ambassadors, and lesser lights. The dinner would be dull, Kathy said, advising them to take off for town and see the night life. It would not be like that in Poltava. Or in Topeka either, for that matter.

*Kathy took Vlada into the embassy for several weeks of convalescence from appendicitis after my departure.

14 / *Harriman Goes North*

In the summer of 1943, news from the Mediterranean was all good. The Germans had been swept out of North Africa. Italy was on the ropes psychologically and militarily. In September, Italy switched sides, the fleet surrendering intact. Very shortly thereafter a demand was received from the Soviets for a division of the swag, even though Soviet military operations had come nowhere near the Italian boot. Quite the contrary, actually. General Mark Clark, commanding Allied forces in Italy at the time, in a letter to a friend commenting on an article of mine about Admiral Standley wrote that: "My government persuaded me to have a Russian mission with my Fifth Army fighting in Italy. Andrei Vishinsky* was the political commissar to the Russian general attached to the Commission of the Fifth Army . . . They caused nothing but trouble and made us wonder at times whether we were fighting the right enemy."

In his letter to me assenting to my use of the above quote, General Clark added a revealing footnote: "Five Soviet Army officers visited the Fifth Army front in December of 1943. They had a couple of generals with them and we felt from their attitude that they thought the fighting in Italy was not severe, and they wanted to tell us about how hard the Russians were being on the Germans on the Russian front. They said they wanted to get a look at our front, particularly from the point of view of logistics. We showed them everything, but I had them taken up to the front in the mountains where they had to leave their jeeps and get on mules and endure some German artillery fire. They had to dismount and hike through the mud. One of them was wounded, and that night they had a completely different attitude toward the difficulty we were encountering in Italy.

*Vishinsky was the prosecutor in the infamous purge trials of the mid-thirties.

The Italian fleet had surrendered in good faith, their ships unsabotaged, on the expectation they might be used in the common effort to end the war and oust the Germans from their homeland. Any Allied effort to parcel out their ships, especially to the less-than-admired Soviets, could have resulted in their being scuttled. So rather than a flat, "No!" with probably nasty repercussions from Moscow, a compromise was proposed: comparable Anglo-American warships in lieu of the Italian ships. Actually, the tradeoff was not so comparable; the Italian battleships were big, new, and powerful, the cruisers sleek and agile. But an offer of Britain's World War I battleship *Queen Elizabeth* and the USS *Milwaukee*, a 7,500-ton light cruiser of like vintage, plus some equally venerable supporting ships, saved Russian face.

To add a bit of sugar coating, Ambassador Harriman himself flew north for the 20 April 1944 turnover ceremonies, the *Milwaukee* having beat her way through to Murmansk in a convoy that had fought off U-boat wolf packs, sinking several of their number. The German lines had pulled back so far that the ambassadorial party—Harriman, Admiral Olsen, Tolley, and second secretary F. B. Stevens—flew comfortably up to Archangel at a decent altitude in a Soviet transport plane. The peril of a chance German intruder was by then slight. Harriman had had his own plane since mid-1943. It was easily capable of such trips, but Navy pilots Lieutenants L. B. Prunier and John W. Holt were kept grounded by personal edict of Molotov himself.

My previous trips north had been business, our socializing with the Russians limited to informal calls involving more vodka than useful information. This ambassadorial affair demanded high protocol, with a lavish spread including all the top officials in Archangel, military and civilian. Keynoter was Rear Admiral Ivan Papanin, roly-poly little Arctic explorer. "*Dvazhdi Geroi Sovietskovo Soyuza*," twice Hero of the Soviet Union, he wore two gold stars on red ribbons, each award equivalent to the Congressional Medal of Honor for his heroic and masterful leadership in 1937–39 explorations. Member of the Party, deputy to the Supreme Soviet, he was currently Director of the Northern (trans-Arctic) Sea Route. It was he who had donated the building housing the American naval contingent in Archangel.

"Hello, Tovarishch Tolley!" he said cheerily, his Charlie Chaplinesque mustache over an always-ready smile. He had used not only the address, "comrade," but had remembered my name from months ago. It was clear why this bustling little gnome had endeared himself to Russian and foreigner alike.

Papanin took us for a ride on one of his powerful icebreakers, stubby and wide of beam like himself, plowing a path through the Dvina's thick ice as effortlessly as a hot knife in butter. This broke up the corduroy road laid

The Russian ensign flying from the stern of the cruiser USS *Milwaukee* (CL-5).

Captain Ferguson, CO of USS *Milwaukee*, with the prospective Soviet skipper.

Ambassador Harriman with Rear Admiral Feodorov and Lieutenant General Andreev at Murmansk.

Admiral Olsen arrives at Murmansk for the *Milwaukee* turnover. In parka, Captain Ferguson, CO *Milwaukee*, facing Admiral Olsen. Captain Frankel is beind Olsen.

Icebreaker path on Dvina River at Archangel. The board roadway timbers seen on right will be relaid across broken ice and frozen hard enough for truck traffic in a few hours.

on the ice for motor traffic between banks (there was no bridge over the broad river). But it would freeze solid again in a few hours and the road would be rebuilt, while disconsolate but resigned Russians very literally cooled not just their heels awaiting a crossing.

The banquet was all sweetness and light on both sides. The Soviet speeches were as predictable in content as a high mass. Stevens translated both ways with marvelous perfection, swaying like a sapling in the wind, holding onto a nearby curtain for support after all those vodkas. And for a blessed once, I didn't feel obliged to surreptitiously dump mine in the potted palm. This was an embassy show.

As for Navy House, little had changed. The atmosphere of a typical Russian interior was still as strong, the seat on the outdoor plumbing still as frigid. Aside from old reliable Lieutenant "Jack" Harshaw, man in charge, public relations expert par excellence, there were some familiar faces among the Russians who dropped in for a chat, a meal, or a drink. Among them were three or four young ladies far above the cut of the "sawmill blondes" who frequented the Interclub to dance with foreign seamen. There had been a succession of candidates for steady guest at Navy House, but in the end a select few had prevailed. One was an engineer, so she said. Extremely intelligent, very pretty, statuesque, without the familiar potato-sack midriff, she had a sharply chiselled face that could be hard, the eyes cold, sometimes narrowing to mere slits when she was crossed. Yet she was the best of good company, going far enough, but not too far. Later, she turned up in Moscow, where she visited a Navy friend in the embassy, entering the gate without escort. There is little doubt where "Sasha" (for Alexandra) stood in the scheme of things.

Masha was the opposite pole, with very large, very brown eyes, a wide mouth that smiled often. Pleasant and compliant, she cheered up Harshaw, a man twice her age, giving him good advice on how to cope with Russian intransigence and with an ulcer that flared up on those rare occasions when he succumbed to Russian insistence that he join in a toast. It is not improbable that Masha served Navy House as the Moscow second secre-

Two Archangel lasses, among the dozens popularly known as "sawmill blondes," who came to the International Club to dance with foreign seamen.

Sasha, a girl at Archangel, an engineer in the port. She was a frequent visitor at the U.S. Navy house.

tary's ballet friend did him—go-between in matters too delicate to negotiate face to face, diplomatically and unofficially making known to a foreigner in a strange and alien culture the path to common ground—without Harshaw's ever being aware of it. At Murmansk, the *Milwaukee*'s classic prewar lines stood out in grey relief against the still wintry sky. Scurrying all over her like children on a picnic, Russian sailors and officers made themselves familiar with their new charge. The ceremonies were short and simple, like a bang of the hammer at an auction. Thus, the *Milwaukee*, veteran of China, the West and East U. S. Coasts, Central America, Hawaii, and latterly the South Atlantic, became the Soviet ship *Murmansk*.*

American sailors helped the new owners read strange nameplates. In the offices, grinning, chattering Soviets ground pencils down to the erasers, trying out that new marvel, the pencil sharpener. At last they had a ship-borne radar in their hands. The big wire dishes rotated on masts or director towers while fascinated Soviets crowded around to watch those little bugs appear, then fade, on the greenish luminescent screens. In the cabin, jolly old Captain William H. Ferguson, weatherbeaten, aquiline, wreathed in smiles most of the time, closeted himself with his relief, a

*Returned to the United States by the Soviets in March 1949, she was sold for scrap in December of that year.

moon-faced captain second rank. There they communicated in the universal language of sailors: sketches, gestures, fractured attempts in each other's lingo, some of the nautical part close enough to be mutually understandable. Skipper Ferguson twanged away on the guitar at evening song and coffee sessions, charming the Russians by his easy informality. The *Milwaukee* wouldn't change the war's course, but she certainly had welded some friendships, however fleeting.

The *Milwaukee/Murmansk* clearly was the star that eclipsed any others, to the extent that Harriman was just another civilian in an area where the predominant theme was blue and gold. But he had exercised his considerable charm and good fellowship to advantage with the civilian officials, no less Soviet than their Moscow counterparts perhaps, but a bit more ingenuous.

Shortly after Harriman's return to Moscow, he was presented with an enormous polar bear skin, a record specimen perhaps meant to remind him of his northern adventure. The ways of diplomacy are devious, if not obscure. As amateur psychologists we middle rankers spent some time philosophizing on the motive behind the gift. We agreed there had got to be such a thing as ordinary generosity with no strings attached, even in the Soviet Union, as the Russians personally are a generous race. Harriman had just been to polar bear country. Was this a thoughtful offering as a memento of past adventures for Harriman's declining days, slouched before a crackling fire, his feet resting on the bear? Could anything be that simple? The Russians are a conspiratorial lot, bargaining with their hands up their sleeves. So was it a subtle inference to, "Watch out, brother! The bear has sharp claws, big teeth, and is very, very large." (Not mentioned would be that the little black nose, which he can cleverly hide with a paw while sneaking up on an unsuspecting seal, is very keen at sniffing out something rotten. Such as something cooking in Washington.) Good God! Had we been in Russia too long? Was there a bug under every bed, a communist behind every bush?

15 / *Life under the Mission*

Actually, if the Russians had been reading Harriman's thoughts—or his telegrams, which was not impossible considering the degree of communist penetration in the U. S. government at the time—they would have felt quite justified in giving him a shaking. In mid-June he told Washington that we had better start taking a firm position or there soon would be a Soviet policy of playing the world bully. Exercise patience, he said, but warned that forbearance was "a sign of weakness to these people."* It appeared he was falling in line with professional diplomat and Russian specialist George Kennan, whose pragmatic views on the Soviets had been surfacing in State Department circles ever since Recognition. These views had remained in low key after his relase from internment in Germany, where he had been on duty at the time of Pearl Harbor. Then, in mid-1944 he went to Moscow, where as minister-councillor he delivered himself of a very long blueprint of the Soviets in general and the postwar picture as he saw it. No punches were pulled on Soviet behavior and mores. On the other hand, he suggested as inevitable Soviet suzerainty over Eastern Europe. This struck State's other senior diplomatic expert on the USSR, Loy Henderson, as a pusillanimous giveaway, but was in fact what actually took place, whether or not Anglo-American measures could have changed things.

In mid-summer 1944, "The Sources of Soviet Conduct," attributed to "X," circulated in privileged government circles, Kennan understood to be its author. Public release came in the July 1947 *Foreign Affairs*. The Soviets scarcely could have been pleased. "For Russia," he wrote, "there are no objective criteria of right and wrong. There are not any objective criteria of reality and unreality. . . . Here men determine what is true and what is false."

**Foreign Relations*, 1944, vol. 4, p. 836.

I had antedated both Harriman and Kennan by a year. In mid-1943, I wrote a tailpiece to a routine intelligence report:

> The present trend of official policy in the USSR, the tone of their propaganda to their own people, and growing Soviet independence and lack of trust should give cause for deep consideration of the potentialities of this situation.

On 9 August 1943, I wrote Major Andrew Wylie, USMCR, who held the Russian desk in ONI, that:

> Every now and then we get the hint that what is really disturbing the local big shots is not the lack of a second front but that there *is* a second front, and not where they want it. They can see the Allies beating them to it in the Balkans. When Germany collapses, it goes without saying that the Balkans would do likewise, with the Reds in a position to jump in their motor cars and tanks and be in every town from Belgrade to Athens in a week. Certainly a hell of a lot sooner than we could arrange it from the sea side, over the mountains. Then they see us (British and USA) piling in at the finish over the western front, at Germany's invitation, while same Germany throws everything she's got to hold off the Red flood until the good old white folks from the west get installed first. If *we* move into the Balkans *first*, their little motor car dash is out. I believe they want everything south of Vienna, excluding Greece, and unless we get there first, they will *get* it, with the help of a lot of people in the countries concerned.

The intelligence reports I wrote were routed to the White House. It would be presumptuous on my part to consider that they would influence policy, both in view of my modest position, and in the face of such pro-Russian and powerful figures as Mrs. Roosevelt, Harry Hopkins, General James Burns, and of such individuals later accused of being communist agents as Harry Dexter White and Laughlin Currie. But it is possible that *somebody* of importance in the White House may have seen these reports, perhaps Admiral William Leahy, the president's influential chief of staff.

My reports in the beginning were the best estimates I could make of Russian character and behavior as we experienced it on trips, where we were in a position to swap drinks, tell long tales, and meet numbers of people unencumbered by NKVD interference. But in spite of expressions of deep friendship and sympathy on their part—that we would meet in Moscow, call them up, come see them—when the time came, they were gone. They were sick. They had been transferred. They had made the sad discovery that even in such times of supposed wartime brotherhood, association with foreigners was poison.

Basically, we found these "strangers that pass in the night" to be dedicated Russian patriots. Indoctrination since childhood had produced an evident scepticism in accepting our explanations of life outside the USSR. But the basic hospitality and conviviality inherent in Russians generally overrode the kindergarten primers that contained such passages as, "Oh, Vanya! There goes a foreigner. You watch him while I go get a militiaman."

As my reports continued, I became a little more sophisticated, reading the message traffic from "upstairs," and being a member of Ambassador Standley's mess, where diplomatic happenings of the day were discussed. It became apparent that any sort of "détente," as it is now called, or any softening of the Russians toward ourselves was a fairy tale, a fantasy. It would never happen; the Russian idea was to receive as much as they possibly could, giving as little credit as they possibly could. It clearly indicated the fallacy of our thinking that one could bank good will; it was strictly *quid pro quo*, there being no treasury of merit.

Throughout all this, we in no respect lost our affection for individual Russians—liaison officers, members of the ballet and theatre, embassy employees. I like to think that my friendship for my opposite number Commander Michail Kostrinsky, "Mike," was wholly reciprocated. Except for his unshakable trust in Stalin, like most Russians he was happy to discuss any subject at any length. Mike was an ex-"byezprizorni," a waif left homeless and parentless by the Revolution. Living in drain pipes, wearing rags, scrounging for food, thousands of them roamed the Russian cities until rounded up and put in government institutions. Mike had been educated, put through the Naval Academy, then eventually sent to England as assistant naval attaché for three years. He had started off as a homeless ragamuffin, he told me. Now he was, not to boast, but simply speaking the truth, doing an important job that fitted his talents. How could he not love his motherland?

In a few words, a honeymoon in relations simply never existed, a state of affairs well understood in the very beginning by the Russians, but not for some time by the Americans.

We did continue to "meet the Russians." Lieutenant Colonel Grey, U. S. Army, over on temporary duty to check the performance of U. S. tanks, came back from several weeks at the Gorky tank repairworks. He was shocked at the lack of tools and facilities. In some cases the tools were there but carefully boxed up, while workmen continued to remove nuts in the Russian fashion: with cold chisel and hammer. The tanks were lying around with no effort made to protect the guns. Most appalling of all were the sanitary arrangements. A three-holer had long since filled up, had overflowed onto the floor, finally into the yard, and at the present juncture the men were climbing on top of the frozen pile.

But as usual, the "Rooskies" were hospitality itself, giving him the

Mike Kostrinsky with Vlada, Olga, and Liuba in my apartment.

best they had to eat, including plenty of meat, normally a rarity. All expressed amazement that he should want to live at the works instead of at the hotel in town, ten miles away, and that he should get out there and dirty his hands. *Russian* officers didn't *do* that!

Grey, a big, jovial, outgoing fellow, continued to exercise his charm after his return to Moscow. He, his date, and another couple had attended the circus, where lacking a match for his cigarette, he asked an officer in the neighboring seat for a light. Grey admired the cigarette lighter, made from a cartridge case. This led to a conversation that developed into the new friend's accompanying the party back to our apartment in Mokovaya. The Russian colonel was one of those rare and highly venerated birds in the

USSR, a Hero of the Sovit Union, the gold star on his chest a passport to far greater freedom of action than that afforded the ordinary comrade. It was a wonderful evening of good fellowship for all concerned, Curly Cram at his best with the piano, old Marusia the maid skittering around flashing her stainless steel teeth, passing out caviar sandwiches. There was plenty of vodka, but not too much. At a late hour, the colonel departed after affectionate bear hugs of farewell. There had been only one other time in his life when his heart was so full, the Russian said, and that was when he received his Hero award. Next morning a package arrived for Grey. In it were six copies of the cartridge cigarette lighter. He couldn't bring it in person, a note explained; he was rushing to be off for the Far East. A week later, a telephone call came from the colonel at Khabarovsk, 4,000 miles away, wishing us all well and repeating how much he had enjoyed our company.

Unfortunately, the scenario did not always reflect the same friendship elsewhere. In 1943, Constantine Oumansky, former ambassador at Washington, not a friend of the United States, was transferred as minister to Mexico, center of Comintern activities in Latin America. In 1944 a flood of reinforcements, Soviet "diplomats," headed that way, numbers out of all proportion to Soviet interests: 27 to Cuba, 53 to Mexico, 22 to Colombia, 26 to Uruguay, from which the shape of things coming could well be inferred.

Although all naval attachés and assistants at the U. S. embassy in Moscow had been additionally designated as "attaché for air," none of us were aviators. So Vice Admiral John McCain, the flyer's airman, decided that the naval delegation in Moscow needed a proper fly boy. A sterling choice was sent, Captain Harry Donald Felt. Small, with sharply cut, handsome features and a trim figure, he was firm and demanding, but with what had to be intuition rather than experience, he hit it off with the Russians right down to the ground.

Don Felt's introduction to the Soviet scene was an eye opener. Along with Commander Charles J. Zondorak, my prospective relief, Don flew from Teheran to Moscow in a Soviet plane in wondrous amazement. There were no seat belts. Mounds of baggage and packages were not tied down. People and cases of Iranian vodka jammed every bit of space.

Again, the inscrutable Russians performed according to plan. It took 30 days for Felt to get an interview with anyone familar with his trade. Then matters miraculously improved. He was invited to make a trip south to Taganrog, near the Black Sea, to visit a Soviet air base. There, he was the first on record (and as far as can be determined, the last) to get the seat of his pants in the pilot's cockpit of a Stormovik, the sturdy Soviet dive bomber, and fly it. As was generally the case with Soviets in the field, his hosts were overwhelmingly hospitable and open. Clearly, Felt had made a hit. On one occasion when he went out to the men's room, his fellow traveler and interpreter, Lieutenant Joe Chase, overheard the Russians discussing Felt in his absence. The gist of it was that they had expected him to be like a Britisher, austere and hard to talk to. "But he isn't," they agreed. "He's just like a Russian!"

Felt also looked in on the shuttle base at Poltava, although it was purely a U. S. Army Air Force operation. Don was not too impressed with the arrangements on the ground to protect the field, noting that at least two of the defensive fighter pilots were women. His assessment was not far off, as we shall see later. For a month he took over in Archangel, while Jack Harshaw came to Moscow for some repairs to his innards. Most of the ships in the convoys at the time were British. Felt noted with interest that at the Red Navy parties held for the merchant skippers, the two groups didn't mix much.

Through one of the Mokovaya regulars who was connected with the musical world, we gave a little and took a little. The Moscow Symphony was approaching a crisis: their wing collars to go with their nonproletarian tail coats were in near tatters. Could we get them some? As a patriotic Russian, Leila, Curly Cram's girl friend, who accompanied him in duets on the piano and elsewhere, reflected some of the mortification that was felt by those magnificent fiddlers, bassoon artists, and bass drum bashers at this demeaning request from the musical super elite of a great country. But war is war, we told Leila. Indeed it was logical that Soviet tailors should be making something more warlike than wing collars. We would be happy to get them. And wing collars there were, by diplomatic air pouch. If Chief Pay Clerk Lane, ONI's expediter, had time to wonder about this new secret weapon, he was justified.

In return for our largesse, we picked up scintillating bits of intelligence from the musical world. Leila had been at a gathering where the well-known composer Prokofiev was present. He said that he and several of his associates were busy writing up a Soviet anthem to replace the Internationale, France's national anthem and international revolutionary song that in 1917 had been preempted by the Bolsheviks. It was incongruous now that great Russia should be coasting along on somebody else's theme song. Especially if that somebody not only was no longer revolutionary, but entertained a thick overlay of those hated Nazis. Four possibilities that had so far been tried out before the Big Shots all sounded pretty much like the old Imperial, "God Save the Czar." What next? we asked ourselves.

As for our own collar problem, we solved it with paper ones for our blue uniforms. Sam Frankel, the irrepressible practical joker, sent half a dozen of them to the Spasso laundry, where they of course disintegrated into mush, to the utter horror of the help.

Continuing past practice, FDR was acting as his own secretary of state, relying heavily on the Navy communication system and ciphers. Now that we Navy types no longer enjoyed the intimacy of the Spasso mess as we did in the Standley days, we still were able to keep in the know via the message files. Such juicy items, for example, as Stalin's having declared that, "They [the Germans] are fools to have attempted a great war without a great fleet." He added that he also had in mind a merchant fleet, which of course could not exist without a great navy. Here, indeed, was a blueprint for the future. Harriman wanted to get back to Washington, having messaged Harry Hopkins, FDR's alter ego, that with the end of the war in sight relations with the Soviets had taken a startling turn, evident during the last two months. "They have held up our requests with complete indifference to our interests and have shown an unwillingness even to discuss pressing problems . . . There is every indication the Soviet Union will become a world bully wherever their interests are involved."*

As late as October 1944 there is documentary evidence that Roosevelt (and Harriman in return) did much of their communicating via the Navy's facilities. "For speed, security, and your convenience," Harriman radioed FDR, "I have been using your Navy channel of communications for all reports both political and military of the Prime Minister's visit here." Then he plaintively added as a postscript what clearly indicated the dicky seat to which the State Department had been relegated: "May I assume that Secretary Hull is being kept informed?"†

At the other end of our Russian world, Vladivostok, Lieutenant Commander George Roullard, stout fellow that he was, seldom complained or called for help. In his clandestine role as consulate general clerk, he and his little band of four or five marooned Americans were not relieved of boredom by the intense activity and fairly free contact with Russians that were enjoyed by the Murmansk and Archangel contingents. Their freedom of action and association were tightly constricted, 19 kilometers from the city being the limit of their travels.

The majority of vessels carrying Lend-Lease cargo to Vladivostok were Soviet, so that no liaison efforts were required. However, on one occasion Roullard prevailed on his Soviet Navy contact, a very decent chap, to allow him to visit one of these Soviet vessels. They embarked in a Red Navy

Foreign Relations, 1944, vol. 4, p. 988.
†Ibid., p. 1010.

Lieutenant George Roullard in civvies and beard at Vladivostok. This photo was used on his official Soviet identification papers until after the USSR declared war on Japan. He was then allowed to wear his uniform, but was severely restricted in his movements in the Vladivostok area and was always kept under surveillance.

barge, really smart looking, although they could just as well have made the trip by motor car to the ship's dock. Obviously they wanted to do it up right, complete with sideboys, even though the ship was civilian-manned.

George was ushered into the captain's cabin where the Old Man was chatting with his wife and some civilian visitors. The routine pouring of vodka immediately commenced, complete with sakuska, fruit, and American chocolate. In short order the vodka carafe was empty. "We've sampled the contents of No. 1 hold," said the skipper. Now they would try No. 2. It then developed that the ship was loaded with "spirt," grain alcohol. After the sample of hold No. 3, feeling no pain, George inquired just how many holds there were in the ship. Whatever the number, (he understandably never could later recall how many), he was assured that since he was inspecting the ship, it was, of course, expected that he would sample them all. By this time, both consulate personnel and Red Navy staff on shore were commencing to worry over George's long absence . . . and that of their flag barge. The party was at last broken up when a couple of NKVD lads came aboard to request that George accompany them back to the consulate in their car, while the liaison officer took home the boat. It was one of those rare occasions when George was genuinely happy to see the NKVD. As for the "spirt," it was in due course offloaded into tank cars, eventually to be cut with water and aged ten minutes to become vodka for the parched throats of comrades all the way west to Lake Baikal.

As for Roullard's throat, it was doing very well, thank you. The Vladivostok consulate general was allowed occasional shipments of foodstuffs, clothing, and other supplies, including alcoholic beverages, shipped via Soviet vessels along with Lend-Lease cargo. The R. C. Williams Co. in New York, purveyors of comestibles to the embassy for some years, informed their customers when, in that era of general scarcity, some choice items were available. Such was the case with a large stock of Corgo brandy they had acquired. At that time there were about ten on the consular staff, so each ordered from four to six cases. Time passed, and as people were transferred, each would jokingly say, "Goodby, Roullard. If that Corgo brandy ever arrives, you may have my share." More time passed, more people were transferred, until one fine day the Soviet customs people phoned that they had 50 cases of brandy for the Consulate General. Please pick it up at once, as they were concerned over pilferage. That is how Roullard came onto a rather large stock of drinkables.

Roullard essentially was a proper Navy man of action, wanting to get out and do things as he had in Archangel, where he had been boarding ships, untangling Red tape, greeting Russian friends, even to the point (by his own admission) of becoming mildly pro-Soviet. Vladivostok changed all that; he was, in effect, under close to house arrest. What of another view? Vice consul McCargar had arrived in the USSR about the time I did. In Moscow he joined me in squiring Vasya and Zena around. Then he was transferred to Vladivostok. Mac was liberal, aesthetic, mildly scoffing at authority and decorum, all quite the antithesis of a professional military man. What did *he* think of Vladivostok? He wrote me from what he called, "the timeless land." His doctor there had ordered him to live quietly for a while. Mac told him he thought he could arrange that, as his visit to him had been the first really sound cause for him to get out of bed since arriving. "Actually, the staff of the American Consulate General does get up every morning, but they're not fooling anybody." Mac wrote. "Since there is no hot water or heat in the building, we may even dispense with getting up during the winter."

Continuing, he said that, "The situation is rather peculiar here, and calls for considerable resourcefulness and morale. The town itself is on the whole very pleasant. It is an interesting place. You have the feeling that perhaps after all there is a lot of life here, and you want to get out into it. You want to know what is going on, who all the people are. You'd like to smile with the girls and argue with the men. But you're stopped. It's like seeing Vladivostok through some tourist's camera, having just that much depth and warmth. You're forbidden to go here. To go there. People are afraid to talk to you. 'Bzzzz . . . Eugenia Semyenova got ten days on a Kolkhoz for walking down Leninskaya with Joe Blow from the American consulate.' etc. etc."

"There is very little to do. Some work in the office, swimming if the weather is good, an occasional ride in one of Ward's [the consul general] boats. Maybe a trip to the 19th kilometer, which is as far as we are permitted to go. Like a damn fool I sit out here thinking that somehow, someday I'm going to get some good information, or be able to write a good report. . . . "

His trip out had been a mixture of boredom and interest in a different way of life. He had got to know everybody in the international car excepting an Air Force major general, who carefully avoided him, although he did send a warning to Mac to keep his door locked. Midway across Russia, vodka went on sale in the dining car; producing a riot. Windows were broken, doors torn off, and a bust of L. M. Kaganovich knocked from its niche over his quotation that Soviet citizens traveling on trains had the duty of preserving genuine Soviet culture. Only one man was wounded. No dead.

16 / *Homeward Bound*

It was time to go home. Zondorak had been on hand to relieve me long since, while the Navy Department, on Admiral Olsen's urging, allowed me to delay and delay, hoping that OVIR, the Bureau of Visas and Registration, would give Vlada her exit visa in time to accompany me. The embassy had made overtures to this end over the preceding six months. Finally, my departure date at last set for early June, Minister-Councillor Maxwell Hamilton had a long chat with Vishinsky on the subject.

Such cases should be taken up via OVIR, said Vishinsky. That is precisely what Admiral Olsen had done, replied Hamilton, but they had informed Olsen that they could not receive foreigners; that one should apply to the Foreign Office, which he, Hamilton, was now doing. What were the underlying Soviet concepts concerning denaturalization of Soviet citizens, Hamilton wanted to know. He said he would like to turn aside for the moment the particular case of Mrs. Tolley and speak in generalities as man to man.

Vishinsky let his hair down to an extent unusual for this scourge of Russians of questionable reliability. His neat grey mustache, horn-rimmed glasses, and rather handsome, kindly looking grandfatherly face belied a nature that was anything but. Perhaps Mr. Hamilton would be interested in the historic background, said Mr. Vishinsky. At the time of the Revolution, he continued, many of the upper classes and a large part of the aristocracy had fled abroad, as had been the case in the French Revolution. Emigrant circles had grown up in neighboring countries that had been inimical to France in the nineteenth century and to the Soviet Union in the twentieth century. This had had much influence in shaping Soviet traditions and thinking on the subject. Hamilton was grateful, he said, for these views. The reverse was true in the United States, he added. It was easy to divest one's self of American citizenship, but difficult to acquire it. Vishinsky apparently was pleased at this admission, welcoming Hamilton's candidness. Now, continued Vishinsky, saying he was speaking entirely unofficially and on a personal basis: after the Russian Revolution, living conditions were extremely difficult in the Soviet Union, demanding much suffering, toil, and sweat. Some people had tried to avoid this work of building up the Soviet state by marriage to a foreigner, many of whom had come to the USSR as engineers, a number turning out to be saboteurs. (Vishinsky had tried some of them.) Those women who married foreigners for the sole purpose of getting out of the USSR were looked on with contempt as shirkers. Certain laws were passed in this atmosphere, with traditions deeply ingrained. They were difficult to change quickly. The real test, Vishinsky concluded, was, had the marriage been culminated because of love—or a desire to divest one's self of citizenship?*

After passing on to me the details of his chat with Vishinsky, Hamilton had an afterthought: "By the way, Commander Tolley," he inquired. (He was a stiffly formal fellow, addressing me by rank.) "*What* does 'D-Day' mean?" Obviously the date of launching the invasion of *Festung Europa* had been received and was imminent. It had not appeared in message traffic, so such a colossal super secret must have come by other means. We had already warned the Soviets that the Germans were reading some of their top codes, and we probably suspected they might be having equal success with ours.

The second of June was a very special day, marking the first flight of U.S. heavy bombers, 73 of them, using the Poltava shuttle base on which such enormous effort and persuasion had been exerted—thousands of tons of marston matting, gasoline, spares, bombs. Lieutenant General Ira Eaker, Commander of Allied Air Forces, Mediterranean, accompanied the flight, then attended a huge party given by the Harrimans for Soviet officers involved in the project. It was probably the high point of the whole war in U.S.-Soviet relations. Eaker had brought along top American decorations for the Air Force chief, Marshal Novikov, and the project officer and air staff operations officer, Colonel General Nikitin. Both were prime favorites of General Deane, especially Nikitin, who in his estimation was top Russian of all he had known. From the first night he met them, Deane was sold. "I found [them] as well as the entire air staff, sympathetic to and understanding of our problems and willing to stick their necks out as far as they dared to help solve them.†

I had already left Russia when the sad blow fell on the night of 21–22 June 1944. A German snooper had followed a group back to Poltava that

**Foreign Relations*, vol. 4, p. 878.

†John R. Deane, *The Strange Alliance* (New York: The Viking Press, 1947), p. 108.

afternoon. At midnight, a huge flare dropped on the field lighting it up like day. Then for two hours the Germans bombed and strafed. Fifty U.S. heavy bombers were destroyed. Lacking radar, both the Russian AA and night fighter defenses failed miserably. Not a single enemy plane was brought down by the 28 thousand medium and heavy AA rounds or the 4 out of 50 YAK fighters that managed to get aloft. This was the end of the shuttle project. Eighteen strong attacks had been made on important targets that otherwise would have been immune. But with the front rapidly moving westward, the bases were becoming too far behind the lines. The whole affair was a glowing lesson in Russian psychology. For those who do not read General Deane's book, it is educational to set down his views on the Poltava experience, as a guide to the future.

> Starting with Novikov, Nikitin, the entire air staff, and extending down to the women who laid the steel mat for our runways, we encountered nothing but a spirit of friendliness and co-operation. We lived, planned, worked and played together—the only discordant notes being those struck from above which perforce reverberated below. Starting in the other direction and working on up through the General Staff, the NKVD, the Foreign Office and the party leaders who lurk behind the scenes as Stalin's closest advisers, we found nothing but a desire to sabotage the venture which they had reluctantly approved.*

This was the pattern as predictably uniform as that on a roll of wallpaper. The weather exchange, commencing in the winter of 1943–44, so strongly pushed by Captain Knoll and his Soviet opposite number, Lieutenant General E. K. Feodorov, a most likable and cooperative chap, was doomed from the start simply because the top political echelon saw nothing in it for the USSR except prying American eyes. There was no definite, "Nyet!" but the same sort of roadblocks and obfuscation in providing visas, communications, priority for shipment of equipment, accommodations, and access to instant decision makers. With the exception of Stalin himself, whose frankness bordered on brutality, straight answers were in short supply in Moscow.

In early June 1944, almost exactly two years after setting down at Baku for a welcoming breakfast of boiled plums, I was back again, after two adventurous years, on my way out. My seat mate was a good friend, twenty-year-old son of the Iranian amabassador at Moscow, Johnny Ahi. During the night's layover, we spent the evening at the opera, where as had been the case a year earlier with Admiral Duncan, I was the center of attention, sitting in a box just off the stage dressed in that short-lived

*Ibid., p. 124.

creation of Admiral Ernest J. King, the "stack-color gray" uniform. In Russian eyes the only gray uniform under the 1944 sun was German.

Teheran was a far cry from its lethargic 1942 format, when I had been stared at in my khakis and helmet liner headpiece. Now, foreigners and jeeps were everywhere, Americans and Russians predominating. Motor cars required constant guarding; a tire brought one thousand of those specially marked dollars that could not be spent in the United States. Soviet roubles were available by the suitcase full at 75 to the dollar, versus the diplomatic rate of 12 to 1 or the official rate of 5 to 1. The only trick was getting them into the USSR, which a number of the lesser embassies were known to be doing via diplomatic pouch.

As time passed in the USSR, we all had become accustomed to the austerity and drabness of life, forgetting the openness of the Outside, so that on arrival at Teheran it was like climbing up from a dank, dark, spider-webbed cellar into the pure sunlight of a world where birds sang, flowers bloomed, and people had smiles on their faces as they laughed and talked on the street. My first night at the hotel was one of reveling in the ability to sit at a real bar, pay real money, and get a real drink; in being able to look out over a sea of tables filled with U.S. Army nurses in chic uniforms, laughing, dancing with whomever asked among the passers-through—officers with the Persian Gulf Command, aviators delivering planes, transients such as myself.

"I've spoken to exactly two American girls in the last two years," I said, approaching a table of four or five laughing and joking nurses. "Could I just sit down and say nothing; just listen to you all for a while?" It was such an experience for me that the name of my neighbor still sticks: Miss Tripodi, lieutenant, a black-haired, black-eyed, striking, dark-skinned, buoyant Italian girl from New York with a most delicious Bronx accent that was more beautiful to me at the time than music from Heaven.

For two years I had not had an orange or banana, moved without the specter of the NKVD always in the shadows, or seen a bright advertising sign. To hell with the war! I was going to take a vacation after two years without one. This was June. My ship, the fast battleship *North Carolina*, to which I had been ordered as navigator, was overhauling at Bremerton, Washington, not ready to sail until September.

That first night in the hotel bar at Teheran was an emotional experience. Not generally known as a sentimental type, it was a reaction attributable only to an abrupt switch in scenery. Perhaps it was the *smell*, an *American* smell—of feminine perfume, Camel and Lucky Strike and Chesterfield cigarette smoke instead of Russian mahorka, a hum of conversation akin to that in a stateside restaurant, calls of, "waiter!" instead of "boy," or "ofitsiant," or "garçon." My God! What was it all about? *America*! How I *loved* it. I can recall only two times in my life experiencing such overwhelming sentiments. One had been aboard the cruiser USS *Houston* moored in Shanghai's Whangpoo. Steaming in from sea, the big old Navy transport USS *Henderson* hove around the bend, past the long line of foreign merchant ships. Her bright new set of oversize colors whipped in the wind against the dirty, leaden Chinese sky. As she drew almost abeam of *Houston*, the thin, shrill call of the bugler sounded "Attention," followed by one blast for "Hand salute." Then the *Houston*'s band burst forth in a crashing rendition of the "Star Spangled Banner." It was a thrilling piece of America. The *Henderson*'s rail was lined with green-clad U.S. Marines, replacements for the 4th Regiment, Shanghai's pride. Yes, I had felt like that then.

The second time was in Manila, the occasion a full-dress military ball held at the huge Santa Ana cabaret, the only place in town big enough for such an event. Big as half a football field, Santa Ana sparkled with Chinese lanterns, the hall ringed by tables filled with merrymakers. Then came the *pièce de resistance*, about two hundred Filipinos, officers from the Philippine Scouts in full evening dress of white mess jackets, dark trousers striped with corps colors: infantry blue, cavalry yellow, artillery red. Gold epaulettes, buttons, and medals shot back points of light. Their ladies were in the sweeping, bouffant-sleeved ball gowns patterned on Spanish court costumes of two centuries earlier. They were doing a sort of mass quadrille, the orchestra playing a selection that rolled like peals of musical thunder off the vaulted ceiling. Looking down from the balcony on this magnificent scene, my heart welled up. It was with the same thoughts that must have come to many a Britisher over the centuries. For me, that thought was, "This is our Empire—a powerful, unstoppable empire—*the American Empire!!*" Such, one supposes, are the dreams and thoughts of glory that strike us all under one circumstance or another, tightening our throats, filling our hearts with pride and our eyes with tears.

Johnny Ahi and friends took me in charge the next busy week. We made excursions into the dusty countryside by day, and partied by night at the homes of wealthy Iranians. All spoke English, French, or Russian. Magnificent rugs sometimes were piled six deep on a floor. "That is our bank account," explained Johnny. "In good times we buy more rugs. In bad times we sell them."

On one such evening I had drawn out two U.S. Army jeeps from Camp Amirabad. Driving the lead jeep on the way home, I noticed that the second jeep, Johnny driving, was no longer following, an awareness that came naturally after several years of NKVD tailing. So turning back with my two or three Iranian passengers, we found Johnny and his jeepload stopped by two Russian soldiers, rifles in hand. Johnny's Russian was perfect, but he was getting nowhere with these two obviously dangerously drunken peasants in baggy Red Army blouses and clumsy boots. They wanted to go to the railroad station and they wanted that jeep.

"It's just some damned foreign general," one said to the other, noting my gold chin strap. (In the USSR, only flag and general officers wore gold chin straps.) "Get those Iranians out of there!" shouted one of the soldiers to Johnny, thrusting his gun muzzle in the direction of the several terrified girls in the jeep. The two soldiers obviously were in no mood to be pushed around. "Look here, comrades," I said calmly. "I just came from Moscow. I know how splendid is the morale of the real *frontovik*. You are *frontoviki*. Death to the Germans, but for our friends and allied, *ourah!*. I'm your friend. The Iranians are helping us. You do not fight your friends. What would Comrade Stalin think?" The soldiers turned toward each other. "Did you hear what he said, Ivan Pav'lich? He called us 'comrade!' " They let their rifle butts drop to the ground. "We are sorry," one said. "We didn't know you were friends," and stuck out a calloused paw in firm handshake.

The Soviets themselves took a dim view of peccadillos on the part of their people. Not long before our own little encounter, a Soviet officer had been caught raising hell in a restaurant, threatening to shoot up the place. An American military patrol subdued him, then handed him over to the sentries at the Soviet embassy gate. Next day the Americans sent word to the Soviets that they didn't intend to press charges. "That's immaterial now," they replied. "The offender died in his cell last night."

Judging from the fairy tales of my youth, Baghdad had to be an exotic spot: curved daggers in the market, lightly veiled dancing girls, flying carpets. The Baghdadi houri from that Manchurian train, "Nefertiti," came to mind—green eyes, long neck, high cheek bones glowing with color. Not an Iraqui at all, but a Baghdadi just the same, probably the descendant of a Khazar princess sent down from the Volga to the harem of the Caliph in the eleventh century. Or, less in the realm of fancy, granddaughter of a Jewish family down from Imperial Russia a hundred years ago, but yet, like most Russian Jews, of Khazar origin—people who galloped in from the Asian unknown before the word "Russia" was invented, drinking their horses' blood, black beards flying in the wind. In Teheran, lying back in the bunk after a night on the town, strains of semi-oriental music filtering through the open window, it was easy to dream up dreams like that. Obviously, Baghdad would be the next stop. It was more or less to westward, the direction I was headed.

The British military transport plane taking me to Baghdad was loaded with assorted boxes, bales, and military personnel strung out in bucket seats the length of the cabin. On one side of me sat a British lieutenant colonel, on the other a WAAF (Women's Auxiliary Air Force), a pink-cheeked, busty, no-nonsense beauty of the type one saw pictured in hunting kit in British sports magazines, striding over the moors, exercising a pack of eager beagles.

It was almost impossible to talk over the roar of the motors in the thin air. We were at well over ten thousand feet, clearing the mountains in what must have been an unpressurized cabin. As we progressed, it seemed our WAAF had assumed a most casual, un-British position, torso between knees, head almost at deck level. My! what a sound sleeper, I thought to myself. Poor kid probably had a rough send-off last night. Then it dawned on me she had passed out from lack of oxygen. The colonel and I stretched her on deck, head downhill, unbuttoned her blouse and bra and put her arms back over her head. In a few minutes of deeply heaving chest she was awake, somewhat flustered over her state of *déshabille* and where she found herself. She sat up, got things buttoned, then thanked us veddy, veddy much, having assured herself that we were indeed the two good Samaritans who were responsible for the striptease.

As we coasted downhill to heavier air, I was able to communicate more easily with the colonel. My plans were to stay at the U.S. legation, I told him. But in the event the minister was out of town, I would go to a hotel.

Where was he staying? "At the Miramar Hotel," he replied.

"Perhaps I could stay there too, if my plans fall through," I said.

"Oh, no! I'm sorry you can't do that," he answered, in the most perfect, clipped Sandhurst English. "You see, I'm an Indian, with the Indian Army forces. We have our own hotels. The British officers have theirs. It would not be considered proper for you to stay at the Miramar."

I realized then that his deep tan was not from the desert sun.

Happily, Minister Loy Henderson was "in residence." He picked me up at the airport after a telephone call to the legation. Then we rode through rows of low, white-walled, flat-roofed houses sprawled helter-skelter along the dusty streets to the legation, a serene, garden-surrounded sanctuary that looked a little more like some of those tales of Scheherazade.

Loy was burning for news, isolated as he was in a sort of diplomatic backwash. While in Washington and Moscow, his straight talk on the Soviet specter's increasing loom had been felt by the administration to be against the best interests of Russo-American amity. In the old days, a troublesome diplomat or politician could always be appointed as envoy to China or Russia. This convenient deep freeze no longer pertaining, Iraq was a "safe" post for such a potentially obstreperous fellow as Henderson.*

Loy was greatly disturbed about the turn of events in the Middle East *vis-à-vis* the Russians, very soon in the game having read the signs,

*Later ambassador to India, ambassador to Iran, see, *Who's Who* for a dossier on a man with probably greater experience in Russian and Middle Eastern affairs than any living American—at the time of this writing, over 90 and very much alert.

reinforced by conversations with the Iraqui foreign minister. The latter had assured him Iraqui patience was wearing thin and that the Iraquis would turn to Russia if we persisted in our pro-Zionist course. Henderson was so fearful that his alleged anti-Russian reputation in Washington would lead them to believe his reporting suggested a Russian conspirator under every bed that he sent off a personal telegram to "Dear Wallace" (Murray, Chief of the Middle East Section, Department of State) explaining that his dispatches voiced not only his opinion, but the joint views of his own staff plus those of the local OSS, OWI, and military attaché. The Soviet game, said Loy, was to detach the Arabs and their oil from the Anglo-American camp, but he feared his warnings were only a thin voice from the far wilderness.

While I was having these fascinating discussions with the United States's best Russian expert, we learned that by now Max Hamilton in Moscow must have got the full import of what D-Day meant; the Allies had landed in Normandy. If I was not to miss the war, it behooved me to get going.

Roughly 500 miles west of Baghdad lies Damascus, oldest continuously occupied city in the world. About 1934 the French had established a motor bus route across the desert. There was no road most of the way, only cairns of stones to mark the track along camel trails worn by the feet of animals and Arabs for millenia.

The British chaps responsible for transportation at Baghdad were reluctant to charge my $230 bus fare to reverse Lend-Lease. Clearly, a bird in hand, feathered with dollars was preferable to one in the Lend-Lease bush. But protestations of poverty, appeals to brotherhood, and downright shaming them at last prevailed. I walked out with a ticket aboard one of the biggest buses in the world—70 feet long, 11 feet high, articulated amidships with a tractor up forward. There was storage for 15,000 pounds of baggage for first- and second-class passengers in air-conditioned comfort. There was a pilot, copilot, and a third driver in rotation, plus steward and conductor. One could loll back in the luxury of reclining seats or call for a table at mealtime or for games. Huge balloon tires carried the vehicle so steadily that wine rode safely in wide-bottomed glasses. It took about 24 hours for the crossing, most of it through desert scrub.

Damascus had been badly mauled in the fighting between Vichy French and de Gaulle's Free French forces, who captured it in June 1941, but things had long since been set to rights. The Street Called Straight, mentioned in the Bible (Acts 9:11), a mile-long corridor roofed over with sheet iron to protect it from the broiling summer sun, had been restored and was swarming with peddlers, merchants, shoppers, idlers, and at least one tourist, myself. Stacks of rugs, showcases of curved, inlaid daggers, ancient coins, filigree silver-work, copper, jewels, medals, and orders from the Imperial age in Europe, gold, richly embossed leather, all to be haggled for over small cups of sweet, bitter coffee. My purchases were modest: a filigree silver dish and a red fez with black tassel, ample excess baggage for a recent bachelor traveling light. The whole picture could have been 1944, 1044 or 0044. The only incongruous note for the earlier dates would have been the occasional soldier in modern khaki, with an almost modern rifle.

The lingua franca was French, the hotel luxurious, the food and wine Parisian. A guide hired for the day at a piddling price took me to an Arab cafe for lunch. The musicians had been twiddling and tootling away on their instruments for a long while, assailing the ear with the most dreadful squeals and clangs. "When are they going to quit tuning the instruments and play something?" I asked my guide. "They have been playing Arab songs all the while, Monsieur!" he replied in an injured voice, sipping away on a "raki," a licorice-flavored concoction that turned milky like wood alcohol when mixed with water and tasted very much like cough medicine.

Clearly, help was cheap. It was more convenient to take a taxi the fifty miles to Beirut, Lebanon, than fly. A daylight trip over the jagged mountains provided superb sight-seeing, plus solid confirmation that Arabs definitely were sold on the theory of fatalism, judging by the character of the driving.

Beirut was far more French than Damascus, the Lebanese more French than French themselves in their abbreviated bathing suits, their flashing eyes, and bubbling gayety. Dark-eyed, mascaraed, bright-cheeked girls at boardwalk cafe tables made extravagant Gallic gestures to emphasize their chatter in liquid French, all the while flirting outrageously with everybody around. "Don't tangle with the local damsels unless you've plenty of money to spend!" advised an old pro at the British resident detachment. "This place is not just gold plated. It's solid eighteen carat. Banking center of the Arab world. Specie covering of its currency highest on earth outside Switzerland. So just look and enjoy."

Hops to interesting places down the coast were conveniently spaced at 50-mile intervals: Tyre, Haifa, Tel Aviv, Jerusalem. Tel Aviv was worth two or three days luxuriating on the sun-drenched beaches, having a fill of those luscious Jaffa oranges. British units were in each city, allocating quarters to transients and giving fatherly advice on the wide prevalence of venereal disease, fast buck artists, and even faster women. It was a favorite recreation area for His Majesty's forces in Africa and the Middle East.

On the Tel Aviv beaches, sturdy Jewish girls gamboled and swam, laughing and shouting in many languages—German, French, Arabic, Hebrew, Polish, Russian, English—a polyglot nation-to-be like our own once was.

Along with many other khaki-uniformed men and women, I made the 14 stations of the Cross. One was reminded in a mild fashion of the taunts, jibes, and thrusts received by an earlier traveler that way by the heckling of the multitude of would-be guides, touts, peddlers, beggars, and others who impeded one's progress.

At the King David Hotel, later to be blown up by Menachim Begin's terrorists, I encountered one of those rarest of God's creatures, a girl whose pulchritude rates 4.0 on a scale of 4. There had been only two others before her in my wanderings: Natalie Synnerberg, daughter of the Finnish manager of the Palace Hotel in Shanghai, and Linnu Toom, an Estonian. Natalie was so beautiful it was embarrassing to take her to a public place; stares and open-mouthed silence accompanied her passage. As for Linnu, there was equal frustration. I was stag-lining it in the Tallinn Yacht Club. After the fashion of those parts, I went to the table where she was sitting and asked her escort for permission to invite her to dance. He replied to my Russian in excellent English. Standing up rather unsteadily, he said that something had disagreed with him to the point he felt quite ill. Would I please be so kind as to sit with his lady while he went out for some fresh air? He obviously was Jewish, certainly not drunk, but clearly in distress.

I sat down with gratitude in my heart that the Good Lord had made Jews, like Japanese, a race not well known for an ability to handle strong drink. Then I looked across at that vision of loveliness, first trying Russian. Then French. Then English. Woe and alack! Her languages were Estonian and German only. We danced in silence or sat at the table where I sweated out what little German I could muster, phrase book sentences designed to keep the traveler fed, bedded, and watered in the Nazi Reich, my headquarters. Then her escort came back, refreshed and grateful, while I withdrew with mixed emotions. Our friendship, if not romance, sputtered on a few months via mail, in German, through the sympathetic help of my Riga landlady, an impoverished old Baltic baroness, her prose probably inspired by memories of her own youthful loves. Then the correspondence languished, fading into memory.

Now, here was Number Three, receptionist at the King David, 4.0, a blonde, blue-eyed Jewish goddess whose fetching accent in English caused me to ask more questions than I really needed answers for. That is the end of the story. As a happily married man, the trail stopped there. It was on to Cairo!

There was no desert bus to Cairo, so I flew. Certain hotels stick in one's memory, through personal experience or their having been a major prop in some very special movie: the Wagon-Lits in Peking, the Palace in Shanghai, Hongkong's staid Peninsular, Singapore's Raffles. In Cairo it was Shepheard's, since burned and rebuilt. On its wide, open porch all the important people in Egypt, if not the world, could at some time or another be expected to pass, including the Egyptian king, Farouk. I shared a huge room with a British colonel, a red-tabs—staff officer, complete with military mustache, pink cheeks, and swagger stick. Mosquito nets as big as squad tents were draped over the king-sized beds at night, revolving overhead fans swishing and creaking in the darkness, lulling one to sleep.

Conviviality was the watchword on the verandah, where all gathered for a whiskey & splash at sunset. The colonel was sympathetic with my having just come out of two years of near exile—no newspapers, no radio, our only source of world happenings month-old copies of news magazines, which if their general coverage matched their reporting of the Russian scene, must have been largely fantasy.

The colonel briefed me in clipped, staccato sentences, like machine-gun bursts of words, with thoughtful pauses between while he sucked his briar or had a sip of drink.

"We've had to keep a blahdy good rein on the Wogs," he said, referring to our Egyptian hosts. "They have a tendency to jump in bed with the victors (Pause, Puff! Puff!)—place full of intrigue, lot of German sympathy in the black days of Rommel." King Farouk was not his hero. "The blighter has a keen eye for the ladies," said the colonel. (Puff!) "Was bellied up to the bar in some posh bistro a while back—sidled over to try on a chat with a good-looking Yank nurse—then he pinched her fanny or squeezed her titty or some such; chap with her, Ameddican bloke, let the old boy have it right in the chops—knocked him flat on his fat arse. Haw! Haw! Blahdy good shaow, that!"

The Yanks were catching on, he thought. Took a "blahdy good pasting" at Kasserine Pass, though, before they got the hang of it. "Those Heinies are no blahdy patsies, y'know!" Yes, the Yanks were an irreverent lot when it came to protocol, and a bit informal with rank. "But not a *patch* on those blahdy Aussies! God! Those Aussies! What a caution! Did more damage to Cairo than the Huns and their bombs. Pub owners quailed at sight of them. But what scrappers! Absolute wildcats."

The colonel was a strong proponent of moving into the Balkans. The British had agents all over the place, he said. It was superb guerrilla country, where every man was a stout ally against the Huns. If we didn't take it, the Rooskies would, and they'd never let it go. "Your man Roosevelt wants to move into southern France," the colonel complained. "He simply hasn't got the long view. Believes everything that blackguard Stalin tells him." (Red-tabs must have picked up some of the fallout from the Teheran conference.)

As for the "Eyeties," those "spaghetti benders," the colonel had only scorn and derision. "Jolly decent chaps personally," he admitted, "and a few damned gutsy ones—frogmen, for example, but pity any race that could put up with that clown Mussolini." This reminded him of a story told of a pre–World War II dinner, where Churchill was conversing with Hitler's bully-boy foreign minister von Ribbentrop, a pure straight-man. "Ah! Things will be different in the *next* war!" Boasted von Ribbentrop. "In the next war the Italians will be on *our* side!" Churchill's best pixy grin appeared. "That is only fair, Herr von Ribbentrop," he said. "*We* had to take them in the *last* war."

The colonel had a good laugh at his own joke, then reddened. "That pig von Ribbentrop! That wretched champagne salesman turned diplomat. Do you know what he did? When he was received in formal audience by the king, he marched up the red carpet, stopped three times, and each time he stopped he stuck up his hand in a Nazi salute and yelled, 'Heil Hitler!' "

Like almost everything else, Red-tabs had strong views on the French. There weren't many of them around Cairo, which suited him just fine. They were a money-grubbing, grasping lot, he thought, reflecting on his Paris holidays in prewar days. "What can you expect of anybody who refuses to speak English?" he said indignantly. "They are constantly at loggerheads with themselves and everybody else. I've never seen any two French officers in identical uniforms. They can't even agree on *that*." I don't believe he was really angry about it all. Rather more sympathetic toward a race he felt had fallen on bad times, and whose shortcomings could be endured as one does the tantrums of children. In time, all these things pass.

Also in Cairo was a genial U.S. Navy Reserve commander, who in civilian life had been a "bone digger." His primary assignment was squiring VIPs to the pyramids and like curiosities, explaining with an archeologist's expertise what it was all about. There being no VIPs in town at the moment, he kindly offered to practice on me, a pleasant change, he said, from the princes, generals, senators, presidents, and so forth. They all were sort of uptight, he suspected, never paying much attention to his spiel, generally preoccupied, talking to their accompanying staff about affairs he felt were better discussed in more discreet surroundings. This included not only military matters but areas of Cairo activity about which the less said the better.

For my part, Cairo was "yes" and "no." It was fascinating to hear the commander say that one could scarcely stick a spade in the ground anywhere in upper Egypt without turning up some artifact perhaps a thousand, or even five thousand, years old. On the other hand, there were the flies and the multitude of urchins pestering one to an extent that walking on the street was a burden. It was a standing joke that a couple of German spies beautifully disguised in burnoose and keffiyeh had given themselves away by brushing the flies off their faces instead of allowing them to crawl into ears, nostrils, stomp on eyeballs, or buzz into an open mouth as was the general custom amongst the natives.

Aside from enlightening myself on such intelligence nuggets as the camaraderie of the bars provided, there were several commissions for me to accomplish. Moscow was wholly devoid of any source of feminine unmentionables other than those black atrocities lamented in an earlier chapter. A long list, including dimensions, had been furnished me, items to mail back from Cairo. The several sales ladies in the boutique obviously were curious about the background, delicately avoiding any direct questions, the whole thing probably suggesting a gentleman outfitting his harem. But as an obvious non-Moslem? I wanted to be sure of the sizes, I insisted. These things were going far, far away, to Moscow. "Ah! Indeed!" they chorused, now on safer ground. "Then we must be sure," they agreed. "But what about that bra?" Was I *sure* it was inches and not centimeters? "You stand at the door," one said, "and when somebody passes by who looks like that, sing out." A couple of British WACs meanwhile had popped in. Like any normal woman spotting a male in this singular type of distress, they were all sisterly help, even offering their own rather ample bosoms for comparison, and were rather crestfallen at being counted out. We all stood in the doorway watching the passing throng. "How about *that* one?" hopefully offered one of the WACs. "Not a patch on it." I said. "Blimey!" breathed the WAC. "'E means it!" In due course half a dozen likely candidates, some of them very generously equipped, passed in review. None, however, filled the bill. Or more accurately, the bra, to the extent my memory suggested. You must be right," sighed the saleslady. "It is inches and not centimeters."

As ships pass on the sea, a Moscow-bound officer crossed my course at Cairo: Commander Charles Marmaduke Parker, (MC), prospective relief for Doc Freddy Lang. I had heard of Charles Marmaduke on the Yangtze, where as a gunboat officer he had been learning to play the Chinese flute. The noise emanating therefrom was so devastating that he found it expedient to employ a hole in his stateroom wall that led to an adjoining stateroom, through which the business end of the flute could be thrust. Charles Marmaduke was like that all the way: ebullient, carefree, a bachelor in name and deed. He viewed my purchases with interest as a sound clue on which to build his own collection for whatever emergency that might arise. "You can add something useful to this in Teheran," I advised him. "Take some Iranian vodka with you. It's the only negotiable currency in Russia." Later reports from Moscow suggested that Parker had overshot the mark. Not knowing that an Iranian case contains 48 bottles, and that the bottles are liters, he ordered three or four cases delivered to the plane at departure time, too late to amend the lading. He had found the winter warm, I later learned.

Having exhausted Cairo's capabilities, I went down, or rather up, to Alexandria as guest of a British three-striper who was happy to share the lovely war he was fighting with five-shilling-a-bottle scotch while enjoying the gorgeous beaches. The war was already far away, battleship sinkings by Italian frogmen in Alexandria harbor only a memory. It would have been nothing less than gross negligence on my part, I thought, to miss a place named for a man dead over two thousand years ago, with odd bits of that legacy still around.

Algiers, next stop, was a totally European-looking city, climbing in gently rising terraces from the breakwater-enclosed harbor. Streets were wide, well planned, bordered by big, substantial stone and brick buildings. Even the traffic and people on the street looked far more sophisticated than in any city on my route so far.

The place was simply bursting with Allied military. In the hotel dining room, scarcely a chair was empty. The air was smoke-filled, the clientele almost exclusively male, in uniform, mostly Army and Air Force, British, American, and French. Tin hats were lined up on the cloakroom shelves. Americans were in neckties. This was George Patton turf. He had been in this same dining room not long before. Transcending the din, he had cast his piercing, high-pitched voice entirely across that wide space to direct some unfortunate officer to get the hell cracking out of there and put on his necktie, then report himself to headquarters as having done so.

My Naval Academy classmate Commander J.A. "Joe" D'Avi was in port aboard a repair ship. He had resigned a year after graduation, then been recalled during the war. His was the first U.S. warship other than the USS *Milwaukee* at Murmansk that I had laid eyes on in over two years! What a huge treat it was to go aboard for dinner in a quiet, peaceful atmosphere of Navy blue and gold, smell ship smells, climb up on the bridge for a look at new gadgets not yet invented when I last went to sea. Yes, I had better hurry.

If Algiers was a sort of Marseilles, Casablanca was Hollywood movie sets *cum* Palm Beach, *à la Arabie*. Alongside a blue, blue ocean under a turquoise sky, the chalk-white houses stood in fields of green, surrounded by palms. It was easy to see why it was an appropriate place for Ingrid Bergman and Humphrey Bogart.

Fortune smiled my way again; another classmate who had resigned early had been recalled and was now a lieutenant commander in charge of local Allied logistics. This included a chateau of noble proportions for his sole use, with ample guest accommodations. There were servants galore, transportation on call, and membership in the posh swimming club. Thus, when the beaches were too stormy, one would not have to undergo the hardship of being unable to observe lissome bodies in close to the raw as an appetizer for lunch on the terrace nearby.

My friend had spent considerable time in France after resigning, so he was able to communicate freely with the French-speaking-only young lady who went with the chateau. Her hair in bouffant style, chic in dress as just the French can be, piquante in manner, svelte and beautiful, one could only breathe a heartfelt, "Vive la France!" by evening's end. My friend and I agreed that things had come a long way since he and I had sat uncomfortably on the very edges of our chairs at the same table in the Naval Academy mess hall, answering stupid questions put by upper classmen.

17 / *Through the Other End of the Telescope*

Major Andrew Wylie, USMCR, held down the Russian desk in ONI. Descended from that special genus, "The Cliff Dwellers," hereditary Washington society as opposed to the transient political breed, the Wylie clan long had been established in a large red-brick mansion on Thomas Circle, where—other than a couple of well-established family ghosts known to be about—Andrew was the last of the family in residence.

During my month's debriefing in ONI, Andrew very kindly put me up, filling me in meanwhile on his rather adventurous past. Well-heeled in his youth, he had spent considerable time rattling around the planet. After extensive Asian travels, he had wound up in Moscow in the mid-thirties, equipped with a large red beard and a lively curiosity. The U. S. Embassy had signed him on as a sort of doorman, an excellent spot to exercise his interest in intelligence. This had led to further activities along the same lines in the U.S. Marine Corps Reserve, when after about six months he left Moscow for home. Considered slightly eccentric by some, bachelor Andrew and I had established a good rapport through a copious exchange of correspondence, in my case, conveying information better not set down in a formal intelligence report, very much as I had done in China.

I abused Andrew's hospitality only once—by inadvertently revealing to the Soviets his secret weapon. It was at a ceremony at Annapolis, wherein our Navy turned over some torpedo boats to the Soviet Navy. Twelve or fourteen Red Navy officers, some with wives, were at the lunch that followed. Having translated several windy speeches back and forth, I remembered some festive occasions in the USSR where the Russians had grouped together, full of vodka and friendly feelings, to sing folk songs, some rollicking and gay, others brimming with pathos and deep sentiments, reflections of Gypsies, the wild Caucasus, and the wide Russian plain. Our guests accepted with good-humored alacrity the suggestion that they "sing for their lunch." For an hour the Soviet group held us enthralled by those soul-twisting melodies with an ability an outsider never ceases to marvel at—that its being produced by such a scratch group, something that we Americans in the best of our barbershop chorus tradition cannot even remotely approach. One of our own party from Washington was so moved that she could not resist joining. I had taken her to Annapolis on her plea that so far in her ONI experiences she had never met a real, live Soviet. She was a tall, slim Navy lieutenant, Andrew's Russian translator, pert, vivacious Irene Holmes, a Harbin Russian aristocrat who had married a National City Bank man in the thirties. He had died and Irene came to the States, joining the WAVES when war erupted. She was in the same category as our friend Olga in Moscow: a Russian blue-eyed blonde with Chinese features, legacy of the Tartars. Her eyes narrowed to slits when she smiled. Her cheekbones were high and pronounced. Altogether, in her white WAVE uniform she was a stunning girl, speaking fluent Russian, English with a delightful accent, with an ace tennis player's trim figure. I did not dream that a year hence she would be my assistant. The Soviets were entranced and made desperate efforts to induce her to ride back to Washington with them, to no avail. Andrew was furious.

All might have been sweetness and light in Annapolis, with torpedo boats being turned over to the stirring strains of "Stenka Rasin and the Countess," "Dark Eyes," or "On Manchurian Plains" (Russo-Japanese War). But unfortunately the same could not be said for the Soviet Far East.

Why the Soviets were reluctant to allow foreign penetration of their Siberian ramparts might be explained partly by what two adventurous young American sailors discovered. Lieutenant Commander George Roullard, already in the USSR for over four years on the working level, had encountered more Russians under broader circumstances than any single American, his activities stretching from Kuibishev, to Moscow, to Archangel, to Vladivostok. He had got to know all classes and ranks. George was a small-town boy from Idaho. He smiled easily, enjoyed the outdoors, could stand cold weather, and was wholly without pretense, all in all a natural for his assignment. However, patience has its limits. At the end of the line, Vladivostok, patience broke. George's cook had quit for reasons unstated. Preparing his own grub over an electric hotplate, he begged, threatened, and sweet-talked the NKVD and his Red Navy liaison officer to find him a cook and give her the necessary clearance to work for a foreigner, all in vain. "Frankly," he wrote me, "all my time in the great SOVYUN I've never been up against such a bunch of bastards. I'm afraid I turned a bit pink up in Archangel, at least toward the Red Navy, but boy, it is all out of me now. I don't know who I hate the most, the Japs or these guys." George had taken his Archangel translator with him, a most efficient and amiable little Greek-American, Irene Matusis, who claimed American citizenship, but was not allowed by the Soviets to leave the country. Irene disappeared.

George might have been a good hater, but he also was a good sailorman as well as Russian expert. He knew that a letter to the Soviet diplomatic agent would be answered in not less than two weeks, if at all. Any enterprising sailor knows that the way to accomplish anything is to radio your boss that, "Unless otherwise directed, I intend to . . ." Then, straightaway go do it before he has time to reply. So George wrote the dip agent that "If no objection is received by six o'clock this evening, a station wagon, license plate 01-01, in the custody of two Americans will be driven along the Primorsk highway from Vladivostok to the American Weather Central at Khabarovsk." Then he confidently loaded up the Navy's identical second station wagon, license number 01-02, with provisions, spare gasoline, and tires. Next, about 5 P.M. the really Machiavellian touch was laid on; George rushed a note over to the diplomatic agent that, regretfully, a mistake had been made; it was car 01-*02* which would go to Khabarovsk. (Hopefully, the agent would have left for his evening vodka and herring by then.) At 7:30 that evening, Yeoman Ted Grason and Storekeeper Klopovich apprehensively set forth, armed with official Navy orders in English and Russian, plus a *putyovka*, the essential travel permit from one's own organization, impressively embellished with fancy seals and ribbon. They were entering territory where Americans were previously forbidden to go, by means even the Soviets might envy in their deviousness.

As expected, they were soon aware of a little black car following. There was no mistaking the NKVD vehicle, but the fact that there was only one car following suggested that car 01-01 was getting more attention and diverting the effort, although it still was in the garage at the consulate. Once on the open road, the big American car soon shook its watchdog to begin a 450-mile adventure that occupies ten pages of Ted Grason's journal.*

The nub of the whole account is that between two of the major cities in the Soviet Far East, no road in the literal sense existed. Little more than a track wandered unmarked over ramshackle bridges, some in such atrocious condition that detours had to be made by fording streams. Checkpoint hurdles were negotiated sometimes by bluff, sometimes by bribery of cigarettes, all marked by indecision, confusion, and inefficiency on the part of the sentries in the face of an unprecedented situation.

The whole operation was sufficiently Byzantine in its conception and execution, the Soviets so patently gulled, so much face lost, that there were

*An unpublished book manuscript by Theodore Grason.

no repercussions. But the diplomatic agent was not seen again, being replaced by another. As we have mentioned several times before, Soviets who dealt with foreigners were in a high-risk profession. One strike was "out."

Shortly after Roullard's caper in the Far East, his old Archangel/Murmansk boss, Captain Sam Frankel was being mentioned in secret dispatches. When he had been detached at last as officer-in-charge at Murmansk in early 1945, Admiral Golovko in his farewell note expressed his appreciation, enigmatically adding that he could accept his departure with the knowledge that his future assignment would involve their common interest. Shortly thereafter, Sam received an open-ended set of orders authorizing travel "in connection with naval matters, as directed by none other than Admiral Ernest King." The assignment was to proceed to Alaska, join a Colonel Ericson, U.S. Army Air Forces, and a Major General Jones, USA. They would be measured for Soviet uniforms preparatory to entering Siberia for a survey of prospective areas of operation for American air forces in the contemplated opening of hostilities between the USSR and Japan. They could not take a chance on American uniforms; spy reports could bring on a preemptive Japanese strike for which they were not yet prepared. Alas! This bizarre scheme died aborning, as had so many during the "collaboration" of the two wartime allies, a term that one suspects is more appropriate in quotes.

While Frankel and Roullard were engaged in their private hassles with friends, I was occupied by a more serious confrontation against the Japanese. It was war at sea in all its ramifications: wallowing in typhoons, watching great flights of carrier aircraft take off at dawn, then anxiously counting them as they came back hours later, the air waves filled with urgent requests for priority landing from wounded pilots or planes low on gas. Sometimes the sky was laced with a crisscross of tracers converging on kamikazes boring in, with an occasional great geyser of smoke and flame when one crashed on a ship. Off Iwo Jima, we watched through binoculars at Marines a mile away charging Japanese bunkers, while our own 16-inch guns pinpointed Japanese positions with salvos that thumped our chests like a blow of a baseball bat, the air thick with acrid powder smoke. Then the war got closer and closer to Japan, until we were bombarding the very coast itself. This was the enormous Third Fleet: 100,000 men, cruisers, eight battleships, fifteen carriers and dozens of destroyers—the whole formation when in line stretching a hundred miles.

Since the end of 1943 this great fleet, Task Force 58 or 38, same ships but different commander and staff, operated in the Western Pacific. One of its five task groups withdrew in rotation for rest in one of the captured atolls, while the others steamed constantly, six or more weeks at a time, task group by task group, withdrawing from the battle area at weekly intervals to replenish underway from tankers and storeships.

Mail was sporadic. Letters came in batches from Moscow, where the blank, unsmiling faces at OVIR gave the familiar refrain to Vlada: "No, no visa yet. Come back next week." She was living comfortably enough in a hotel, working for OWI, the Office of War Information at the Embassy, subsisting on a Soviet ration card supplemented by the embassy commissary. Jocular friends were cheering her up with reports that the *North Carolina* had run aground, the navigator shot. Tokyo Rose was more explicit; the ship had been sunk at least six times.

In Moscow, with the war receding steadily westward, the tempo of social life had increased. Parties at the various embassies vied with those of the greatly augmented U.S. Military Mission, now with much of its personnel in its own spacious quarters, formerly the residence of the German military attaché. The Mission had formed its own jazz band, widely in demand for affairs at other embassies, carrying the logo, "The Kremlin Crows" on its bass drum head until Molotov himself protested that it be changed. Vlada was widely invited, at one Red Cross party singled out by Yugoslavia's Tito as a dancing partner. He was a fascinating man, light on his feet, she wrote. But like the other war brides, she still awaited most anxiously those weekly visits to OVIR, while apprehensively noting that one by one some of the girls had "gone on visits" not to return.

By April 1945 and the invasion of Okinawa, we had perhaps got a little too cocky. The Japanese fleet had in effect been wiped from the ocean at the June 1944 Battle of the Philippine Sea. But now the kamikazes and *baka* (fool) bombs lethally piloted by suicidal Japanese were starting to rain down.* The action usually began with the sudden crack of a single 5-inch gun, opening fire at perhaps 10,000 years. Two or three more rounds might follow. Then a thunderous crescendo. As the range decreased, the 40-millimeter, then the 20-millimeter joined the chorus, the latter indicating it was high time to take shelter.

But as I said earlier, perhaps we were too cocky. As we majestically approached the coast one day in company with other battleships to bombard shore positions, reports began to come in from picket destroyers that they were under heavy attack by kamikazes, some of them hit, several sinking. More were headed our way. I went out on the open platform abaft the navigation bridge to watch the show, casually failing even to put on a tin hat. From high altitudes the kamikazes started streaking down. The usual tremendous fusillade of tracers and shell bursts filled the sky with smoke

*During this 40-day invasion period, 73 ships were hit by kamikazes, 20 of them sunk, 22 very heavily damaged.

and flame. Then there was an ear-splitting crack, like the sound of thunder from a lightning bolt striking dead close. For several seconds a fog of dust and smoke blotted out the local scene. When the mist cleared, three or four people were grouped around, hands out, braced to catch me when I fell. "What the hell goes on here?" I thought to myself. Then everything turned misty red. Blood had run into my eyes. Reconstructing the picture, a shell, probably five-inch, probably from one of our own ships, had hit a nearby fire control director tower. Shards of steel had sprayed out, from fingernail size to bigger. They had ricocheted around the bridge enclosure, one striking me in the upper forehead, another in the nape of the neck. Like all scalp wounds, both bled profusely. Obviously I had been shot clean through the head, logically concluded the bystanders. How in hell could I continue to stand up? No plan here. Possibly accident. Or Fate. Three others were killed and 44 wounded, some heavily.

In April 1945, spine-tingling news came up from main radio, where our decoding teams broke every message for which we held the key, addressed to us or not. Monster battleship HIJMS *Yamato*, with 18.1-inch guns, a light cruiser, and eight destroyers were headed our way, clearly on a suicide mission. There would at last be a slugging match, the kind that battleships were built for. We left the carriers and peeled off to form a surface battle group with the other heavyweights. *Yamato* was heading straight for Okinawa. (It later was learned she had just enough fuel to get there before ramming herself ashore as a huge, unsinkable floating battery.) Constantly shadowed by submarine and aircraft, *Yamato*'s ever-closing position was plotted on my chartroom situation board. We could hear the hiss of ejection air and slam of dummy projectiles as *North Carolina*'s 16-inch gunners honed their loading skill. With *Yamato*'s superior range and shell weight, early multiple hits on her were imperative. Straight on she came, not even zigzagging. We were closing her and her consorts at close to sixty miles an hour. In a night action it might be anybody's game, this being a type of scrap in which the Japanese had often distinguished themselves. The carriers were rushing north as well, but their reach was longer. Before we could make contact, clouds of planes had torpedoed and bombed the plucky Japanese until only four destroyers were left afloat of that powerful force. It was indeed the end of a great navy that only four years before had ruled the Pacific to the very shores of California.

My own hurt was superficial, soon healed. But *North Carolina*'s was more vital. Without the director tower our invaluable port 5-inch antiaircraft battery was close to wholly ineffective. The war was so far along that *North Carolina* proceeded to Pearl Harbor for repairs unescorted. On board were some 250 officers and men from other ships, passengers going home. Many were survivors from sunken ships, most of them diagnosed as victims of combat fatigue. In outward appearance they seemed normal. But the psychological wounds were deep. At the clang! clang! of the alarm for general quarters drill, even though the war was well astern, our passengers fell apart, diving under tables, screaming incoherently, dashing about aimlessly. And well could we understand. Only two months before, the carrier *Franklin*, steaming just several hundred yards from *North Carolina* was hit by a lone Japanese who dived in out of a cloudy sky. Planes on deck burst into flame as bomb loads exploded with the smoke and fire of an angry volcano. Forced to jump by the fires or blown overboard by explosions, hundred of men in lifejackets bobbed astern in the ship's wake. Others swarmed from below to crowd on the ever more steeply sloping flight deck. By extraordinarily heroic effort, the ship was saved. But like those poor devils riding home with us, many must have received similar psychological scars that would last a lifetime.

The *North Carolina* was back on line by July, ship and ship's company renewed and refreshed, their shooting skill diminished but soon remedied, although airborne targets had become scarce. In fact, opposition at sea had become so feeble that the battleships formed up for night bombardments of shore industrial areas, exercises not without peril from mines or suicide boats such as had been encountered at Okinawa. Apprehensions associated with the foregoing were shared by my faithful steward's mate who brought meals and news of below-deck happenings to my 80-foot high navigation bridge cabin, a sort of eyrie that was my permanent home at sea. He had brought my favorite dessert, a plate of ice cream. "My God, Starling! That must be at least a quart. I can't possibly eat all that!" Not much but his gleaming teeth and the rolling whites of his eyes were visible in the dim twilight. "Commandah, suh!" he explained. "Afteh tonight, maybe you ain't gonna git no mo'. An' anyway, fat men floats bettah!"

Victory in Europe rolled over us without much of a ripple. We had our own private war yet to fight. A million men were mobilizing for Operation Olympic, the assault on Japan. About the only fallout in the Pacific from V-E Day was the addition of some British warships to Task Force 58, released from Atlantic duty to be in on the Pacific kill. But Moscow was different. Even before I left Moscow in June 1944, victory was in the air. All of the increasingly frequent Red triumphs were celebrated in the most spectacular manner with huge fireworks displays. In the still-blacked-out city, the effect was magnificent. Earlier, the fireworks had been augmented by indiscriminate firing, after the trigger-happy Russian fashion, of antiaircraft guns of all calibers, not to mention sentries' rifles and machine guns. This showered the city with shell fragments and bullets that killed a number of entranced citizens, including a couple of generals. The final victory was reported by Vlada as being a day of indescribable joy and

A great victory over the Nazis is celebrated with fireworks in Moscow in 1944. The blacked-out Kremlin is in the foreground, as seen from my apartment window.

elation, city squares packed with people kissing each other and hugging. A spontaneous crowd of several thousand gathered in front of the American chancery under the flag that waved from its balcony outside my old apartment. Several American officers who appeared on the street were tossed in the air by the wildly cheering mob, then passed over the heads of the crowd on willing hands.

In the first days of August, the Task Force, busy softening up the island of Kyushu, received a mysterious directive to withdraw 350 miles off the coast and cease all air operations. Speculation was imaginative. Some suggested we had brought out a quantity of German V-2 rockets from Okinawa for a mass bombardment of the home islands. Others guessed that the Japanese had come up with some fantastic weapon. Then on 6 August we got news that chilled one's blood. Mankind had just entered a new and terrifying age. With mixed awe, horror, perhaps even a little grim elation, we learned that a single bomb had wiped out an entire city with most of its population.

From then on, the war was all downhill. Lengthy English language broadcasts from Japan no longer featured the dulcet voice of Tokyo Rose announcing the loss of one or another American ship for the umpteenth time. In the tortured syntax of a language that avoids saying "yes" or "no," it was clear that the game was up. The war wound down with a whimper, even a bit of humor. "If any Japanese planes appear," personally broadcast Admiral "Bill" Halsey, Commander Task Force 58, "shoot them down in a friendly way."

Something like a kid being yanked from the table just before dessert, I was ordered detached from the *North Carolina* a week before she entered Tokyo Bay for the surrender ceremony. Climbing down at last from the foremast to join the wardroom crowd for dinner, it was almost like peacetime. My last official act was to perch atop a ventilator on the ship's after deck, loudspeaker in hand, giving Japanese lessons to the several hundred members of the landing force scheduled to go ashore at the great Yokosuka naval base. It would have been utter fantasy if not superior clairvoyance to have dreamed that twelve years hence I would be commanding that base myself.

To those who have not experienced a transfer by highline between underway ships at sea, imagine a trip over Niagara Falls on a tightrope. Fifty yards apart on parallel course, the two ships surge, roll, ease in and out, sometimes together, sometimes to a different drummer. Sloshing between is the choppy Pacific, fifty feet below. One sits in a boatswain's chair under a pulley that is managed by ropes from each ship. The chair swings, dips, and surges as the wire slackens or tautens to the roll of the supporting ships. In such a manner I crossed to a tanker, then a few days later to a homeward-bound aircraft carrier. At San Francisco to greet me was my very first serious fiancée, long since happily married, whose farewell fourteen years earlier almost to the day at that very same city had torn my heart before launching on a cruise that would twice girdle the earth.

What next? My request for shore duty had been as naval attaché China, strongly recommended by the current incumbent, old friend and once fellow Yangtze "River Rat," firmly seconded by my one-time mess-mate in Moscow, war-whooping General-Ambassador Patrick Hurley at Chungking. But again Fate proved to be a capricious master. Almost overnight the accent had changed from just-vanquished Japan to Russia. Early in the war, Commander in Chief Ernie King, akin the girl in the song, "What Lola Wants, Lola Gets," had opted for his own private ONI, wholly apart from the venerable institution that had generated so much internecine strife in the immediate pre-war Navy Department. Currently it was being run by a man I had marked for flag rank ever since we had been midshipmen together, Captain W. R. Smedberg II. "Smeddy" needed a "Russian," and I was "it." His directions were characteristic of this outstanding officer: "Go where you want, talk to whoever you think is appropriate, and give me the answers I need."

My flat, on Rhode Island Avenue near Connecticut, was ideal for entertaining. It once had been the public rooms of a turn-of-the-century mansion, with Italian carved marble fireplace mantels and crystal chandeliers, Persian rugs, and excellent antiques. The pantry was stacked with Limoges china. But there was no bedroom, which enormously piqued the curiosity of those wives among my guests at parties who took a personal interest in the more intimate affairs of acting bachelors. To have revealed that I slept on the *takhta* would have spoiled the game.

The news from Russia was not good. OVIR was wholly noncommittal on a visa. In October and November of 1945 there had been a flurry of telegrams between Washington and Moscow on the visa problem. Harriman, by now a firm convert to the hard line, said the whole thing was "an expression of arrogance of Soviet secret police, and of their confidence that the American individuals will never really have the backing of higher levels of our Govt . . . " Such certainly was not the case. Vishinsky had been approached on the subject by Minister Kennan. Then the ante had been upped; Secretary of State Byrnes told Harriman the department was under constant pressure. *Do* something! "Navy Secretary Forrestal has requested Dept to make strong representations to Soviet Govt with regard to case of Mrs. V. I. Tolley . . . " Senators were getting into the act, urging the State Department to start throwing its weight about. Secretary Byrnes, attending a foreign ministers' conference in Moscow, brought up the subject with Molotov.* But nothing happened. At OVIR, it was, "Perhaps later. Come back later."

In Washington, there was the same division of Soviet officers into eligibles and ineligibles as had been the case in Moscow. Half a dozen shy fellows I had met at Soviet embassy receptions were always "out," or "on a trip" when I telephoned an invitation to dinner. But one cocky little captain-lieutenant could always be counted on to show up, willingly donning one of my stock of tails-out Russian shirts, dancing the *gopak*, squatting while kicking out his heels, jubilantly shouting "yah! yah! yah! yah!" in time with the music, in general the life of the party. His sketchy knowledge of the sea and ships clearly suggested his real colors.

The naval attaché, an amiable chap wearing a captain first rank's broad stripe and thus locally called "commodore," also was available, but without comrade wife. Once, he turned up with an old friend in tow: Rear Admiral Ramishvili, our host at Baku when we visited the Soviet Naval Academy. He was his usual outspoken Georgian self. "Keeping Vlada in the USSR is the stupidest thing I ever heard of!" he exclaimed heatedly. It was typical of some of the hamhanded, counterproductive things Moscow perpetrated, he said. Alas! A few months later Ramishvili left the USA closely escorted by two of those characters in the black suits and celluloid collars. Perhaps some of his comments had reached less friendly ears. He eventually wound up as a by-lined commentator for *Newsweek*.

My other contacts with Russians were with defectors. As the only Russian-speaking officer in the Navy Department (Frankel had been lent to help set up the CIA) I was called upon to conduct a preliminary interview to guide detailed debriefing later by experts in the defector's particular line. Three widely diverse types are represented in the following notes I took at the time.

Victor Kravchenko had been invalided out of the Soviet Army and in 1943 came to the USA as a member of the USSR Purchasing Commission, listed in his passport as a civilian. In April 1944 he defected, starting a chain of claims and counterclaims that reached as high as the president and Molotov. He was a military deserter, the Soviets said, and must be returned. He was civilian, said the State Department, and could be tried, possibly be deported, but by U.S. law any deportation would be to a country of the deportee's own choosing, a process taking months or years. It was typical of the ambiguity of Soviet demands and requests. I interviewed Kravchenko in a room in the House of Representatives, U.S. Congress, where he was pushing his case. "*Kravchenko*," I wrote, "is a dynamic,

*This extensive correspondence is on pages 1157–59, *Foreign Relations*, 1945, vol. 5.

self-centered, single-minded individual who would make good in any country by sheer will power and application. His personal revolt I believe is due to an unwillingness to have his potentialities cramped by the Soviet hierarchy and system, to put up with the win-all, lose-all possibilities of the high Soviet official. It can be boiled down to an expression used to me by Kravchenko himself: 'I'll show those Kremlin bastards what I can do!.' "

Next came Lieutenant Colonel Leon Volkov (alias Kotov), late of the Soviet Air Force: "He is the salt-of-the-earth, country store cracker barrel sort of fellow you would find a counterpart of in a Maine small town. He is a hard-headed, practical type who reasons things out, laboriously perhaps . . . but thoroughly. If there were any question of who might be a plant, "Volkov" would be my choice, though I consider the possibility small. His usefulness to the Soviets certainly has been outweighed by his damage to their cause through publicity in the United States. I think he ran away partly because he is lazy and partly because he was tired of being pushed around by what he considered to be inferior intellects."

Of quite another breed was Alexeiev, late of the Soviet embassy in Mexico City. He was a mouse. Educated, and having a considerable amount of information, he obviously was dominated by his flashing-eyed, black-haired, confident wife, who looked like a Georgian—Gypsy or Jewish. The poor man obviously was more afraid to obey the order recalling him to Moscow than he was to run away.

Barsov and Pirogov were Soviet Air Force lieutenants, the latter definitely the leader, answering all questions put to the pair. Barsov acted and looked like what the Russians call a "Vanya from the derevnya," Johnny from the country, a rube, who was talked into this escape caper by cleverer Pirogov to buck up the latter's resolution. The pair was given a grand tour of the eastern United States, after which Barsov elected to go back to Russia, with wholly predictable circumstances—a propaganda whirl, then oblivion. He simply missed his barracks crowd, his vodka and herring, Russian girls with some meat on their bones. Violent change of habitat for a man of simple intelligence, background, and taste generally is a wrench too great for his personality to cope with. Front man Pirogov remained, writing articles, generally well adjusted to his new home.

There must be a compelling reason for any Russian to renounce his homeland. It is naive to assume that the freedom of America is sufficient lure. Actually, it leaves many defectors bewildered and insecure. A hundred years ago, Dostoyevsky clearly expressed it in *The Brothers Karamazov*:

> If I run away, even with money and passports, and even to America, I should be cheered by the thought that I am not running away for pleasure, not for happiness, but to another exile as bad, perhaps, as Siberia. I hate that America, damn it—already! How shall I put up with that rabble out there,

> though they may be better than I, every one of them, damn them, they are not of my soul. I love Russia, I love the Russian God . . .

Today, the "Russian God" is a skillful blend of the immortal God in Heaven and the current leader of the party, who, self-glorified to the point of near deification, takes his place as one of the long line of "little fathers" who protect and direct the motherland.

Many of the defectors of today are not Kravchenkos, Volkovs, Alexeievs, or Pirogovs, but independent thinkers who have been forced to leave the USSR, rather than being sent to Siberia as in czarist times, or shot by Stalin. The onus of guilt by association has eased, but then that never has been a Russian monopoly. By the end of 1945 a considerable number of ex-Muscovites were in Washington: news correspondents, State Department personnel, ex-military and naval attachés, Red Cross, OWI. The holiday season seemed like a good time for a get-together. Why not Stalin's birthday, 21 December? About a hundred and fifty of us were at the Army and Navy Club to reminisce over vodka and zakuska. Next day the Washington papers carried articles about a "crowd of Stalin worshippers" gathering to toast "that villain . . . " It was an ironic reminder that no monopoly was held by *Pravda* ("Truth") in which there is no truth, or *Izvestia* ("News") in which there is no news, as quipped by irreverent Muscovites.

There still were parties in Moscow, too, in spite of the deepening East-West chilliness. At an Afghan embassy affair, Minister George Kennan pointed out to Vlada a wizened little man in gray diplomatic uniform. "That is Dekanozov," he said, "deputy minister for foreign affairs. One of his roles is passport and visa management. Why don't you have a chat with him?" Vlada poured out her tale of woe and frustration. Obviously, there had to be an appropriate proverb. "Obyeshyanovo tree goda zhdoot!" observed Dekanozov by way of comment. ("That which has been promised you must wait for three years.") "But it has been almost three years exactly!" pleaded Vlada.

On Vlada's next visit to OVIR, expecting the usual "Come back later" routine, the answer was positive. In another ten days she was on a Stockholm-bound plane. She was among the few lucky ones. Half a dozen others who had remained after their spouses had at last departed in despair disappeared one by one, letters to them unanswered.

Thus, for Vlada and myself, this story can have a happy ending. For Dekanozov, one cannot say the same. By 1947, a second Great Purge was under way, taking those who had been war prisoners, who had worked for or with foreigners, or in some obscure manner had incurred the enmity or suspicions of Beria's secret police. Zoya Feodorova, our lighthearted guest at many parties, got eight years in prison. Embassy employees disappeared.

Dekanozov and many others were shot. So fared alike architects of victory, scoundrels, prisoners, and innocent bystanders, once more filling the camps and mines that in wartime had spilled out millions for cannon fodder or stevedores at the ports, expendable in one-way missions. That was Stalin's way, the grotesquely twisted legacy of Marx, Engels, and Lenin.

From the other end of the telescope, to have regarded the Russian leadership as "just like Americans" and to have so treated them was folly. If our spurned efforts turned sympathy and love to suspicion and hate, let us now at last grow up sentimentally, remembering that since Russians came down from the prehistoric trees, their policy has been based on well-founded suspicion, European-style total self-interest, a keen appreciation of the power vacuum, and an oriental stoicism regarding brutality, suffering, and hardship.

Let not the seeming harshness of the above indictment suggest a dark and hopeless prospect for our future relations. Temper it with the thought that sixty million Great Russians stand surrounded by some Union republics of dubious loyalty. They are allied with unwilling satellites, while *one billion* unpredictable Chinese line a 4,000 mile border. Concurrently, another quarter billion unfriendlies, the Americans, combine with a like number of NATO allies. As for the Soviets, it is not what *we* think, not what *we* think *they* think, but what *they* think that must be cranked into any peaceful solution—take that mile walk in the other fellow's moccasins. Hopefully, there will be another Dekanozov, and that he will not be shot for his efforts.

Appendixes

A / *Letter from Admiral H. E. Yarnell to Admiral William D. Leahy*

Vladivostok, U.S.S.R.
1 August 1937

My dear Leahy,

The AUGUSTA and four destroyers arrived at Vladivostok on Wednesday morning, July 28th, and will leave today for Tsingtao and Chefoo. A rough passage was experienced on our way up, as we were on the edge of a typhoon.

Upon arrival I called on the officials in Vladivostok. These consisted of (1) the Commander of the Far Eastern Fleet, who wears the stripes of a vice admiral, named Kirdiv; (2) A Commander of Division (rear-admiral) who is the garrison commander and has command of all army air forces and coastal fortifications of this vicinity. His name was Eliseev; (3) The Mayor, a civilian named Ogarov, an inoffensive looking young man about 32 years old; (4) The Commissar of Foreign Affairs, named Tihonov, who wore an admiral's stripes but was not senior to the Commander of the Far Eastern Fleet, and (5) an Army Commissar of the 2nd rank named Olgunev, who did not wear a uniform. As far as you can make out the commissars are the members of the government who watch over the naval and military officers. These calls were returned the same day. The remainder of the time has been given up to dinners and entertainments for the officers and men. I gave a luncheon for the leading officials and also a reception yesterday. Lieut. Colonel Faymonville, U.S. Military Attaché at Moscow, was in Vladivostok to assist in the visit. He has been of the greatest assistance due to his knowledge of the Russians and his ability to speak the language. I also brought Lieutenant Taecker up on the AUGUSTA. He is a Russian

Admiral Harry E. Yarnell (in whites, center, front row) with U.S. and Russian officers, under the 8″ guns of the USS *Augusta* (CA-31) at Vladivostok 28 July 1937. Those present and identifiable: (front), 2nd from left, Army Commissar Okunev; Ugarov, Mayor of Vladivostok; Admiral Tihonev, commissar; Vice Admiral Kireyev; Rear Admiral Eliseyev, garrison commander, Vladivostok; Captains Cherneschok and Orlov; (rear), Commander Deyo; fourth from left, Captain Faymonville, USA; 3rd from right, Captain McKittrick; 2nd from right, Captain McConnell. (Courtesy Mr. and Mrs. Philip Yarnell)

language student and speaks it very well. Very few of the Russians speak any language except their own.

The visit of this force evidently has meant a great deal to these people and considerable preparations were made for our reception and entertainment. As far as I can make out they are quite friendly to the United States and did everything in their power to show this friendship.

The officials are a rather mediocre looking lot and if they have much ability it was not apparent. The one exception was the Commissar of Foreign Affairs, Tihonov, who looked as though he had some ability and was a typical communist in appearance. He was about 35 years of age.

I was told that there are about 200,000 people in the city—an increase of 100,000 in the past five years. On the whole they are a drab, untidy looking lot of people. A well dressed person was the exception. Just what they all do for a living I could not make out, as Vladivostok is not a commercial port to any extent.

The city itself is rather imposing from the anchorage but once ashore it is a sad disappointment. There are two main streets paved with cobblestones and the remainder are dirt roads. The buildings are unkempt with evidently no attempt at upkeep. I was told that there has been much building going on and some of it was evident in the shape of apartment and living quarters. Sanitation in the city is at a low ebb. Colonel Faymonville tells me that this town is not typical of others, since little has been done to build it up. We were shown a very elaborate "fifteen-year plan" for the development of the city. This was on a very elaborate scale and will probably never get much beyond the paper stage.

There is little commerce from this port. The Russians run a steamer to Shanghai occasionally. Also, a Japanese steamer comes over here about twice a month. The shops in the city are rather pathetic from our standpoint. The goods are few and of very poor quality. They are also very high in price. The official exchange rate for the rouble is 5 roubles for one U.S. gold dollar. I was told, however, that bootleg roubles could be bought from 30 to 50 for the dollar. An ordinary looking pair of shoes was priced at 200 roubles. A moth-eaten silver fox fur was priced at 3000 roubles. Even at the bootleg price of roubles goods are high in price.

The officials are very secretive about any details of their defense or armed forces. There is a navy yard here and from our anchorage we are able to see about fifteen submarines tied up, some of them rather rusty looking. During our stay one submarine arrived and one left. I would judge they were about 1500 to 2000 tons. They have here also a destroyer about 25 years old called the STALIN, and three smaller torpedo boats. I was given to understand that during the summer their submarines are operating from ports to northward. Just how many they have altogether I could get no information. They refused to let us visit the navy yard, saying it would be necessary for them to get authority from Moscow, and that there was not enough time to obtain this permission. There are large numbers of naval enlisted men on the streets in Vladivostok. They are very clean in appearance and are a well-built lot of men. There were no troops in Vladivostok itself except some of an engineer regiment. We are unable to obtain much information about their air force. The only planes I saw was a flight of twelve fighters over the city one day. I understand their main airports are not in this vicinity.

It is, of course, not possible to generalize about Russia from what is seen of this one city. However, I can not but believe that while general conditions here are worse than they are in other sections of Russia the general appearance of the people and the attitude of the officials is perhaps typical, and if it is, God save us from communism. In order to make a success of this form of government the following requisites seem to be necessary: first, kill off all the intelligentsia of the country; second, destroy all churches and deny all religion; third, discourage family life; fourth, have one half the people watch the other half.

While this visit has been interesting and instructive I do not care to repeat it and would not advise its being made at other than infrequent intervals. A full report on our visit will of course follow in due time.

Very sincerely,

/s/ H.E. Yarnell

B / *Naval Attachés in Imperial Russia and the USSR Through WW II*

Ward, Lieutenant Aaron, Paris, Berlin, and St. Petersburg, 1 March 1889–1892

Rodgers, Lieutenant Commander Raymond P., Paris, St. Petersburg, and Madrid, 1 October 1892–1897

Sims, Lieutenant William S., Paris and St. Petersburg, 30 April 1897–1900

Harber, Commander Giles B., Paris, St. Petersburg, 1 June 1900–1903

Smith, Lieutenant Commander Roy Campbell, Paris and St. Petersburg, 5 August 1903–1906

McCully, Lieutenant Newton Alexander, St. Petersburg, 15 March 1904–1905

Fremont, Captain John Charles, Paris and St. Petersburg, 22 August 1906–1908

Chapin, Lieutanant Commander (later Commander) Frederick Lincoln, Paris and St. Petersburg, 13 January 1908–1911

Hough, Lieutenant Commander (later Commander) Henry Hughes, Paris and St. Petersburg, 20 January 1911–1914

McCully, Captain Newton Alexander, Petrograd, 6 October 1914–1917 (?)

Crosley, Commander Walter Selwyn, 1917–1918

Nimmer, Captain David R., USMC, Moscow, 1933–1934, accredited as assistant naval attaché. No naval attaché assigned.

Duncan, Captain (later Rear Admiral) Jack Harlan, Moscow, April 1942–1943

Olsen, Commodore (later Rear Admiral) Clarence E., Chief, Naval Section, U.S.Military Mission (naval attaché disestablished)

Maples, Rear Admiral Houston L., Naval attachés reestablished. May 1945– August 1947

C / *A Sample of Lend-Lease Lading to the USSR via the Northern Convoys: List of Cargo Loaded on SS Puerto Rican*

Aircraft		*Tons*
Curtiss Wright	15 planes	107
Douglas A 20B	8 planes	77
Aircraft parts	456 cases	56
Tanks		
Medium tanks with guns mounted	20 tanks	522
Medium M.I. tractors	5 boxes	42
Light Army tanks with guns mounted	3 tanks	34
Vehicles		
Motorcycles and parts	12 cases	30
Willys auto parts and tools	120 pkgs	18
Willys 4 X 4 trucks	9 trucks	12
Auto parts for recce trucks	29 cases	7
Guns and Ammunition		
TNT	8,000 cases	205
75mm H.E. cannon ammo	19,503 rounds	221
81mm H.E. cannon ammo	8,820 rounds	45
37mm cannon ammo	20,000 rounds	45
37mm H.E. cannon ammo	19,920 rounds	42
20mm Oerlikon	92,540 rounds	28
37mm solid projectile, tracer	10,000 rounds	22
Cannon powder for 90mm AA	2,208 drums	150

Guns and Ammunition		*Tons*
30 cal. ball, A.P., tracer	24,000,000 rounds	138
45 cal. ball cartridges	1,974,000 rounds	42
50 cal. A.P. cartridges	266,600 rounds	37
Various		
Rubber pontoon carrying cases	91 cases	20
Aniline oil	290 drums	56
Dredging buckets, luffing crane	73 pieces	80
Power press	2 cases	41
Vertical hydraulic piercing presses	15 cases	36
Grinding wheels	143 cases	22
Hydraulic surface grinders	9 boxes	17
Power plant type C–173	40 cases	7
Air pumps	15 boxes	4
Semi-automatic 1½ thread milling	1 case	1
Cold rolled screw stock steel	1,247 boxes	562
Cold finish steel bars	655 boxes	308
Steel bars	174 bales	235
Hot rolled chrome-silicon steel	158 bales	214
Nitralloy aircraft annealed steel	331 pieces	142
Assorted steel stock	650 boxes	315
Copper cable	131 reels	88
Steel billets	316 pieces	80
Steel wire	1,075 bundles	168
Iron bars	55 bundles	51
Brass wire	220 barrels	49
Rubber sheeting	697 boxes	43
Hard copper tubes	300 cases	26
High grade piano wire	46 drums	24
Copper tubing	145 boxes	21
Sulfanilimide USP powder	68 barrels	10
Galvanized steel aircraft cord	33 reels	7
Brass wire cloth	25 boxes	4
Dibutylphthalate	638 drums	148
Tinplate	336 cont.	145
Phenol	234 drums	53
Innersole leather	205 bundles and 100 bales	43
Pneumatic truck tires	1,400 tires	43
Dimethylaniline	200 drums	51
Truck tires and tubes	1,200 tires	35
Dyphenilamine	172 bbls	24

Various		
Insulated copper wire	252 reels	20
Finders bends	120 bales	19
Sox, shoes, trousers, helmets, jackets, hat covers, mittens, coats	78 cases	10
Telephones and spare parts	60 cases	9
Spark plugs	39 cases	3
Canned meats	9,209 cases	296
Canned pork sausage	1,999 cases	42
Canned lunchmeat	1,334 boxes	38
Vegetable seed	690 bags	16
Miscellaneous		30
For U. S. interests		
Mail	339 bags	7

No one class of items was loaded in a single ship, so that the loss of a ship did not wipe out entire categories of material. SS *PUERTO RICAN* carried almost 1,000 tons of high explosive, quite enough to ensure obliteration in case of a good torpedo or bomb hit. Most ships were similarly loaded.

D / Intelligence Report of a Visit to the Soviet Destroyer Razumny

On 13 January 1944, Rear Admiral C. E. Olsen, accompanied by Commanders F. R. Lang (MC) and Kemp Tolley, and Lieutenant Commander E. W. Yorke, visited the destroyer *Razumny* at Polyarnoe.

The general impression gained was that this ship, built in 1937, was inferior in every respect to a contemporary American vessel; that her effectiveness in battle would be not greater than that of a World War I type U. S. destroyer. Her design is not good and there seems to be little understanding of construction measures to reduce fire hazard. The artillery was in excellent condition but far from a modern installation. The rest of the ship was in poor material shape and reflected poor operating discipline.

Ships of this type are used as escorts for arriving and departing Anglo-American convoys and for escorting the few Soviet ships using the Barents Sea. There is little indication that they have been used in landing operations or in offensive action against German naval forces which might have been found along the Norwegian coast. The endurance of all Soviet vessels is so poor that any forays the destroyers indulged in would of necessity be limited to very minor operations.

Razumny was formerly in the Pacific Fleet, having joined the Northern Fleet four years ago via the Northern Sea Route. Her present commanding officer, a captain-lieutenant (equivalent to a senior lieutenant USN) has been in her at least that long, having served in her in the Pacific.

The commanding officer stated that she carried 225 men, which appears to be an abnormally high number for such a small ship, but in view of the short times they are at sea, probably never more than a week, this overcrowding may be put up with. It has always been Russian custom to allow part or all of a ship's company to live ashore in barracks when the ship is in port, particularly when laid up for the ice season.

The main battery guns are of the standard Soviet type. Proportion of length of barrel forward of trunnions is greater than in American guns, this muzzle heaviness being countered by a large weight surrounding the breech. The trainers' and pointers' controls are duplicated on each side of gun, so that either may fulfil both functions if one man or the gear one side of the gun is knocked out. A plate attached to the slide seals at any angle of elevation the aperture for the barrel through the gunshield. Maximum elevation is estimated to be 50 degrees. Semifixed ammunition is used. There is a shell-loading rack attached to the left side of the after end of the slide. This swings in abaft the breech, so that the shell, previously placed in this rack and held from slipping back by a pawl, may be rammed by hand rammer into the breech without danger of damaging the screwbox. The rack may then be swung out to clear the way for loading and ejecting the powder case. Narrow slits in the forward side of the shield on each side of the barrel accommodate the two telescopic sights.

The shield is all-welded, about half-inch plate. Shield roof extends several feet abaft breech, the forward gun having a blast shield extending some four feet in addition. Shields are roomy, but in view of lack of remote control gun laying gear, power loading or director control, the space surrounding the guns is enormously cluttered up and indicative of inefficient design.

Shells and powder cases are passed up by hand through tubes from the magazine to a point behind the gun when the latter is trained in. There was no apparent stowage for ready ammunition.

Salvo fire by bridge control or local control with individual fire is used. There is a range computer on the forward side of the bridge, in the open, which transmits range and deflection to the guns by dials at the sightsetting positions.

There is no radar and the commanding officer and the chief of staff of the Northern Fleet both expressed a keen desire to have such equipment. They also mentioned that nothing would please them better than to have the vacant spot on their U. S.-built minesweepers filled with the radar equipment meant to go in it.

(In connection with the above, Captain First Rank Suhiashvili, superintendent of the Naval Academy, told me that the cruiser *Molotov* was equipped with radar, as she used to warn the area of the approach of German planes when he, Suhiashvili, was commanding a marine brigade near Novorossisk, Black Sea.)

The torpedo tubes may be controlled locally or by the torpedo directors, one on each side of the bridge. The tubes are very little longer than the torpedoes and do not have a projecting, folding overhang as do American tubes. The lower, outboard end of the tubes curve downward to avoid breaking off the tail on launching. The two outboard tubes in a three-tube nest can each be worked out fifteen degrees for firing a spread. Launching is by powder impulse charge. No spare torpedoes were seen. All tubes were loaded.

Single mine tracks ran on each side of the main deck from the break to the stern. No mines were on board.

Ten 125 kg. depth charges were stowed in two rows in slots in the fantail. These slots are of a depth of about half the depth charge diameter. In this case, the charges were more or less surrounded by ice accumulations from snow and sleet storms and possibly washing down, and could certainly not have been launched without prying them loose with a pinch bar. There was no "Y" gun, but on either side of the after deck, some 40 feet forward of the stern, was a gun for launching a single charge to that side only.

The navigation bridge is open, with a waist-high screen as the only protection. This bridge surrounds a combination chart house, plotting room, and wheel house about 10 feet in diameter. This space has about a dozen 8-inch portholes framed with heavy curtains, and would not be a satisfactory navigating or battle conning station due to poor visibility. Battle ports are of light metal, dogged down with wingnuts.

Next above this bridge structure is a rotatable tower about eight feet in diameter housing two coincidence range finders and a vertically mounted spotting glass. These instruments appeared to be very well cared for, as was all the ordnance equipment.

On each wing of the after part of the upper bridge structure was a 50-caliber machine gun, and on the lower deck of this structure, two 37-mm automatic AA guns firing shells in clips, one gun on each side. The last gun aft on the fantail appeared to be about 3-inch 30-caliber AA.

Degaussing gear was installed. The CO said they ran over the degaussing range once every three months.

Gaskets throughout the ship were in fair to good condition and not painted over, although painting in general was careless. Dogs were of a light type and were in bad shape. There were no quick-closing doors. Doors into deck house appeared to be non-watertight. There was a good supply of timbers for shoring bulkheads but no wedges. Doors and hatches were not marked to indicate that any damage control system was in effect.

The galley, in the after deck house, had three 20-gallon steam kettles and a five-foot range. The diet, judging from the galley facilities and from the food we received aboard our cruise in AM-114, was largely soup. The galley was superficially clean, but dark and dingy and not one where deficiencies in sanitary measures would be readily apparent. Messing is on portable table much like ours. A mess being set up while we were passing through around noon indicated extreme simplicity, each man with a soup bowl and spoon, a pile of black bread stacked on a bare wood table.

There are three boiler rooms in line, each with one boiler operating on a maximum of 350 pounds. Abaft these are two engine rooms, each with a separate and complete entity for one shaft. They are crowded and suggest poor planning. In the engine room visited, minor overhaul was in progress. Overhead cork insulation was hanging down in strips, and had obviously been in that condition for some time. In a number of places, tin cans hung on wires under pipe flanges to catch a drip. The general impression of both engine and fire rooms was that upkeep was sloppy.

The engine and boiler control point is a compartment about six feet deep running across the after end of the forward deck house, on the main deck. There is no other control except local individual control at each engine and boiler. The gauges in this control room, some of them over a foot in diameter, had glass covers. Overhead lights were enclosed in large ornamental white china shades about a foot and a half in diameter. This type of fixture was also found throughout the living spaces, and although the CO said they were removed during cruises, the ship was then lying where German airfields were 15 minutes away by bomber.

Officers' rooms and the wardroom were elaborately furnished with overstuffed leather chairs, the bulkheads covered with plywood paneling and the beams enclosed in wooden casing. Nowhere was the ship's skin available to quick access for repair of battle damage. There were heavy curtains in many places, and ports were framed with bulky and ornamental hangings.

Decks below were all linoleum covered. Weather decks were bare steel with small mounds of steel applied by spot welding, to improve the footing.

The wardroom was on the main deck, under the bridge, running the full width of the ship. Four powerful lights at the four corners of the wardroom table made it adaptable for an operating table, something not fitted in the sick bay.

Officers' rooms were abaft the wardroom on the port side and amidships. On the starboard side, from the wardroom aft to the break in the deck, there was a clubroom for the crew, with small library, a big table, musical instruments, and a few newspapers. The bulkheads were plastered with violently colored caricatures and illustrations calculated to whip the crew into a high state of enthusiasm for the war effort. While considerably smaller, it was almost as comfortably fitted as the wardroom. As the crew numbered over two hundred, it obviously could accommodate only a fraction of them.

The crew's quarters were chiefly forward and below officers' country. Bunks for about half the crew were installed and the remainder either swung in hammocks or hit the deck. Chief petty officers were quartered and had their mess room below the main deck under the after deck house, and were comfortably accommodated. There were nine of them.

The ship's office and sick bay were in this area also, the sick bay having bunk space for two patients. Sanitary conditions and facilities in sick bay were of a low order. On opening a box containing operating instruments, a squad of cockroaches dashed out, this being typical of the whole atmosphere of the place. The medical officer was a "feldscher," one having had but three years medical training and not qualified to perform operations.

Those of the crew encountered in the inspection appeared to be alert and more intelligent than the average soldier, as is generally the case in any country. Their state of physical cleanliness was not all that could be desired, some of them nothing less than filthy.

As to the small things that go to making an impression of a ship and her efficiency, one could give an average of about 3.0 on a scale of 4.0. The boats were in fair to good condition, but showed no signs of much use. Boat falls were sound and well stowed. Electrical gear throughout the ship was clear of paint, switches were clean, and bus bars bright. The gangway watch was on hand when we arrived, but couldn't be found when we left, and he didn't look particularly neat or dressed for the occasion. The colors were two-blocked, clean, and never fouled. There was a good deal of oil wiped on topside surfaces, apparently as a preservative. Hatch coamings and hand rails on ladders were dirty and greasy. Weather deck hatches were covered by badly rigged, ragged canvas hatch covers. Paintwork, in general fairly clean for wartime standards, was scrubbed pretty thin above decks; down to bare metal in some already rusting spots.

Ladder treads, mats, handrails, and fittings subject to much wear were all worn to a point where they would have long since been replaced in our Navy, for efficiency as well as appearance's sake.

There was no indication that any special preparations had been made for our reception. The ship was in her everyday condition.

It must be remembered that the USSR has been scraping bottom for a long time as far as materiel is concerned. That the ships are operating at all is more wonder than that they are in such poor condition and her sailors dirty. Yet it is certainly not the whole story. There are ships in the USSR Navy which even now compare with the best standards of the peacetime U. S. Navy. The submarine *K-21*, for example, is an indication that war or no war, a Soviet ship and her crew can be maintained at extremely high standards. The rank and file of their officer and enlisted complement scarcely measure up to the pace set by Hero of the Soviet Union Lunin and his *K-21* however, and are certainly well below the average found in our navy. Individually, they have proven brave to the point of being spectacular, particularly ashore as marines. But their concept of naval organization, planning, and an appreciation of the use of sea power show markedly the same shortcomings which have made German naval performance second rate whenever they meet a first class opponent, even though in most cases the Germans were aboard superior ships with superior equipment.

Soviet shipbuilding, as reflected in this destroyer, shows a tendency to follow the lead of Imperial Russia: more concerned with the comfort of officer personnel than with the battleworthiness of their ships, either unaware of or not valuing the most primary principles of damage control and fire prevention measures.

Technical development is far behind that to be found in the major navies, with little use being made of foreign developments which obviously are available to them.

There is little doubt that the Soviet Navy is ambitious. It will surely expand after the peace and reconstruction have made materials available, but not for many years does it appear in any respect to be a rival for any of the great naval powers.

Kemp Tolley
Commander, U.S. Navy

E / Tolley Report to ONI: Discussion of Situation in the Soviet Union

1 December 1942

During the last six months, a number of foreign visitors have come to the Soviet Union for conferences, fact finding, back scratching. Their impressions frequently influence in no small way the conduct of our international relations and the war effort. It appears of interest therefore that O.N.I. be in a position to fully evaluate the views and decisions of such visitors through a knowledge of Russian psychology and the peculiar conditions existing in the Soviet Union. This discussion is intended to present the views of one who has had wide experience in oriental countries and long association with Russians of many political complexions.

It is unquestionable that a newcomer to Russia generally views the Russians as of a totally "white" and European country. This basic initial error is supported after arrival by the superficial similarities existing between foreigners and Russians in manner and custom, particularly among Russians whom a casual visitor will most likely encounter. The visitor who prolongs his stay, particularly one who does not speak Russian, invariably experiences a feeling of frustration and disillusionment growing out of a lack of appreciation of existing conditions and facts.

Two of these facts which chiefly affect the mores of contemporary Soviet Russians are: 1) they are ruled body and soul by a bureaucracy maintained by power and fear, and 2) there is a strong and often controlling oriental influence in the average Russian's psychological makeup.

The ruling bureaucracy is unfortunately staffed only too often with men of much animal cunning but little real intelligence, imagination or training. Initiative is stifled due chiefly to fear and secondly to lack of knowledge. The awful penalties of a fall from favor are such that the average

American can scarcely appreciate the Russian official's eagerness to hew the line. It may appear trite to mention the huge numbers of Russians now in concentration camps or dismal outposts of the Far North and East, but this picture is always before the Soviet citizen, affecting his every move.

To anyone well acquainted with the Chinese, certain behaviorisms of the Russians are not surprising. To the average American who expects a straight reply to a straight question and direct action when direct action is promised, the procrastination and evasiveness of many Russians are exasperating in the extreme. With a bland smile and a straight look in the eye, a Shanghai tailor will promise your suit ready tomorrow, when you and he both know it will take at least a week. Similar performances on the part of a Russian (and there are many) generally evoke surprised annoyance and anger at this "unexpected" lack of cooperation.

This practice of "letting you down easy," part and parcel of asiatic mentality, is never appreciated by the visiting general who wants to do it *NOW*. Coupled with the above are qualities of cold, animal cruelty which are peculiarly oriental, evidence of the Tartar and Mongol blood which is so freely mixed in so many Russians.

There are undoubtedly a tremendous number of Russians who believe wholeheartedly in the present regime, particularly industrial workers and certain of the peasants. They are unquestionably better off than under the Empire. The younger generation of course knows nothing else. There are, however, a considerable number of petit bourgeoisie, intelligentsia and ex kulaks who realize the generally sorry condition of the Soviet picture and the fear under which many people suffer a lifetime. It is incredible to one who has not lived in Russia to witness the ignorance of the multitude. Practically no one seems to know that the United States participated in the "First Imperialist War." None seem to know that there are enormous colonies of Russians living all over the world. Few have ever heard of such things as an electric refrigerator, vacuum cleaner, portable radio, automatic record changer, string beans, corn, mayonnaise dressing, cigars, chewing gum, two pants suits, the game of golf, hundreds of everyday things that we have come to look on as necessary parts of our life. Most, when told, simply do not believe that there was one car for every five people in the U.S.; that one could walk into stores everywhere and buy anything required, even a pair of five rouble silk stockings. (Present price in Russia, 500 roubles). This extra-ordinary attitude is largely the result of "education", plus being entirely cut off from any contact with the outside world. Very occasional and carefully selected American movies (three or four a year) bring crowds blocks long.

A recently published Anglo-Russian dictionary (1937) had the following item in the errata sheet: "Evict" . . . as, 'to evict the workers from their flats for nonpayment of rent (in America)' . . . change 'America' to read, 'in capitalist countries'."

A phrase in a Soviet primer: "Oh, Vanya, there goes a foreigner!! You follow him while I go look for a policeman!"

Russians may occasionally be talked into visiting a foreigner's apartment or coming to dinner. The precautions they go through to escape being followed or observed are truly remarkable. I know of two girls recently arrested, presumably for associating with foreigners, so perhaps these precautions are indicated. (In Vladivostok, foreigners are practically quarantined.) When walking with a Russian on the street, they are continually looking around to see if they are being followed and if such appears to be the case, there is always a very keen uneasiness apparent until the cloud has disappeared or been shaken off.

I have had a number of individuals very openly express themselves along the lines that, a) they would be better off under the Germans, b) if it had been the British attacking instead of the Germans, there would not have been much support from behind the front, c) express the hope the Allies will come in after the war and "straighten things out", d) that many of the citizens who stayed behind in Moscow after the October 1941 mass evacuation were putting on their best finery in preparation for the German entry. There is, of course, no doubt that some of these informants were "plants", endeavoring to obtain information on our attitude but many cases were spontaneous and under conditions of place and circumstance that guaranteed sincerity.

An interesting question is the refusal of the Soviets to allow foreign military observers or attaches to accompany Soviet troops. There have been several cases where well stage-managed trips to the front have been accorded attaches and press representatives but this can be classified as scarcely anything more than a gesture.

Two explanations suggest themselves. The first, supported by a parallel attitude in other matters, is that the Soviets are actively thinking about the next war, and/or intervention . . . and are not exposing anything of possible value to a future opponent. The second, suggested by alleged statements of Soviet soldiers and of hints in newspapers, is that methods of discipline in the battle areas and the treatment of prisoners (when any) are such that foreign military officers might be astonished, if not aghast. There are various rumors which indicate that direct and extreme measures are taken to insure that the front is held on those occasions when the tactical situation demands it. Troops are influenced by the stationing of NKVD detachments in their rear, and officers remember that occasionally there is a "purge", such as at Rostov in 1941, when the High Command considered the loss of that city unjustified.

The above is meant solely as an explanation of the point in question, and not to detract from the tremendous effort and bravery of the great majority of the Soviet troops, who are activated by a lively hatred for the Germans and by love of Russia, no matter who is running it.

In evaluating the performance of the troops of various powers, one should bear in mind that in most cases, the home life of millions of Russians is quite as primitive and little more comfortable than life at the front. In wartime, they are certainly much better fed than the civilian population in the rear, which is now on rations which unquestionably are resulting in general malnutrition verging on starvation.

The average official visitor is impressed by the cleanliness of the streets (nobody has so much as a matchstick to throw away), the excellent food in the hotel (regular diners eat cabbage soup and grits), the elegance of the official guest house, (no heat, frequently no lights or gas in most Moscow residences), gushing official hospitality (if you stay too long the food deteriorates, and paralyzing official procrastination sets in), people warmly bundled up against the freezing cold (a fur overcoat, if obtainable at all, $1,000; shoes, $50, average salary $60 monthly).

It simply adds up to the fact that superficially, the Soviet Union impresses one as a normal Great Power, whereas beneath the surface there actually lies a huge, roiling mass of dissatisfied, fearful, anxious citizenry, not knowing from which direction their next plague will develop. Suspicion of everything and everybody has been instilled for years: capitalists, foreigners, the secret police, neighbors, every small indication and action that is not clearly understood.

The NKVD rules the roost, a country within a country, with thousands of plain clothes operatives, hundreds of thousands of infantry, cavalry, air force, and artillery, control of many factories and sources of supply and forced labor. With them and with the Army lie undisputable power to shape the future, barring foreign intervention. There is being built up a military hierarchy of professional officers who are more and more assuming the trappings and prerogatives of a military caste. The political commissars have been (temporarily, at least) put aside. High officers go about in smart uniforms, occupy the best accommodations everywhere, dress their wives in attractive clothes and fur coats, are rumored to be soon re-establishing shoulder straps and epaulettes. The soldiers dress in baggy tunics and clumsy boots, ride three tiers deep in "40 & 8's", as they did in Imperial Russia. There doesn't appear to be much left of that facet of communism which preached equality.

There does not seem to be any alteration in the position vis à vis foreigners comparable to the other moves to the right. The only news or information of any sort that the public receives consists of the news communiqués of the war, issued by the various allied news services and Tass.

It is truly pathetic and certainly illuminating to see the wonder and enthusiasm exhibited by the average intelligent Russian on being shown a foreign magazine, such as, "LIFE", or "VOGUE". They are simply enchanted at seeing things almost as if coming out of a book of fairy tales. They are always lavish in their appreciation of American superiority and openly apologetic for the shortcomings of the Soviet Union. This attitude is particularly noticeable in the north, where foreigners are generally much more freely accepted and associated with than in other regions. A great many of the people there are evacuees from the Ukraine and Leningrad and after the sufferings of the past year, simply don't care a damn any more what happens to them. They have had an opportunity to see the great quantities of supplies and equipment arriving from the northern convoys, something the average Russian knows nothing about. They have been befriended by men from the ships and have lost a lot of the suspicion which beclouds the foreigner in other parts of Russia.

It is perhaps unfair to wholly blame communism for a state of affairs we Americans consider appalling and in many ways, inhuman. Since the dawn of Russian history there has always been the equivalent of an NKVD, and people have been sent to slavery or death for speaking their minds too freely. Under the Imperial regime, foreigners were subjected to close scrutiny and accepted not without suspicion and reservation. Imperial Russia was one of the very few countries in the world requiring a passport for entry or exit. Jews and minorities were treated no less cruelly than have been certain elements the Soviets have considered undesirable or dangerous. It seems to be the "russkaya natura."

Summing up, the Soviet Union and its people should be approached warily, subjectively, keeping in mind that a white skin sometimes conceals a Mongol or Tartar or trans-Caucasian psychology that does not function in the Kansas fashion.

Bibliography

Abbasia, Patrick, *Mr. Roosevelt's Navy: The Private War of the U.S. Atlantic Fleet, 1939 to1942.* Annapolis, Md.: Naval Institute Press, 1975.

Academy of Sciences of the USSR. *A Short History of the USSR.* Moscow: Progress Publishers, 1965.

Bailey, Thomas A. *An American Faces Russia.* Gloucester, Mass.: Peter Smith, 1964.

Barron, John. *KGB.* New York: Bantam Books, Inc., 1974.

Bemis, Samuel F. *A Diplomatic History of the United States.* New York: Henry Holt & Co., 1950.

Berthelsen, Bert. *Tin Can Man.* New York: Exposition Press, 1920.

Braisted, W.R. *U.S. Navy in the Pacific, 1909–1922.* Austin: University of Texas Press, 1971.

Carse, Robert. *A Cold Corner of Hell: The Story of the Murmansk Convoys.* New York: Doubleday & Co., Inc., 1969.

Cumming, C.K., and Pettit, Walter W. *Russian-American Relations, March 1917–March 1920.* New York: Harcourt, Brace & Howe, 1920.

Custine, Marquis. *Journey for Our Time.* New York: Pelligrini & Cudahy, 1951. (First published 1843.)

Dawson, Raymond H. *The Decision to Aid Russia.* Chapel Hill: University of North Carolina Press, 1959.

Deane, Major General John. *Strange Alliance.* Toronto: Macmillan, 1947.

Department of State. *Foreign Relations of the United States.* Government Printing Office, various volumes, 1933–1945.

Duranty, Walter. *Stalin & Co.* New York: William Sloane Associates, Inc., 1949.

Engle, Eloise, and Paananen, Erki. *The Winter War.* New York: Charles Scribner's Sons, 1973.

Ergang, Robert. *Europe in Our Time.* New York: D.C. Heath & Co., 1958.

Grason, Theodore. Unpublished book manuscript on his World War II experiences in Vladivostok and immediately postwar in Odessa, USSR.

Graves, Major General William S. *America's Siberian Adventure, 1918–1920.* Cambridge, Mass.: Harvard University Press, 1967.

Halliday, E.M. *The Ignorant Armies*. New York: Harper, 1960.
Hardman, Richard. *Fifteen Flags*. Boston, Mass.: Little, Brown & Co., 1968.
Harris, John. *Light Cavalry Action*. New York: William Morrow & Co., Inc., 1967.
———*Farewall to the Don: The Russian Revolution in the Journals of Brigadier H.N.H. Williamson, RA.*
Herring, George C., Jr. *Aid to Russia*, 1940–1946. New York: Columbia University Press, 1973.
Ironside, Lord Edmund. *Archangel, 1918–19*. London: Constable, 1953.
Kennan, George F. *Russia and the West under Lenin and Stalin*. Boston, Mass.: Little, Brown & Co., 1961.
———*Memoirs, 1925–1950*. Boston, Mass.: Little, Brown & Co., 1967.
Krasnoff, General P.N. *The Unforgiven*. New York: Duffield & Co., 1928.
Lockhart, Robin Bruce. *Ace of Spies*. New York: Stein & Day, 1968.
Loubat, Joseph F. *Narrative of the Mission to Russia, in 1866, of the Hon. Gustavus Vasa Fox*. New York: Appleton & Co., 1873. Reprint by Arno, N.Y., 1970, under title, *Gustavus Fox's Mission to Russia, 1866.*
McCully, Lieutenant Commander Newton A. *The McCully Report: The Russo-Japanese War, 1904–05*. Annapolis, Md.: Naval Institute Press, 1977.
McGinnis, John. Unpublished book manuscript on his two years in wartime Russia.
Maynard, Major General C. *The Murmansk Venture*. New York: Arno Press, 1971.
Miller, Wright, *Russians As People*. New York: E.P. Dutton & Co., 1961.
Morison, Samuel E. *John Paul Jones*. Boston, Mass.: Little, Brown & Co., 1959.
Olsen, Rear Admiral Clarence (Ret.). "Full House at Yalta." American Heritage, vol. 23, pp. 20–25, June, 1972.
Pavlovsky, Michel N. *Chinese-Russian Relations*. New York: Philosophical Library, 1949.
Rambaud, Alfred. *Russia*. New York: The Cooperative Publication Society, 1874.
Riasanovsky, Nicholas V. *A History of Russia*. New York: Oxford University Press, 1963.
Richards, Guy. *Rescue of the Romanovs*. Greenwich, Conn.: Devin-Adair, 1975.
Riis, Sergius M. *Yankee Komisar*. New York: Robert Speller & Sons, 1933.
Rubenstein, Alvin Z. *The Foreign Policy of the Soviet Union*. New York: Random House, 1966.
Schofield, B.B. *The Russian Convoys*. New York: Ballantine Books, 1964.
Shields, Henry Seward. *A Historical Survey of United States Naval Attachés in Russia, 1904–1941*. A thesis presented to the faculty of the Defense Intelligence School, 1970. Defense Intelligence School Library.
Snyder, Louis L. *The War, a Concise History, 1939–1945*. New York: Julian Messner, Inc., 1960.
Standley, Admiral William H., and Arthur Ageton. *Admiral-Ambassador to Russia*. New York: Regnery, 1955.
Stevens, Vice Admiral Leslie C. *Russian Assignment*. Boston, Mass.: Little, Brown & Co., 1953.

Strakhovsky, Leonid I. *Intervention at Archangel*. Princeton, N.J.: Princeton University Press, 1944.
Sutton, Anthony C. *National Suicide: Military Aid to the Soviet Union*. New Rochelle, N.Y.: Arlington House, 1973.
Tarsaidze, Alexander. *Czars and Presidents*. New York: Obolensky, 1958.
Thompson, Valentine. *Knight of the Seas: The Adventures of John Paul Jones*. 1939.
Treadgold, Donald W. *Twentieth Century Russia*. Chicago: Rand McNally & Co., 1968.

Index